31 TREATS
AND A MARRIAGE

LYNN FARLEY-ROSE

Esmeralda
PUBLISHING

Paperback ISBN 978-0-9934711-0-0
Kindle ISBN 978-0-9934711-1-7

Cover design by Jo Dalton room59.co.uk

Typeset by handebooks.co.uk

Published in the UK and USA
Esmeralda Publishing

60treatsandmore@gmail.com

Dedicated to the memory of Nicky Briffa
(1951-2014)

For helping me smell the roses

When you've had a long, happy marriage and you reach your fifties together, you expect life to be settled…

When you've spent years raising a family and they're now grown up, you hope that life will get easier…

When the husband you love, has been life-threateningly ill and recovers, you would think that everything would be wonderful…

Well…it's not necessarily so.

PROLOGUE

Sitting on the balcony of a friend's villa on the Cote d'Azur, the sun toasting my toes, I decide that I really am in dire need of some treats.

I gaze across the Mediterranean, toy with the flaky crumbs of a croissant, and contemplate with pleasure the lazy lunch I'll be enjoying later in the local crêperie. I'll be happy to sit there for a few hours, eating, drinking and chatting as the midday sun beats down and the stays jangle against the masts in the marina. But by three o'clock I'll be sleepy and will need a siesta, so I'll return to the villa. Then, this evening, we'll take a drive along the coast and eat moules in a beachside bistro while the air cools and the sky darkens.

Some treats. Yes, that's definitely what I need.

I run through the possibilities. Maybe a Hermès Birkin bag in ostrich hide, with goat-skin lining. Pink? Red? Perhaps baby blue? That would go well with a pair of statement earrings in amethyst, my February birthstone. I could set it all off with a Lotus Evora in velvet red with ivory leather seats, perfect for driving to a cosy hotel for a weekend tucked away in the Cotswolds. A leisurely cruise would be a welcome break, too, taking in a few Caribbean islands. Reliable sunshine, fire-spiced food, languorous swimming and plenty of time to rest and read. On the way back I could stop off at—

No, no, no—stop. This isn't what I mean at all. The truth is that I rarely have more than one handbag at a time, and I prefer cheap earrings. That way I can have lots to choose from and I'm not bothered if I lose one. My old car starts reliably and is undemanding. A Cotswold hideaway and a cruise would probably be quite enjoyable, but right now what I need most is something that will engage my brain and revitalise me. Then there's the problem of how to pay for these trifles. Whilst I can't claim to be penniless, I'm not awash with spare cash and am

3

only enjoying this French holiday thanks to the unexpected generosity of a friend.

Most of my adult life has been dominated by two roles. Twenty-eight years a wife and twenty-three years a mother. Give me a fractious toddler, a grumpy teenager or a stressed-out husband and I'll manage. I can soothe, reason, cuddle, transfer money between bank accounts at short notice, and provide lifts in the middle of the night. What I can't manage so well is knowing what I want out of my own life.

I start working out how long it is until my sixtieth birthday. It takes a while. There's a lot of scribbling, crossing-out and double-checking, but at last I have my answer. In 2749 days I will be sixty.

2749 days. If I want them to, then each and every one of those days could contain something new and satisfying. For years, ideas have popped into my head, but because it's been filled with other priorities, they've popped straight out again. Now I have a chance to really think about them. I manage to stop my enthusiasm from hijacking me. *Every* day is probably too much excitement for anyone, but it's not unrealistic to believe that *some* of those days could surprise and reward.

A librarian from Sittingbourne made the news recently during the journalistic wastelands of the early summer. Lesley Evans wrote a list of sixty things that she wanted to do in the year leading up to her sixtieth birthday. These were not marathons, parachute jumps or exotic holidays. Instead, she listed simple pleasures that meant something to her. They included sending an email to Test Match Special, drinking a glass of Sambuca, protesting on behalf of 'Save our Libraries', and visiting Weston-super-Mare. The full list was published in a newspaper article. I looked at it with interest but couldn't relate to any of her enthusiasms. Why would anyone want to hold a tarantula or drive a fork-lift truck? These choices may mystify me, but I'm intrigued by the complex webs of likes and dislikes that make us all unique. Ask thousands of people, and they'd each come up with a completely different list of things they want to do.

I could make a list.

2749 days is just over seven and a half years, so I've got quite a bit of time, if I'm lucky. But of course I don't know if I'll be lucky or not. Nor do I know which obstacles will get in my way. Experience has taught me that. During the past few years my family has fallen off a metaphorical ladder. We had a run of bad luck and the fallout from this changed us in all kinds of ways, some of which I'm still struggling to understand.

Up until six years ago, things were going pretty well. My husband, Shaun, was a partner in a London law firm and commuted every day on the train. Home was a comfortable house in East Sussex where, with our four children, Will, Emma, Henry and Molly, we enjoyed a large garden, dogs, cats, chickens and various other animals. Life was busy, noisy and full of young family chaos.

I knew I was fortunate. But I never questioned quite what that meant until our comfortable way of life fell apart. First, in the space of a few months, Shaun's firm faced some serious crises and we were ensnared in these. Each day seemed to present a daunting new tax bill, or some other demand on our resources. Gradually, an unpalatable truth became obvious. With a big mortgage and no savings, we had no option but to sell our home.

We all loved it in our various ways and the loss of it happened so quickly that we were in shock. The new owners were desperate to complete the purchase as fast as possible so we had only three weeks to clear out the clutter accumulated during nine years of disparate hobbies and part-finished projects. I went backwards and forwards to the tip and the charity shop and managed to find emergency homes for all kinds of things. There was an automatic chicken feeder, piles of curtain material, boxes and boxes of books, and Shaun's precious collection of wood that 'might just come in handy for something.'

Shaun didn't express his feelings but I knew that he was

already mourning the loss of this fount of our family memories and symbol of his professional success. I understood this, and found the loss of security frightening, but at its most fundamental level, to me the house was just bricks and mortar. We were all together and my focus was on going forwards. We moved to a rented house in a nearby town, took a deep breath and started to make it a home.

Then Shaun came home with the devastating news that he'd lost his job. It was another painful blow to his confidence but he faced the difficulties and decided to set up his own company. He dealt with the legal side of things and together we worked on the marketing. Finding clients was not straightforward, though, and after six months without any income, we had to cut our costs, and downsized to a flat. Just over a year later, when our landlord sold up, we were on the move again. In little more than three years, we had four different homes.

Yet these calamities were not the worst. For Shaun was diagnosed with a life-threatening disease. He nearly died three times.

During all of this he dealt with the three litigation cases in which he was entangled, and I went back to college to retrain so that I could contribute to the family finances. I felt like we were caught in a huge ball of knitting wool. Whenever we made some progress, we'd get to an impassable knot. Then we'd have to retrace our steps and figure out another route. New treatments, new health crises, new business leads, new financial demands, new teenage vicissitudes, new removal crates to pack and unpack, new qualifications to get, new essays to write, new intimidating and contentious faxes... new hopes, new disappointments. It went on and on. In between we somehow managed to get on with family life and gradually many of these problems got resolved. As I sit in the sun things are relatively steady and have been for the past six months or so.

Some treats. Yes, that's definitely what I need.

I resolve to draw up a list of sixty things I want to do before my next milestone birthday. I want each one to enrich me and expand my mind. I don't know yet what they'll be, but I'll be surprised if they include any tarantula petting. There's been much in my life so far, that I'm glad to have experienced. I'm proud to say that I can trim a goat's hoof, clip a chicken's wings, and I've eaten sausages from pigs I've reared myself. I can address a roomful of people, knit very, very fast, and I have a PhD. Most of all I'm thankful to be the mother of four thoughtful and interesting children. Somewhere along the way, though, are things I seem to have missed out; yawning caverns in my knowledge and experience that make me feel ignorant, curious or shut out from the pleasures of shared culture. Perhaps everyone feels like this? After recent events I'm desperate to reverse this agonising feeling that my personality is being washed down a great big, swirling plughole. I need to remember who I once was and find out who I've become.

It takes me several weeks to work out which ideas are important enough to include. During this time I keep a notebook with me as sometimes I wake up in the night with a new inspiration. Other times they come to me while I'm driving. Then I have to repeat them over and over again so I don't forget them. At last, though, my list of sixty treats is complete. It includes visits to places both near and far, learning new skills, watching films, taking some very long walks, and reading books. There's also a bit of magic in there.

I think hard about why I've wanted to make this list now. Is it because I want to have some fun? Is it about learning new skills? Is it about finding out what I'm good at? Yes, to all of these but I know there's something else that underlies my need.

One of the most famous list-makers ever, was the British physician, Paul Mark Roget. His professional life was successful but his private life was peppered with sad events. Both his father and wife died young and there was much mental illness in his family. One of his uncles died in his arms after cutting his throat with a razor. Roget found that making lists provided solace and helped prevent him from sinking into the depression that afflicted so many of those around him. His enduring gift to the world was his eponymous thesaurus with its lists of synonyms.

Am *I* seeking to avoid depression? Not exactly. But I think I *am* wanting to fill a void at whose rim lies a difficult question. I've spent most of my adult life raising my family. That job is nearly done. Three of my children have more or less left home. What happens next? What am I for?

I type out my treats in no particular order, and stick the print-out to the wall above my computer. As I do this I wonder what the next seven years might bring. Will I be a grandmother, perhaps? How will Shaun have fared? What will I have learned through my treats? I could never have predicted the ride that led me to where I am today but I'm reassured by the knowledge that I've not only survived but have learned along the way to take pleasure in small things. The pink highlighter that will mark my progress, remains as yet, unopened, and the list sits pristine, the black type on the white paper, so full of the promises I've made to myself.

One thing's for certain. Like it or not, by the time this sheet turns pink I'll have discovered what happens next.

And it won't all be good.

AUTUMN 2011

ONE

THE VIEW FROM UNDER THE TABLE

I wake up and immediately remember I'm not in my own bed but in a cheap hotel at John Lennon Airport in Liverpool. Henry is in the twin bed next to me. Today he starts university. Although he's the third of the brood to go through this, I dread it each time. When Will went, and then Emma, there was the realisation that family life would change and our relationships would be different. This time when I get home there'll be just Shaun, Molly and me. Will has recently gone to teach English in Estonia and Emma has stayed in York after graduating.

I wake Henry and we're having a cup of tea when there's a very loud noise. The fire alarm has gone off. There's always the moment when everyone thinks 'it must be a practice,' but we decide to play it safe and set off down the corridor. Doors open and people peer out blearily, trying to judge what to do by looking at everyone else. We assemble outside where it's cold and windy. Lots of people are still in their pyjamas. A couple of minutes pass, then two fire engines arrive. If Henry had been small it would have made his day. As it is, he's feeling slightly edgy about university. I remind him how he loved his fireman's helmet when he was three. He gives me 'a look'.

The firefighters jump down out of the engines and go into the building. We wait and wait whilst growing extremely chilly. There's no exciting unloading of hoses or other equipment, though, and it turns out to be nothing more than a false alarm caused by someone with a cigarette. Eventually, the fire engines leave and we're allowed back in by an efficient blonde woman wearing a fluorescent vest and carrying a megaphone. I'm disappointed that she doesn't use this, but she does thank us all individually for our patience, and offers everyone a free coffee. We decline as we've got a plan for the morning and I'm keen to get going.

We've been told to arrive at Henry's hall of residence between 2 and 3pm so this gives us a few hours to fill. I know Liverpool quite well as Will also studied here, and I've made many journeys to either deliver or retrieve him and his paraphernalia. For a long time, I've hoped during one of these trips to go to Tate Liverpool but have never managed to find the time. Henry is also keen to do this, and we've agreed that this is how we'll spend our morning.

TREAT #1

We've only just got inside when we see a colossal table with four colossal chairs. By the American artist Robert Therrien, and called 'Under the Table', it's an exact replica of a dining room table and chairs, but on a massive scale. My first reaction is puzzlement, but as I walk below the table and look up, I'm unexpectedly moved. I've not been able to walk upright beneath a table and look at its underside since I was tiny. I can see the hidden texture, rough and bare, another view entirely when compared to the upper side which is dark brown and lustrous with polish. The bits I really like, though, are the corner joints. Seen from under the table, perfectly positioned and holding everything together, they have a purpose and solidity that would not be apparent from any other perspective. Being able to interact with this sculpture challenges my relationship with it. All the parts are reproduced so perfectly that it's easy to slip into a fantasy. I feel like I'm in a children's book; perhaps I've turned into Alice, Mrs Pepperpot or one of the Borrowers. Other people are wandering under the table, smiling broadly. We've all escaped the adult world and returned briefly to childhood.

Henry is under the table too and I wonder what he's thinking. I hope that memories of his childhood make him happy; my own recollections of being young are less than sunny, set against a wintry backdrop of parents who rowed constantly, and threw things quite a lot.

I put this treat on my list because I like the way modern art provokes disagreement and debate. If everyone could immediately see what it's about then perhaps there would be no point to it. I've had a lot of logical thinking in my past. Ranging from the banality of matching up socks and cajoling unwilling children through their maths homework, to knottier problems such as how to protect them from adult knocks like life-threatening illness and dwindling finances. I welcome the chance to reject logic for a while and to let my mind run free.

One of my favourite exhibits is 'Casserole and Closed Mussels'. This is a casserole pot with a column of glazed mussel shells rising out of it, and a lid on top. The artist, Marcel Broodthaers, intended this to be both abstract and a satire on his native Belgium where moules are so popular. But an artist can never predict how their audience will react, and my response is different. For me, it evokes powerful memories of a holiday we spent in the Loire Valley. Henry had just discovered the joys of moules frites and ordered them at every opportunity. Recalling this makes me smile, but I'm more ambivalent about mussels than Henry is. They annoy me in the same way that globe artichokes do—there's something most unsettling about finishing a meal and appearing to have more on your plate than when you started.

Henry and I drift around, meeting up occasionally and exchanging comments ranging from wild enthusiasm to utter bafflement. We see so much that after several hours we agree we've got artistic indigestion. This is a good point at which to admit defeat, so we go to the café for coffee and cake.

All too soon it's time to climb in the car and get Henry started on his new life. He's very quiet for the last five minutes of the journey and says he's feeling 'excited but nervous.' On arriving, we see dozens of second and third year students, all in identical yellow T-shirts, and each doing their bit to ensure that Freshers are welcomed and know where to go. One of them zealously slaps a post-it sticker on the windscreen and tells us that it's very busy today and we only have half an hour to unpack the car. As we wait in a long queue for keys to Henry's room, a friendly student introduces us to John, the hall porter, who is apparently 'an excellent shoulder to cry on' and 'always has pear drops.' I hope that Henry will need neither of these.

Then it's up and down the three flights of stairs a number of times, arms full and chin resting on various piles of this and that. There's the constant sound of doors slamming shut on echoing, concrete corridors. I suppose it won't be all that long before the end of term when we'll be doing this again, but in reverse. At last the car is emptied and Henry's suitcases, posters, electric guitar, amp, and mini fridge are in his rather sparse room. It feels very rushed, but perhaps it's best this way. I give him a big hug and manage to get out without shedding a tear. It's different, though, once I'm on the stairs. I can't make eye contact with other parents but I do take in the randomness of the items they're carrying. There's a huge drying rack, a pale pink pedal bin and the most enormous plastic crate of tortilla chips. No-one else seems to be sobbing and I feel ridiculous.

Once in the car there's time for a quick raw weep and then the post-it note reminds me that I have to go. I set the sat nav and head off on the four-hour drive home. By the time I reach the M62 about twenty minutes later, I've recovered. But a couple of hours further on I put some music on. It's 'The Best of the Smiths' and I sob again as it reminds me of Henry. He's always fitted in, uncomplaining and easy. Life will be less colourful without his quirky sense of humour, teasing, and regular offers to make me a cup of tea. What I won't miss will be his three-hour soaks in the bath, my constantly empty purse, and the strange things I find in the fridge. The latest was an unsuccessful experiment that involved steeping gummy bears in whisky.

It seems apt that today I enjoyed the first of my treats. It amused and mystified me, made me remember what it's like to be small, and expanded my mind. I'm a bit tear-stained—but it's a promising start.

MINCE PIES AND OTHER AVERSIONS

Later in the evening I take the lid off the highlighter pen and make the first mark on my list. I strike through 'Visit Tate Liverpool' and then stand back. From a distance I can't see the detail of what's on the paper but it's clear from the layout that it's a list. My own list and completely unique to me.

I've made lists all my adult life. Strings of 'to dos' whose creation is always accompanied by the comforting but misguided faith that each item will be addressed comprehensively and effectively. Some occupy a prominent place and become embellished with smug ticks and crossings-off. Others have a less illustrious existence on torn-off corners of paper that live as forgotten confetti at the bottom of my bag.

Very few of my lists make it to list nirvana, the equivalent of a bingo full house, and there are some that have *nothing* ticked off at all. I'm well aware that being the proud owner of a list doesn't, on its own, cause anything to happen, but having enjoyed my first treat so much I'm determined that this new list will get plenty of attention. I want every item to have its moment, when a line of pink highlighter confirms its metamorphosis from a prospect to a memory.

While I'm standing there I reflect on what it is about lists that I find so appealing. I'm clearly not alone in this. They're very big business and the bookshops are full of them. There are some predictable and reasonably appealing examples: places to visit before you die; films to watch; music to listen to, and so on. But I have trouble with a book called '101 Things To Do Before You Die'. I consulted this when I was making my list but I didn't seem to be in tune with the compiler. The suggestions include 'getting into the Guinness Book of Records' which is too competitive for me. I don't care if I never manage to be present when 'my country wins the World Cup' and I'm simply too old for 'throw a house party while your parents are out'. Maybe I could do this and shock my children instead. As for '101 Places To Have Sex Before You Die', I'd just be worrying about all the other people I might bump into there, all eagerly clutching their lists and ticking them off.

My head is full of lists. Amongst those that preoccupy me most are the ones that cover my family's likes and dislikes. This knowledge comes in handy when buying presents and it's helpful too in resolving emotional crises. I know that Shaun likes philosophical ideas, being active, and dark chocolate. He doesn't like letting people down and loathes horseradish. Will, our eldest son, now 23, loves mince pies, words, anything pickled, and travelling, especially in Eastern Europe. He hates bananas and gets upset by clowns, particularly when they ride unicycles. Emma, 21, loves going to the theatre, shoes, Spanish food, India, and being busy. She's phobic about sharks and worries about being short of money. Henry, 18 loves blues music, his friends, toasted cheese and ham sandwiches, and Dr Pepper. He hates mince pies and snobbery. Then there's the baby of the family, Molly, aged 13. She adores tennis, the Beatles, dolls' houses, and clothes. She loathes jelly and injustice and is terrified of rodents.

This is all useful. At times it's even quite interesting. The trouble is that for years my head has been so filled up with this kind of information, that there's been very little room for remembering what's important to *me*. On the one hand I've always loved black and white films, family meals, the smell of roses, and long walks. On the other, I've a lifelong aversion to Jaffa cakes and hate being cold. But somehow that doesn't seem a lot to show for my fifty-two years. I'm sure I can be passionate about many things but I juggled like a demented children's entertainer for such a long time that I managed to forget what they are. My individual patchwork of enthusiasms was started many years ago and was put on one side for a long time. I'm glad to have threaded my needle again.

TWO

A Little Planning

A basic premise of my list is that I've no idea how, or when, each treat will become real. If this was about goals then I'd plan them in minute, strategic detail. Treats are much more laid-back. I'll need to take *some* action to make them happen, but as far as possible I want them to sit in the wings of my list like characters in a play. I'll think about them and get to know a bit about their background. Then when the time is right, they'll make their entrance.

The seeds of my second treat are sown unexpectedly when I take Molly to see 'One Day' at the cinema. I loved the book, but find the film disappointing. The location, however, is beautiful, and clearly affects Molly. Emerging into a dark and rain-twinkly Sunday evening she asks, 'Where's that? Is it Oxford?'

'Edinburgh,' I reply.

'Well, I'm going to university there,' she said.

'Aha', I think. *'Take Molly to Edinburgh* is on my list.'

'Shall we go at half-term?' I suggest.

Within ten minutes of getting home we've booked cheap train tickets and found an economical serviced apartment by the waterfront at Leith. Now we're going to have to wait six weeks, but the anticipation is half the fun of any trip. A bonus comes when we tell Emma about our forthcoming adventure and she says she'll take the train up from York and join us.

TREAT #2

The Wednesday of half-term arrives at last, and armed with sandwiches, crosswords and magazines, Molly and I set off. Sitting watching the autumnal countryside rush past is just what I need after a frenetic few weeks and it's a thrill to see the sea flash into view just north of Newcastle.

Edinburgh is getting dark as we arrive. Commuters dash into the station on their way home as we make our way uncertainly, trundling our suitcases and tripping people up. We decide it will be much more fun to go on foot rather than getting a bus or taking a taxi. It proves a long walk but it's an excellent way to remind myself why it was that I wanted to bring Molly here. The buildings are grand and quite different from other Georgian cities like Bath and York. Those places seem feminine, whereas Edinburgh's refinements have a masculine reserve that make it handsome rather than pretty. It's a joy to see Molly inhaling it, and within minutes she's said, quite unprompted, 'I love it!'

Clutching our instructions we eventually reach Leith. Huge blocks of flats have appeared since I was last here, and the roads have names like Ocean Drive which seem more appropriate for California than the east coast of Scotland. After checking in at reception, we open the door of our apartment and are startled. The hall, alone, is twice the size of an average hotel room and there are five doors leading off it. We've got two bedrooms, two bathrooms and a compact little kitchen with a dining table and living area. And all for less than the price of a couple of rooms in a budget hotel.

I sleep well in my enormous bed and the next morning we discover that the bus terminus is only two minutes from the apartment. It's a relief that there's a bus there already as the wind is sharp and bites at our cheeks. We climb the stairs and with the front seat all to ourselves, we enjoy a cinematic view of the city at the start of a new working day.

Our original intention was to start with some culture, but the attraction of the huge John Lewis is irresistible. It sucks us in and we spend a guiltily enjoyable hour browsing bags, shoes and knickers before setting off to see some Edinburgh sights. First, there's the Royal Mile. We wander all the way to the Palace of Holyrood which stands in baroque splendour behind black railings. The Scottish Parliament building, opposite is a different kettle of fish altogether. The concrete has impressions in it, like handprints, and there are perplexing, rickety, bamboo structures stuck to the outside. It reminds me of one of the 'stickings' that the children used to bring home from nursery school.

The rest of the day passes in cheerful, meandering exploration and in the evening we go to Waverley station to meet Emma from her train. She recently decided to give up the office job that she's had since leaving university this summer. Today was her final day as she wants to move south and explore something more creative.

I succumb to another glorious night's sleep, sprawled across my massive bed and after breakfast we all set off again at the top of the bus, in our favourite front seat. Once we reach the city, we start at the castle and wander round the outside looking at the imposing views. The tickets to go inside are rather expensive, though, so we give that a miss.

Emma has heard that the Camera Obscura and World of Illusions attraction is fun. I've no idea what a camera obscura is, but it's only a few paces down the Royal Mile so we go there next. What a good recommendation it proves to be. There are dozens of fascinating surprises, spread over five floors and we start in a maze of mirrors. It's disorienting and very hard to navigate. Just when you think you can see the way out, you go smack into your own reflection. We spend a happy ten minutes here bumping into ourselves and one another. However, the *raison d'être* of the whole place is the camera obscura. It dates from the 1850s when a mirror was first mounted on top of the building. This can be moved so that it picks up reflections through a full 360° and these are then directed onto a round, white, wooden table. We make our way up to the top floor to see a demonstration. About twenty people huddle into the small room and the guide puts the light out. He begins to explain the camera obscura and suddenly there on the table we can see remarkably clear, detailed images of what is happening outside. We watch people milling around outside the castle, and cars crossing the Royal Mile. Then the guide does his party trick. He slides a small piece of card onto the table and appears to pick up one of these small, ant-like people. Then he bends the card to make a small bridge and the cars are 'made' to drive across it. It's like watching a film, but there's no gadgetry, just a series of mirrors. It can all be explained by fourth-form physics but must have seemed like a modern wonder of the world to the Victorians. It seems pretty phenomenal to me too.

There's so much in the building to keep us amused that we stay over two hours and for the first time in my life I manage to tune into a magic eye picture. I stare and stare, and suddenly from within the pattern, three sharks jump out. It's addictive. The display says that magic eye images rest the brain and I'm clearly suffering from acute mental exhaustion as I feel drawn to it again and again.

Next, I stand in front of a heat-sensitive camera. It shows a thermal image of my body and I wonder what would happen if I had a violent hot flush. It could be interesting; it might explode or set alarms off. But Sod's Law prevails. On the one occasion when it would be fun to have one, I remain stubbornly cool.

A bit later we have a pleasant wholefoody sort of lunch in the crypt of St Giles Cathedral. Then, wondering what to do next, we have a short debate and opt for a visit to the ancient underground streets which run under the Royal Mile. These form part of a slick attraction called 'The Real Mary King's Close' and we join a guided tour along with seventeen elderly ladies from the West Country. I heard on Radio 4 only last week that the collective noun for finches is a 'charm'. That for elderly ladies on a day out is surely a 'twitter'. They chatter, giggle, and prod at things just like seven-year olds on a school outing. One hands out sweets, and very generously includes us.

The guide, dressed in seventeenth century costume, takes us down narrow passageways and into rooms where earlier

Edinburgh residents kept cattle. The Close was badly hit by the plague and was, at times in its long history, a very unpopular place to live because of this. Several families would live in a room, no bigger than our sitting room at home. They had a toilet bucket in the corner and twice a day the contents would be tipped into the street. Our Leith apartment would be big enough to house at least a dozen families. Home means a lot to me. Growing up, poor, in a house that frequently had ice on the inside of the windows, I've appreciated the warmth and cheer of the homes I've created with Shaun and the children. Having to sell our house and uproot ourselves so many times in recent years has unearthed deep insecurities.

At the end of the tour the 'twitter' poses for an official group photo. The brisk guide asks if we want one too. Emma replies very politely, 'I think we're alright thank you.' This is clearly much too diffident for the no-nonsense Scotsman who retorts impatiently, 'Well do yae want one, or don't yae?'

As we blink and clamber back into twenty-first century Edinburgh, Emma receives a text. She's clearly upset. One of her favourite university tutors died from breast cancer a few hours ago. She was in her early forties. I reflect on how this is the first time that Emma has lost someone she knows well. How different that could have been. Less than a year ago, Shaun was having a serious relapse. We all felt pretty desperate then but nearly a year on, he's doing well and is currently in Spain on a business trip.

I realise with surprise at the end of our stay that I've felt truly happy for the first time in a long while.

THREE

THE NOTE THAT CHANGED EVERYTHING

I'm settling an old score by watching Brideshead Revisited. For nearly thirty years I've been incensed by the mere mention of it. Reviewers always seem to say when describing a new drama, 'the best since Brideshead,' or 'if you loved Brideshead you should watch this'... and maddeningly it seems that everybody *did* love it. It's a cultural landmark and I feel cross to have missed out on something so important.

I decide this is a nice easy treat to start as the autumn evenings draw in, so order the DVD. It drops through the letterbox and when I take it out of its padded envelope it says 'Brideshead Revisited' clearly on the cover. Unfortunately, it also says 'De complete serie. Naar het boek van Evelyn Waugh.' I have somehow managed to order the Dutch version. I need my glasses to make sense of everything these days. Fortunately a sticker informs me in very small print that the Dutch subtitles can be switched off.

TREAT #3

A few days later I settle down to watch the first episode but although I expect to love it immediately, I'm disappointed. The period recreations of Oxford and Castle Howard are gorgeous and the acting undeniably excellent, but it doesn't draw me in. The characters are insufferable.

I stick with it, though, and slowly, slowly, it gets under my skin. By the third episode I'm won over, particularly by the sound texture. Jeremy Irons' narration gives it an aching, reflective quality. Then there's Geoffrey Burgon's music which reminds me how fond I am of brass. Perhaps it's in my blood.

My father was a trumpeter, though I never heard him. By the time I was born, my mother wouldn't let him play. I'm so mad about the music that I watch each episode right through to the end of the credits so I can hear every last note.

There are small details that fascinate me. I can't help noticing that these aristocratic characters never say, 'Thank you'. And I like the way that history has added a new perspective. Waugh mentions in an updated preface that when he wrote the book, people didn't have the same reverence for historic buildings that we have today. Now, our 'heritage fascination' makes the location, Castle Howard, as much a star as the actors. Together with Oxford and the Marchmain family's London town house, it provides a quintessentially English setting. What I'm not expecting is to be taken to so many other places; Venice, Paris, New York, Mexico and Morocco. Some of my favourite scenes are on board a storm-ravaged transatlantic liner.

Thinking back, I've no idea why I didn't watch Brideshead in 1981. But one thing I do know is that it had only just finished its run when I met Shaun. I was living with friends in Putney and had recently broken up with my boyfriend. We were still friendly, though, and when he rang and asked me to a party at a local rowing club I decided that would be more fun than a Saturday night at home. Not long after we arrived, he went off with a noisy crowd of rowers. I didn't know anyone else there so, somewhat disillusioned and a little bit drunk, I turned to the nearest man and said, 'Men make me *sick*.' That was Shaun and we spent the rest of the evening together. When I left the party at 2am he suggested I drop by to see him some time as he was living in rooms above a neighbouring rowing club on Putney Embankment.

I'd found him funny and interesting so had no hesitation in taking up his offer the following week. I chose to call during the day, though, when he was likely to be at work. I was worried that I'd been a bit the worse for wear and that things might be a bit awkward so I wanted to put the ball back in his court.

Even more deviously I'd prepared a note giving him my phone number and explaining that I'd called by whilst he was out. I darted in, found his room, knocked, then, relieved that there was no answer, shoved my note under the door. I was making a hasty exit when I bumped into his friend Marcus, who lived in an adjoining room and had also been at the party. We had a brief chat and I told him I'd left Shaun a note.

When Shaun got home from work, Marcus greeted him with news of both my visit and the note. He went up to his room and looked inside expectantly but there was no sign of any message. So he went back downstairs to check with Marcus who confirmed what I'd said. It was all very puzzling. Then fortunately he had the brainwave of taking up the carpet next to the door. There underneath, was my note, carefully prepared to look like a casual scribble. Shaun rang me that evening, and we arranged our first date.

Very soon, we were spending a lot of time together and I knew I'd fallen for him. He wasn't like any of my previous boyfriends. In particular, he was strikingly bright and full of creative ways to solve problems. Where most people would decide that it wasn't possible to do something, he would refuse to accept defeat. I found his inventiveness both charming and exciting. He came from a background that was different from mine. It was very middle-class, with a father who'd been in the colonial service, boarding at a prestigious public school, and then Cambridge. But importantly, we did share similar values. He was honest, hard-working and believed in treating people fairly. And he made me laugh.

Just over eighteen months after meeting, we married. I was twenty-four and Shaun was twenty-five.

Returning to the topic of Brideshead Revisited, I'm pleased to see that it's ranked second in the Guardian list of top TV dramas. This was compiled by TV writers but despite a great deal of praise, not all the Guardian critics were won over.

Sam Wollaston called Brideshead, 'very slow' and 'really dated.' I disagree. I love it and it's been a great treat to make its acquaintance. That's exactly what I hoped it would be and I have at last turned into one of those annoying people who say, 'You haven't seen it? Oh, you'd *love* it.'

FOUR

A MAGIC KINGDOM

Eighteen months ago, whilst still very ill, Shaun managed to recover some capital from his previous business partners. The legal process had been long, stressful, and expensive, but the successful outcome made a big difference to our financial situation. It was enough to give us a deposit on a house and although our old house was spacious and comfortable, I immediately warmed to this small one which is undemanding and quiet.

My current compact garden with its pots and small beds is a delight and easy to manage. However, one of the regrets I had about our large garden was that I never made compost. It was something I always intended to do, but I just didn't get round to it. For this reason, 'making compost' is one of my treats.

Thinking back to our old house reminds me how busy we always seemed to be, and how we came to choose that way of life. We'd spent the first thirteen years of our marriage living in South London, and during that time we'd had Will, Emma and Henry. We had local friends, cousins round the corner, a good state school for Will and Emma, and Shaun cycled to work. But like many parents with a young family, we had a compulsion to seek out a different kind of life with space for the children, country walks on the doorstep, and animals.

I was impatient to introduce the children to the pleasures of country life and shortly after our arrival I decided to make elderflower cordial from blossom grown in our own hedgerows. I tried to enthuse Will, Emma and Henry as they helped me gather the frothy, heady fronds, but the poor little townies cried and complained that the grass was tickling their bare legs. They soon toughened up. Life was very different for Shaun, too, who now had to spend several hours each day on the train. And I had to get used to being in the car a lot. We had paradisiacal walks on our doorstep but in order to do anything sensible like buying food and getting the children to school, I needed to drive. A delivery driver summed it up when he emerged, hot and bothered, from the confusing network of local lanes. 'I've heard of the middle of nowhere...and this is it.'

Our small house was a squash for the five of us and although our long-term plan was to extend, we had no idea when we'd be able to afford this. Our family was growing, too, as in little over a year, we added a baby, a chocolate labrador called Harvey, and two farm cats. We'd also branched out into keeping animals that would contribute to the family economy. We started with six hens. They made wonderfully contented sounds as they pecked about the garden, and their eggs had sunflower yolks.

The next step on our smallholding ladder came when friends offered us two goats. This demanded a stronger level of commitment as chickens can be easily contained and are mostly biddable but goats are not. Gwyneth was white and angular, and looked like she'd just stepped off the lid of a Swiss chocolate box. Mirabel was quite different. A Golden Guernsey; small, timid and ginger. Wherever Gwyneth went, Mirabel was always there, a respectful six paces behind.

The garden had an old corrugated tin shed in the corner, and at night, we shut the chickens in there to roost. When the goats arrived, it became their shed too. They bedded down there and each morning I led them down to the woods where they browsed all day, munching on holly, brambles, nettles, and thistles, whilst single-mindedly plotting their escape.

We wanted all our animals to be useful and I nurtured romantic notions of having freshly-squeezed goat's milk for breakfast. We didn't fancy getting our own billy goat as they can be both grumpy and smelly, so I rang a local goat farmer for advice about how to get Mirabel into kid. She sounded as though she could single-handedly run an empire, but was friendly and invited me along for a chat about artificial insemination. I was about to put down the phone when she bellowed mystifyingly, 'Don't forget your jam jar and handkerchief.'

I turned up the following week with the requested items. My hostess put me in front of a billy goat, told me to wipe the hankie round its horns, stuff this inside the jar, and then screw the lid on tight. I followed these instructions precisely and then enjoyed a tour of the premises. They were spotless despite there being hundreds of goats. I was still no wiser about the jar, though, and when the farmer showed me to my car I asked about it, somewhat tentatively as I didn't want to appear agriculturally clueless. She looked me up and down several times, before issuing instructions to remove the handkerchief from the jar each morning, waft it under Mirabel's nose and observe her tail closely. If she wagged it, then she was in season and ready for artificial insemination.

For the next few weeks I opened up the jar, day after day, but Mirabel's tail remained stubbornly static. Then one happy morning it moved tentatively from side to side and did an unambiguous waggle. That evening, when the children were in bed, I loaded her into the back of our old Volvo and we set off for the goat farm together. She bleated pitifully all the way, but these complaints were as nothing to the rumpus she made when the farmer approached with a very large syringe.

We waited patiently for five months, to see if Mirabel was in kid. But nothing happened, and with a young baby I couldn't face going through the handkerchief palaver again. After a while we decided to part company with Gwyneth and Mirabel and were delighted when a nearby public school offered to add them to their smallholding enterprise. They went off and we got a report back reassuring us that they'd settled in well. Several years later I was making small talk with an acquaintance and asked where her son went to school. When she told me with an air of pride, I said without thinking, 'Oh, I know it—our goats went there.' I quickly regretted my words which made me sound excessively competitive.

We also kept pigs for a couple of years and marvelled as our first pair of weaners converted a large grassy field into a mudbath. These pigs and the ones that followed were always very cheerful but eventually the happy days would come to an end and the local butcher would turn them into sausages. Sometimes Shaun would give them to colleagues in London. Usually they would ask, 'How can you eat meat from animals you know?' Shaun's standard response was, 'How can you eat meat from animals you *don't* know?' At first the children threatened to become vegetarians but they quickly came to terms with the realities of farming.

Like the goats our first piglet pair were completely different from one another. 'Good Pig' never put a trotter wrong, but 'Bad Pig' gave us many headaches. One such occasion was on Molly's first birthday when we had a small tea party for assorted friends, godparents and babies. I was busy pouring drinks when the phone rang. It was our po-faced neighbour, Catherine, a wealthy City fund manager, who drew up the drawbridge up on her manicured estate when she got home from London, and thoroughly disapproved of our muddy lifestyle. 'Your pig is in my garden,' she announced frostily. I had a party dress on but donned my wellies, grabbed a bucket of apples and headed next door. Catherine had been doing some dainty dead-heading when Bad Pig crept up behind her and snorted. By the time I got there he was grunting greedily and tucking into all kinds of juicy plants. She was standing at a safe distance and shaking a rake whilst he showed disdainful indifference. Fortunately, Bad Pig had a weakness for apples so I waved the bucket under his snout and by trotting along slightly faster than he could, I managed to entice him back to his field. Then I did a botch repair on the fence and was back at the party in time for birthday cake.

There were many occasions on which the animals led us a merry dance and my first proper taste of this came a few months after we'd moved, when my old boss came down from London to witness our rural idyll for herself. We had lunch, then I equipped her with wellies, and we set off to take Harvey, the dog, for a walk around the fields. I'd always admired Pat's urban polish and wanted to present to her an image of an orderly, settled life in which we were at one with our new surroundings. Unfortunately, I hadn't yet mastered the art of controlling the family dog and whilst I told her about our plans for a smallholding, I watched as Harvey rounded up the local shepherd's pregnant ewes and drove them into our stream. I tried to carry on chatting politely but the unhappy bleats of thirty sheep became hard to ignore. Eventually I had to excuse myself. I waded into the stream and grabbed Harvey. The next task was to get the sheep to move and throughout this I could see Pat staring curiously. I was fully-dressed and chest-deep in freezing water, whilst attempting nonchalance with a flock of soggy sheep. Fortunately there was no lasting damage to anything other than my pride.

On another occasion a sheep escaped from the field and careered down the lane. After a lot of dodging from side to side, like a crazy game of netball, Will managed to contain it in a corner with hedges on either side. It looked to the left. Then it looked to the right. There was no escape. After a moment's hesitation it looked up and a wild inspirational light came on in its eyes. Time slowed down and we watched as it squatted down, sprung up and threw itself against Will's chest. Sadly, its bid for freedom was unsuccessful. It was a very fat sheep and greatly overestimated its athletic abilities.

SMALL IS GOOD

During these years our family life was happy but I'm not sure if I was content. Although I loved being a mother and wife, there were so many challenges that I never relaxed. Children are plenty of work. Add in recalcitrant animals, a large garden, a remote setting, and a major house extension, and you've got a hectic life.

Although we now had the garden we'd craved in London, it was not a straightforward pleasure. There was plenty of room for the children to play, but an acre of grass requires regular cutting or it quickly gets out of control. During the growing season it took at least half a day a week to keep it short. That was usually Shaun's job. However, we never had enough cash to get a really decent mower and went through a series of inadequate second-hand purchases, each less reliable than the last. We looked enviously at people who had shiny ride-on tractor mowers with powerful engines. And there were times when we were desperate. We would have one, or sometimes two, broken mowers which we couldn't afford to fix, and we could see the grass growing longer by the second. On the worst occasion, Shaun came up with some of his special brand of problem-solving and asked the shepherd to put his flock in our garden. It was quite exciting to look out of the window in the morning and see several dozen sheep immediately outside. Much better there than in the stream.

Whilst Shaun was in charge of keeping the grass cut, my horticultural role was to tend the beds and to introduce some colour. The garden was still essentially just a bit of reclaimed field and had never been cultivated. I dug enthusiastically to reveal bare earth... and then became progressively less enthusiastic as I realised how much it was going to cost to buy the requisite number of plants from garden centres. So I begged cuttings from friends and regularly attended the plant sale at the local auction rooms. I'd bid for all kinds of things and fill the back of the car. Then I'd get home and find that even this volume of plants was but a drop in the ocean of our large garden. Like the Roman Empire it had become too big to control easily.

TREAT #4

This brings me back to the topic of compost and may explain

why I never got round to making it. If I'm going to put this right now then the first job is to choose my compost bin. I browse in the garden centre and select a black plastic one that looks like a Dalek. Shaun helps me install it in a corner of the garden and I begin filling it with vegetable peelings, torn up newspaper, coffee grounds, and fur from our fluffy cat. I'm careful not to add any cooked food as I know this can attract vermin. This should be an easy treat as I'll simply feed it and leave things to develop. Just leave nature to take its course and there shouldn't be much that can go wrong.

As autumn starts to fray and the onset of winter becomes inevitable I reflect on the treats I've had so far. Their effects have been profound in a way I'd not anticipated. I've started to regain a sense of what I enjoy in my own right. There's a new energy driving me on and I'm looking forward to what comes next.

TREATS COMPLETED THIS AUTUMN	TREATS IN PROGRESS
Tate Liverpool	Compost
Edinburgh	
Brideshead Revisited	

WINTER 2011

FIVE

CHRISTMAS TREATS

An unexpected benefit of my list is that it gives Shaun and the children plenty of ideas for presents I'd like. They've clearly taken on board that I'm serious about these treats, and on Christmas morning I'm delighted to receive two DVD box sets; David Attenborough's 'Life of Birds' and 'Mad Men'. We've bought things for the children, and as they've each done the same for one another and for us, the number of parcels under the tree is approaching polynomial proportions; it's a relief that Shaun is now in well-paid work. My present to him is a leather jacket—it's soft and supple and he seems quite pleased.

This Christmas is different from last year and warrants special celebrations. Then, Shaun was seriously ill. He'd had a relapse and spent much of the holiday period in hospital receiving treatment. We didn't know if he would survive.

Although illness first cast its shadow over our family five years ago, with hindsight the warning signs were there for many months before. Shaun was exhausted a lot of the time and succumbed to all kinds of bugs. I admired the way he kept working, even when he felt awful, but I was worried by his growing frailty and tetchiness. These illnesses were vague and evaded diagnostic labels. They also coincided with our growing realisation that we were in a financial mess and would have to sell our home, so the obvious conclusion was to attribute Shaun's poor health to the stress that choked us like smog. And when we faced the next crisis, Shaun's redundancy, it wasn't any surprise that he felt no better. The demolition of his career was devastating but I did believe that in a perverse way it might bring some benefits. In particular, I hoped that a rest from the punishing regime of commuting and law firm politics would perk him up. Instead things got steadily worse. The day that his new business was launched he developed a chest infection and by the evening he felt so ill that he took himself off to A&E. Within a few hours our lives changed. This was no stress-induced infection. It was chronic myeloid leukaemia.

For the first few weeks there was overwhelming fear—but it's surprising how quickly you can adjust to living with serious illness. Shaun was offered gene therapy drugs and responded very well. These had only been available for five years and offered the hope that a previously life-threatening cancer could be turned into a manageable chronic condition.

Everything did indeed go well for the first eighteen months but then a routine blood test showed that Shaun had become resistant to the drugs. We were called in to see the consultant during his Sunday morning ward round. He explained that a bone marrow transplant was Shaun's only hope. With this he may be completely cured but without it he probably had about a year.

Siblings are the most likely match so the first resort was to test Shaun's brother. Several weeks passed while we waited for the results, but in the end we got the news that he wasn't compatible. Nor did the Anthony Nolan Bone Marrow Register yield any matches, so the search went worldwide. The consultant put Shaun on strong drugs to suppress the leukaemia but, whilst we recognised they were necessary, they made him feel awful. He couldn't think clearly, and this distressed him a great deal.

This went on for several months, but then, when we'd almost given up hope, a lunchtime call from the consultant changed everything. A donor was available, and he had an excellent compatibility rating. It was a one in eleven million match. The experts advised that the chances of the transplant succeeding were 60-70%. Given the hopeless prediction without intervention, this seemed a risk worth taking.

We spent a strange Christmas that year. All the children were at home and we did what people usually do in these situations. We tried to be normal. Shaun was weak but managed to do something special for each of us. He gave me some boots with a fleecy lining. I knew he'd chosen them in case he wasn't around to sympathise about my chilblains.

Towards the end of January, Shaun was ready to be admitted to the Hammersmith Hospital. I drove him up to London and they wasted no time in starting the treatment. As soon as all the paperwork was done, a nurse came into the room and gave him a toxic drug to kill off his immune system. It made him horribly ill. I held his head and stroked him as he moaned with nausea and despair. During the next few days there were more of these drugs until eventually he had no immunity left. His isolation room had a vestibule where people disinfected their hands and put on gowns before going in. There was a steady stream of nurses, doctors, domestic staff, physiotherapists and dieticians who were in and out all day but I was the only permitted visitor.

Shaun was on a strong cocktail of drugs in the run-up to the transplant and these caused hallucinations. One morning he woke up to see three brown sheep sitting on his bed. He called the nurse and explained this to her. She bustled off and came back with some drugs to antidote the ones that were already antidoting something else. These removed the sheep, but they were replaced with strange modern paintings. Shaun could see every fibre on the canvas. It was like being in an art gallery. By moving his head he could get a different view.

One evening when it became clear that his hair was falling out, I shaved it off for him. Then eventually he was ready for the transplant itself and the day before, a member of staff flew off to collect the cells. We weren't supposed to know much about this but an indiscreet nurse revealed that the donor lived in America.

I arrived early on the morning of the transplant and sat with Shaun in his little bubble of a room. We were full of anticipation but when the procedure happened it was astonishingly simple. A nurse came in with a small bag of fluid which she attached to a drip and in forty minutes it was over. Shaun's mouth was terribly sore so I nipped off to a nearby Waitrose for baby food, and then it was a case of waiting for the new cells to multiply.

This stage went unbelievably well and within three weeks Shaun was ready to come home. A team of friends helped me clean the house to minimise infection and then I collected him. He was pleased to be home but those first few weeks were full of anxiety. Any small temperature or other minor symptom might herald the start of an infection that could, within hours, become fatal. We got into a routine of twice-weekly monitoring trips to hospital and I tried to view them as a day out together, and to enjoy them. The woman at the hospital coffee stall became so accustomed to seeing me that she kept asking if I was 'staff' and trying to give me a discount. At first Shaun had to stay away from people, but gradually we got more and more daring and even had a trip to a restaurant one lunchtime. We asked to be seated in a quiet area but it was ridiculously exciting to be out together in the real world again.

We'd been warned to expect setbacks, though, and it wasn't long before we were contending with something major. On Good Friday, Shaun woke complaining of pains in his arms and legs like 'animals gnawing' at his bones. His limbs grew weak and after an awful weekend I drove him to London, feeling desperate as he wept. A succession of doctors showed concern but admitted defeat until at last a neurologist diagnosed Guillain-Barre syndrome, an auto-immune disorder. Numerous complications followed and just about the only doctors who weren't consulted were the obstetricians. Gradually and miraculously, however, all of these problems resolved, and after a year or so, Shaun began to do some work.

For a while life returned to something approaching normal, but this wasn't to last long. The next blip was a mysterious pain in Shaun's hip. Despite several appointments with his consultant, weekly sessions with an osteopath, anti-inflammatory drugs, and ultrasound treatments, he was in great pain and no-one could explain why. Then, after a series of x-rays, scans and biopsies we found ourselves back in the consultant's office. The leukaemia had returned, in the form of a rare, frequently fatal tumour. It was 6cm in diameter and had already eaten away at some of Shaun's hip.

Yet again we tried to have a normal Christmas, but inevitably it was difficult. Shaun spent much of it having radiotherapy in London and was clearly suffering both physically and emotionally. He was also back on the anti-leukaemia drugs and although we knew that he needed them, they were unwelcome. As before, they affected his ability to think clearly.

I was repeatedly surprised by his reactions, which were now quite unpredictable. This person that I'd known and loved for many years seemed to have changed. He said that he couldn't hug me because he 'only liked women with nice-shaped bodies' and when friends invited us to watch the Michael Caine movie, Harry Brown, he left part-way through saying that he didn't want to be married to a 'woman who watched a film like that.'

The donor agreed to provide more cells and Shaun has now had two infusions of these. The consultant is optimistic about his prognosis and has explained that these extra cells are often necessary to complete the changes started by the transplant. During the nine months since his last infusion, he's suffered from whooping cough and a sore mouth, but otherwise he's doing well. There's a good chance that before long he'll be able to stop all the medication.

SIX

THE PURSUIT OF CHOCOLATE HEAVEN

Truffle-making found its way onto my list because of headaches. Migraines run in my family. My father got one most weekends, and my sister gets visual migraines where she has no pain, but loses half her visual field. Nonetheless, up to the age of fourteen, I didn't know what a headache was. The notion of having a pain in your head seemed very curious to me, and when I saw my father suffer I couldn't imagine what it was like. It's one of those things like gout, labour pains and carpal tunnel syndrome that you can't understand if you've never experienced it. However, I soon found out. I started getting the odd headache as a teenager and gradually they became more and more frequent. By my early forties I was having a three-day attack most weeks. Although I was rarely sick, I felt deeply nauseous; like I'd been poisoned. Every movement made my head hurt, I could hardly keep my eyes open, and I was unquenchably thirsty. All I wanted was to crawl into bed and let sleep steal me away until it was over. This was usually impossible with children at four different schools, and a husband with a demanding career based fifty miles away.

I tried all kinds of treatments. A doctor of Chinese medicine prescribed a mysterious mixture of twigs, leaves and bark. I had to boil this in water and drink the vile concoction. Then there was homeopathy, osteopathy, the Alexander Technique, swimming, relaxation, and feverfew. Nothing seemed to help and the migraines came relentlessly. My GP prescribed Sumatriptan but whilst this took some of the pain away, I still felt like I'd been poisoned. Every week I was having to plug the gaps between the Sumatriptan with large quantities of painkillers. I knew they weren't good for me but I couldn't cope without them.

All this time I was sure there must be an answer and read

avidly about research trials and treatments. Then one day I had a breakthrough. I'd always been adamant that my problems had nothing to do with food, but one article made me think again. In the past I'd tried cutting out the well-known triggers like chocolate, coffee, and cheese; all to no effect. But what I hadn't considered was that I might have multiple food intolerances. If this turned out to be the case, then cutting out one culprit but continuing to eat the others would make no appreciable difference. Inspired by this discovery, I did an elimination diet under the guidance of an allergy doctor. For the first week I ate only foods that rarely trigger an allergic reaction; lamb, salmon, turkey, courgette, sweet potato, bean sprouts, pears and turnips. This made for some peculiar breakfasts.

At first I had a pounding withdrawal headache but once that passed I felt astonishingly well and gradually I introduced other foods. Broccoli, chicken, bananas, mushrooms, spinach and green beans caused no problems. Then I tried cow's milk and within a few minutes I could see flashing lights. These were followed by a tight band around my head and then the nausea started. The same thing happened with potatoes. I've avoided cow's milk and potatoes ever since and although my migraines haven't totally disappeared, they are much less severe.

It's eleven years since I made these dietary changes and I'm now completely adept at adapting recipes and annoying restaurant staff. The most difficult of all the adjustments, though, has been chocolate. For long periods I've avoided it. This has been a hardship, as I love it, but recently I've done some tentative experiments and can usually manage if the chocolate is very dark.

Last year my thoughtful friend, Wendy, made some lactose-free truffles for my birthday. She used goat's cream and very dark chocolate, and they were utterly divine. I enjoyed them so much that I put, 'Make good lactose-free truffles' on my list.

The week between Christmas and New Year seems a good time to start this treat, with plenty of opportunity to experiment, and willing testers to give feedback.

I begin by consulting a book about truffles that I bought many years ago in San Francisco. It captured my imagination then, but has spent the subsequent twenty-six years practically unopened, wedged amongst more favoured cookery books, several of which have been so well-used that they're falling to pieces. This book has always bothered me. I hate the idea of possessions that I'll never use. That poignant thought first struck me after my mother died and I cleared her house. She wasn't a hoarder by any means, but there were books she'd bought and never read, wool for jumpers never started, and recipes she'd cut out of magazines and never tried. We all have things like this; full of enthusiasm, we acquire them and then, for a variety of reasons, they're put on one side and forgotten.

I feel a similar sadness when I think of things I planned to do with the children, but never got round to. I never took them to see a ballet, I got stressed if they made a mess cooking so this didn't happen much, and the two metres of pink gingham I bought twenty years ago will never be transformed into a cute pinafore dress for Emma. They're neglected dreams, and lost opportunities that seem all the more poignant now that most of the children have left home. Shaun's illnesses, too, reminded me that one day it will be too late to do the things we dream of.

Mindful of all this, I'm glad of the opportunity to rescue my old book from its ignominy. There are plenty of recipes to choose from. Dublin truffles… Jamaican truffles…Yucatan truffles… They sound exotic but as a truffle virgin I decide to go for the basic recipe. I have to substitute a few ingredients because of my dietary quirks, so the small proportion of milk chocolate gets omitted and the cream is replaced with goat's cream. I gather all the equipment together, put on Radio 4 and get down to work. There are several stages. I melt the chocolate, add hot cream, and whisk in egg yolks and brandy. Then the mixture goes into the fridge to firm up before the lovely, messy bit when it's rolled into balls and coated in cocoa. These go back into the fridge for a bit more firming up and several hours later, following lunch, I hand them round to Shaun and the children.

This first attempt is reasonably successful but I have a problem. I set out to make 'good truffles' and how will I be able to judge when I've done that? One thing I'm sure of is that I can improve on flavour, texture and appearance, so after weighing up a lot of alternatives I decide that my treat will be complete when I manage to produce a batch of truffles that I'm truly proud to offer round.

This is clearly going to need some perseverance.

A CRIMINAL ENCOUNTER

It's New Year's Day and we've been at home for what feels like ages. We've played games, caught up with friends, and eaten too much. It's time to do something different so Molly and I decide to have a day in London.

We enjoy a leisurely breakfast and then as we've made ourselves late, we rush about and are grateful when Shaun gives us a lift to the station. This gets us there in good time and calm is restored. We're looking forward to a relaxing train journey and the last thing we expect is to get involved in a crime.

The station is one of those small ones where the ticket office is frequently closed, so we join a queue to buy a ticket at the machine. Just as the couple in front are about to complete their purchase, a young man appears from behind. He tells them that the machine isn't working and that they'll lose the money they've put in. He leans over and presses 'cancel'. The customer looks surprised and pushes the refund button. Nothing happens and he says angrily to the young man, 'You just made me lose £40.'

'No,' says the young man, 'it's not working, you'd have lost it anyway. That woman there lost her money too.' He points vaguely towards the opposite platform. It all feels very odd. There's a general fidgeting in the queue and people look uncomfortable. I offer my phone number to the customer in case he needs someone to confirm that he really did lose two £20 notes. Deciding not to risk putting my credit card in the machine we get on the train, ticketless.

When the guard comes round and we're buying our tickets I ask him about the faulty machine. Suddenly everything falls into place. He explains rather wearily that this is a scam. The young man who appeared to be helpful, and eager to cancel the customer's transaction, will have glued something up inside the machine to block it. At the end of the day he'll remove this blockage and pocket all the cash that has been rejected, but not returned to its rightful owners. I feel absurdly naïve as I remember how I'd smiled at him and as we settle down to the rest of the journey, Molly ponders out loud about being a criminal. She says she thinks it would be fun, but only if she could help people.

We feel more relaxed by the time we arrive at Charing Cross and as the New Year's Day Parade is taking place today, we set off towards Lower Regent Street to watch it. Molly asks if I know where we're going. Of course I do. I lived in London for eighteen years. Molly is wary from previous days out, though, and knows that my internal compass has been put in back to front. Whatever I do, I consistently turn the wrong way. This makes life very complicated. I often wonder whether my navigational deficiencies come from a childhood spent living at the top of a hill. Up and down were the only directions that mattered, and I could usually get those right. 'Up and down confidence' is not so useful, though, when negotiating the streets of central London. After half an hour of walking we spot a familiar sight. It's Charing Cross station, where we started.

Eventually we reach Piccadilly Circus and the bottom end of

Regent Street. The crowd is eight-deep, though, so we squeeze our way along to Pall Mall. There's a lot more elbow-space here and we arrive just in time for the first part of the parade with its donkeys, Pearly Kings and Queens, miniature steam engines, vintage bikes, Chinese folk dancers, red buses, and a giant rabbit. But my favourite bits are the American high school and university marching bands, some with cheerleaders and dancers too. Colorado, Delaware, Georgia, Florida and Hawaii; they've all come such a long way. Without exception they put on a great performance; the musicians blowing their hearts out, and the others smiling with perfect American teeth. With my passion for the trumpets that remind me of my father, I would stay to the end, but after an hour and a half, Molly gets fidgety. She's cold and a bit bored, so we agree to move on.

TREAT #6

We've wandered as far as Regent Street and are happily window-shopping, when there's a sudden dramatic downpour. Within minutes we're drenched so we take shelter inside the nearest doorway. This is serendipitous as it happens to belong to a large branch of Zara, and *'Buy something at Zara'* is on my list. It's the world's biggest fashion retailer and yet I've never even set foot in any of the shops. I discovered recently that the first store opened in Spain in 1975 and was named 'Zorba' by the owner Amancio Ortega Gaona, after one of his favourite films, Zorba the Greek. Unfortunately, after ordering the moulds for the shopfront sign he noticed that a local bar had the same name. His pragmatic solution was to come up with a new configuration for the letters and each mould could be used more than once.

We're thoroughly soaked and as I try to mop the drips from my hair with an inadequate piece of tissue, we decide to seize this unexpected opportunity, especially as there's a sale on. Molly's very happy to join me as she's always loved clothes.

When she was little, her urgent passions for Brownies, karate and ballet were entirely motivated by the special outfits they required.

We each gather a selection of promising items. Mine is a mixture of jumpers, blouses and a coat, and in the spirit of exploration I include several styles that I wouldn't normally consider. Zara's sizes range from XS to XL and as I'm a size 12, I guess that medium must be about right. But when I finally manage to squeeze into the first blouse I think I must have picked up S or even XS by mistake. My upper parts are both squashed and spilling out. Coupled with my inability to breathe, I decide that, all in all, it's not a flattering look. It takes quite a while to wriggle out and when I check the label, it is, indeed, a medium. This is very disheartening. I try to cheer myself up with the jumpers, but one by one I discard them.

Then I find one I love. It's boxy with broad black and white stripes and a slash neck. I also fall for the black, quilted coat. It's stylishly cut and the furry hood will keep me warm on my morning walks round the park. I like the pockets, too, which are deep and slanting so I can carry my phone and keys without fear of them falling out. Molly hasn't found anything she likes today but she approves of my choices, so I take them off and pay.

We're both feeling tired now and head back to Charing Cross station. I let Molly do the navigation, so we get there refreshingly quickly, and luckily the train is already on the platform. Despite the downpour and our brush with the criminal underworld, the New Year is looking quite promising.

SEVEN

HELP FROM A GOAT AND THREE BEARS

TREAT #5 (CONTINUED)

I've taken a short break from my quest for the perfect lactose-free truffle, but now, I'm ready to resume and am full of optimism. My first experiments have left me feeling that the Californian book is limited, so I've ordered a new, more modern guide to truffle-making. Like Mr Toad I place all my faith in this and feel sure that it will provide me with the definitive method. But I'm disappointed. It's full of clever and sophisticated ideas that I can't relate to, like peppered pineapple truffles.

Gradually, I work my way through a variety of other recipes, gleaned either from my collection of cookery books, or from the internet. It's amazing how many variations there are on a basic theme of chocolate and cream. Everyone who visits during this period gets to sample my experiments. The chocolates are perfectly nice, and my testers are complimentary but I'm still not satisfied.

One batch is too runny. The next ones are too small and don't have the right 'mouth-quality'. You should be able to bite into a truffle, rather than popping it whole into your mouth. Then I overcompensate and the next batch are too large. I try a recipe that includes orange zest. This is horrid. Another batch has too much brandy in it. I'm beginning to feel like Goldilocks.

Although I'm enjoying my truffle treat, I'm also frustrated because with every attempt, something different goes wrong. Then I have a brainwave. As so often in life, the answer is right in front of me, and has been all along. Wendy's truffles were delicious, so I need to find out how she made them. I send an email, and she replies straightaway with instructions. They're very simple. Just equal quantities of chocolate and goat's cream. Other flavourings like brandy or peppermint essence are optional. I try her magic formula, and like she did, I roll half of them in cocoa and the other half in chopped nuts. They're very good indeed. The family seems to enjoy them, and I do too. There's still a small challenge niggling away at me, though, as I want to experiment with chocolate coatings.

Another week passes, and Sunday morning finds me rolling a new batch and getting sticky. I put the resulting truffles in the freezer for ten minutes, then dip them in melted chocolate. They look a real mess and I wish I hadn't bothered. Wondering what to do next, I'm close to giving up when I find a video on YouTube. An American woman explains calmly and confidently exactly how to coat truffles in chocolate. I watch the entire eleven minutes and, abracadabra, it gives me the key. Dip the truffles in chocolate as I did, but then freeze them again for ten minutes and quickly drizzle melted chocolate backwards and forwards over them. This leaves a trail across the surface, and miraculously, they look almost professional.

Friends are coming over on Saturday so I make yet another batch. Later, I feel truly proud to hand round my chocolate-coated, drizzle-embellished, lactose-free truffles. With general satisfaction all round I declare my treat complete. But there's one major drawback. Much as I've enjoyed the challenge of learning this new skill, my craving for truffles is now thoroughly satiated. So much so that the thought of them makes me feel quite sick. I wonder if Goldilocks feels that way about porridge?

IMPERFECTION

It's now several weeks since I opened my Life of Birds DVD on Christmas morning. Ever since, I've been waiting for an opportunity, and at last one evening, there's a chance to sit down and begin to watch it.

This is the first part of a treat that will take some time to complete. I want to see the entire David Attenborough Life collection. This comprises nine series covering all aspects of the natural world from the deepest oceans to the furthest reaches of the Poles and jungles. The first series was shown in 1979 and the last in 2008. There's a total of 79 episodes and they've been repeated many times. So how is it that I've managed to watch none of them?

I've been expecting my choice of treats to reveal some insights and suddenly here is one, camouflaged by the unremarkable wish to watch an engaging presenter who speaks of the natural world with breathless reverence and passes the time of day with silverback gorillas. I realise that the reason I've not seen any of these films, is more significant than I first thought. It's part of a bigger issue. It reflects a need for wholeness.

Somewhere inside I believe that if I can't complete something then it's not worth doing at all. So, if I can't watch all of the episodes then I won't watch any. I put things off, with optimism that I'll return to them in the future. I realise that this mindset contains the seeds of a lot of my treats. Their germination has been delayed throughout my spring and summer. I saw my parents and most of their generation pass on. This didn't create a sense of urgency. Old people die. That's what happens. Having a husband who nearly ran out of time prematurely, was different. I lived and breathed the reality that life is finite. I can't put things off forever.

This desire for wholeness feeds the need to delay. Why do I have it? Is it helpful? If not, then what can I do to shift it? I don't have any answers straightaway. I talk to a couple of friends and am reassured to discover that although we express it in individual ways, the need for completeness is a common preoccupation.

Eventually I come to the conclusion that self-definition is pivotal here. Finishing something creates a change in the way I see myself, albeit in a small way. It's an experience I've had that adds to my knowledge and understanding of the world. Sometimes it just stays within me, but often it provides material for connection with other people. Enthusing over a shared passion, or even a shared aversion, is life-affirming.

But putting these beliefs under this new sharp spotlight makes me realise, that like so many other deeply-rooted human behaviours, this one is based on a faulty premise. It assumes that the mere act of completion will change me. In truth, there are many books, films and plays that I've seen through to the end, but without them making any impression at all. Often I nod off for a few minutes, or my mind wanders to other more tempting or pressing places. On occasion I've even missed the crucial moments that should give the whole experience its meaning. I watched The Usual Suspects whilst engrossed in a particularly absorbing piece of knitting, and I missed the twist at the end. According to my self-definition theory this means that whereas I would like to be 'a person who can enthuse about this ingenious film', I am instead 'a person who sat through it but missed the point because I was knitting'.

During the last few decades I've read hundreds of books, watched countless films and visited many places. Something in me fears that if I don't hold onto a little bit of each of them then they're pointless experiences. That my life is washing over me, leaving no trace. And if it leaves no trace in me then how can I leave a trace in the world?

This pattern I've just untangled goes right back to childhood, when I didn't know any better. I didn't understand shades of grey so it was all or nothing and probably a childish attempt to impose some order into the life where I felt powerless in the midst of disharmony. I'm disturbed to realise that it's stuck with me all these years, uncriticised, and I haven't recognised it for what it is. It's caused me to put off things that I could have enjoyed and it's compelled me to stick with things that I don't really want to do at all.

The first step is recognising that it's maladaptive. But this will only be worthwhile if I can replace it with a new more helpful construct. I take a huge stride forwards when I come across the Japanese Zen principles of wabi sabi. These state that nothing lasts, nothing is finished and nothing is perfect.

The first of these nuggets is the one that I can relate to immediately. In recent years I've often hung onto this when I've felt anxious about security or the pain that Shaun has had to endure. When you're in a good place it's upsetting to remember that nothing lasts. But when things are hard it's a comforting thought.

The second is the idea that nothing is finished. This is new to me, and it's enlightening. I've recognised that I put things off because I don't want to leave them incomplete, but this new aesthetic forces me to redefine what 'completeness' means. If I watch one episode of my Life of Birds DVD then that in itself is a kind of completeness. But then there is incompleteness, too, because I haven't watched the rest of the series. If I did this, then there would be the other eight series in the collection—and then everything else that David Attenborough has ever worked on—and later, every natural history programme ever made—every TV programme—and so it goes on; to infinity and insanity.

Then there's the reminder that nothing's perfect. My watching of The Usual Suspects was certainly imperfect. But so is everything that I ever watch, do or experience.

I think it's time to outgrow these developmental chains. I can take what I want from each experience and be glad of it. Over the next few weeks I work my way through the ten episodes of Life of Birds. I don't knit but my mind is still distracted for much of the time. It meanders along random paths. I ponder what I'm going to give my sons for their birthdays in March, I remember a hat I once bought for a wedding, I do a rough calculation of the distance from Exeter to Inverness, and I speculate about what it was that made the Romans finally abandon Ancient Britain. I also try unsuccessfully to remember the name of my first teacher at primary school and the Latin name for daffodil. In between there are some wonderful bird-related moments that stand out and weave themselves into a tapestry of memory.

I'm particularly pleased to find out about chickens' eggs. Having kept poultry myself, I've often wondered why they only lay once a day, and now I have my answer. The yolk and the albumen sit in the chicken's oviduct, and it takes a day for the glands to secrete enough lime to create the hard shell. My eyes water when I hear about the kiwi bird whose egg is a quarter of its own body weight. That's equivalent to me giving birth to a baby weighing over two stone.

I enjoy watching some grebes. They're attentive parents and make their chicks eat feathers. These line their little tummies and stop them being pierced by sharp fish bones.

One of the most amazing birds is the Australian Superb Lyrebird. I love it and clearly Sir David does too. He chose its call as one of his Desert Island discs. Not only does it mimic the songs of other birds, but it does a mean impression of the sounds that man has brought to its environment; a camera shutter, the whirring of a video camera motor, a brushwood cutter, and a car alarm.

My favourite, though, is the bowerbird, also found in Australia. The male goes to great lengths to attract females. He builds a bower from sticks, positions it vertically, and then decorates the surrounding area with flowers, stones, berries, leaves, and coins or bits of brightly coloured glass if they're available. He then spends hours arranging and re-arranging them, whilst various females go from bower to bower, making their choice.

Another tale that will stick with me is the shocking demise of the passenger pigeon. At one time these birds were amongst the most common in North America. The skies above the prairies would turn black for several days at a time as billions passed overhead. Then the seemingly impossible happened. They became extinct, wiped out through shooting, netting and forest fires. The last one died in Cincinnati Zoo in 1914.

The series was filmed in 42 countries and whilst many of the birds are unfamiliar and exotic, I'm glad that the humble sparrow gets a mention. I learn that they have markings on their feathers, like Army ranks, which denote where they come in the pecking order. There are the privates that have to give way to their superiors, and then there are the colonels with their black bib markings. Everyone defers to them. This finding changes me in one of the small ways that I welcome. Now, whenever I sit at an outdoor table in a café, I'll enjoy the antics of the sparrows even more by knowing that they're not as random as they seem.

My viewing of The Life of Birds has been enjoyable and complete. It's also had the unexpected benefit of being perfectly imperfect.

EIGHT

One of the things I'm most enjoying is not knowing how these treats will work out. When I look at the list on my wall it's exciting to trust that they will all happen eventually, but without having any idea when or how. I've spent most of my life being impatient and trying to plan ten steps ahead. But Shaun's illness and our financial insecurity have forced me to relinquish control. Gradually I've come to trust that as long as we keep doing our best it will be alright. Even when things have worked out in unexpected ways, they've given us surprising benefits which were often better than the route we'd planned.

This week has been difficult, though, as Shaun has been suffering again. We've become accustomed to complications since the transplant, but they're still upsetting when they happen. This one started with a fierce pain above his kidneys on Sunday night. By Monday afternoon, he had an angry rash down the right side of his body and we suspected shingles. This was confirmed by our GP and she gave him a course of antivirals.

He managed to get through the week and even did some work as there's a new client that he's keen to keep happy. It's Sunday, now though, and he's confined to bed, exhausted and worn down by pain. We were supposed to be having our spry 90-year old neighbour in for lunch but it's clear that we'll have to postpone. We don't want to infect her, and as for Shaun he just wants to stay in bed and sleep. He insists that he doesn't need anything except a quiet house, so I suggest to Molly that we spend the day at Greenwich Market.

It's very pleasant to travel by train on a Sunday when the carriages are almost empty and you're not only guaranteed a seat, but have a range of choices: table or no table; facing or non-facing; window or aisle, near the person with the noisy headphones, or in blissful peace.

We sit quite near the toilet, and this proves to be a very fortunate choice as shortly after settling down, I discover that my container of soya milk has leaked all over my bag. Since giving up dairy products I always carry some of my substitute milk with me and put it in small, plastic tubs that my friend, Helen, supplies. Her partner gets them from his local hospital but I've a niggling suspicion that their intended contents might be sputum or something similarly repellent. Although they usually work very well it seems that on this occasion I didn't press the lid on firmly. I tip everything out of my bag. Receipts and other bits of paper are all soaked and sticky, and there's a big puddle of milk. Pleased that we chose a seat near the toilet, I leave Molly mopping up the mess on the table and take my bag there. I lock the door and am busy pressing the red button and wondering why no water is coming out when I hear a disembodied voice inside the cubicle.

'Are you OK?' it asks urgently.

I'm puzzled and mumble that I'm fine.

'It's the driver here,' comes the rather rattled reply. 'Why did you press the emergency button?'

'I'm terribly sorry,' I say. 'I was trying to get some water.' I launch into an explanation of the recalcitrant lid, the spilled milk and my wet bag and then realise that he's not very interested.

'I'll get the conductor,' he says abruptly. And that's the last I hear from him.

By now, I've discovered how to turn on the water and manage to clean my bag. Then just as I arrive back at my seat, I spot the conductor peering into the toilet cubicle and looking like he's lost something, or someone. I decide that I'd better explain. But instead of being reassured he looks unaccountably sad.

'It's very big—and it's got 'emergency alert' on it,' he says.

After arriving at Charing Cross, we walk down to The

Embankment. Molly suggests it would be fun to travel to Greenwich by river bus, so I go to get the tickets. It takes a long time. The clerk and I debate topping up my Oyster card, the pros and cons of singles versus returns, and how to add a child's fare to an adult one. It all seems very complicated but at last we're ready to set off down the gangway to the boat. It's sectioned off by ropes so that the queue can snake along in an orderly way. There are very few people here today, though, and somehow we end up in the wrong bit. A fierce member of staff shouts and ticks us off. I feel disappointed to have had so many communication difficulties on one journey and for a wild moment consider speaking in French, so that I can feign ignorance. But fortunately, I come to my senses and realise that this might confuse Molly who knows I'm not French, and might ask awkward questions.

London looks different from the river. As we potter along on the boat, we pass the Globe Theatre, Tate Modern, and lion heads all along Victoria Embankment. These are mooring points for river craft, but they're also an important part of London's flood warning system. If the river gets high enough to reach their mouths then the Tube system and Thames tunnels are all closed. There's also an eclectic range of smart apartment blocks. I'm just enjoying a romantic fantasy about living and working alongside the river when the boat begins to pick up speed. It sounds like a plane taking off. I'm easily pleased and find this exciting. It reminds me of a washing machine I once had when my horizons didn't extend beyond the supermarket and playgroup. When this washing machine went into its spin cycle I'd close my eyes and imagine I was flying off somewhere exotic. I managed to get to Japan, Bolivia and other fascinating destinations, all for the price of a little electricity, water, and washing powder.

We disembark at Greenwich and go in search of the market. I put this on my list because of its reputation for street food and because I'm partial to markets, in general. Columbia Road flower market in East London is a particular favourite. I've often been there on a Sunday morning to buy plants, do a bit of bartering and enjoy breakfast at one of the surrounding vintage cafés. I was expecting Greenwich Market to be in the open air too, but after a short walk we discover that it's a covered market with its own permanent site.

Lunch is our first priority and we weigh up the pros and cons of all kinds of dishes including sushi, Korean, Ethiopian, goat curry, and paella. Eventually Molly chooses chorizo and potato stew with couscous and I settle for chicken piri piri with rice. We take our cardboard plates and perch on some nearby steps to tuck in.

There are dozens of stalls, and it doesn't take long for both Molly and me to spot a bit of treasure. She falls for a pretty pale grey cardigan with pointy white stars on it and I'm captivated by a small framed picture. It's created from black paper cut into intricate shapes. The shopkeeper tells us that this, and the others in the shop, are all created by his wife who is Chinese and gets her inspiration from European fairy tales. The one I love shows a procession of Lost Boys, walking through woods. Strange monkey-like creatures hang menacingly in the trees. The children stride along purposefully and play at being grown-up. One carries a make-shift flag, another bangs a drum, a third blows a bugle, and several have a rifle slung casually over their shoulder. Touchingly, a few trail their soft toys behind them. It would go very well on our bedroom wall which is still bare because we've been unable to decide what to put on it. There was a time when we would have had no trouble with this kind of decision, but at the moment we seem unable to agree on very much at all. I think there's a good chance that Shaun might like it and resolve impulsively that I will buy it, and that Molly can have her cardigan too.

We're having a lovely day, but I'm aware that Shaun is in pain, at home. I text him a brief rundown of what we've been doing. This is one of the most difficult things to negotiate when someone is ill for extended periods. Shaun wouldn't want us to put our lives on hold but it still feels callous to carry on regardless. Illness can crush the joy out of life and it's hard to get the right balance. Shaun texts back and says that he's been asleep for most of the day. He adds that he's glad we're enjoying our trip.

One of the things I'd hoped to find today is a new handbag, and it's a particularly pressing need after the soya milk incident. I spot the perfect one on a stall filled with leather goods. It's got just the right number of zipped compartments and a special pouch for my lipstick. It also smells gorgeously leathery. While the stallholder is wrapping it up, she tells me that it was made by an elderly man in Hungary. I say proudly, 'My son lives in Estonia.' She smiles but looks a little blank. Later when talking to Will on the phone I'm disappointed to discover that Hungary and Estonia are about a thousand miles apart. I'm also ashamed of my geographical ignorance. Perhaps this is caused by too much 'travel by washing machine'.

There's so much to look at and as well as buying some coffee, earrings and handmade cards we decide it would be nice to get a couple of small presents to take back to Shaun and Emma. Molly finds some soft duck-appliqued socks for Emma, and an organic chocolate brownie for Shaun. I decide on three soothing lavender-scented floating candles that he can burn next to the bed, and a hand-made passport cover for Emma. I tell the stallholder, who makes them herself, that it's for my daughter as she's recently graduated and wants to go travelling. She shows genuine interest, and asks where Emma wants to go. When I say 'South America, particularly Buenos Aires,' she beams and says that she went there during her own gap year. I love this kind of shopping that's so full of human interaction and shared enthusiasms.

We've bought more than I intended and at last we set off for home. As the boat picks up speed I recall the memory game, 'I Went to Market', that we used to play on long journeys. I wind back through our visit. Today I went to market and bought a handbag, a cardigan, a pair of earrings, a chocolate brownie, five birthday cards, three floating candles, two socks, a handmade passport cover, two bags of coffee, a picture and some truly delicious street food. It's been a treat for the senses, and yes, Shaun did like the picture.

A Tale of Tails

Treat #4 (Continued)

I set up my compost bin in the autumn, and ever since then it's been filling up nicely. We've fed it like a member of the family, particularly at Christmas when it got extra rations of Brussels sprout trimmings and cardboard. Poking around inside has revealed a satisfying number of happy little worms wriggling about. I've also checked on progress from time to time, by opening the flap at the bottom. This, too, has been ridiculously exciting as I've seen the contents steadily transform from a mishmash of waste into rich crumbly earth. It's been going wonderfully well—but now we're in February and it's all gone wrong.

I've been vaguely aware that the earth around the bottom of the bin is churned up, but with plenty of things to keep me busy, I haven't given it much thought. Suddenly, it all makes sense when I go to put some compost in the bin, lift the lid and come face to face with two fat rats crunching contentedly on egg shells. I put the lid on quickly, take a deep breath, and hope

I'm hallucinating. I take it off again, slowly and cautiously, but unhappily they're still there and whilst I'd like to compare them to Beatrix Potter characters, they're definitely meaner than that.

Their presence creates a delicate dilemma as Molly is phobic about rats. If she discovers that we have them in the garden then she'll pack her bags and leave home. I do some reading around the problem and find out that weeing on the compost heap is a good deterrent as they don't like the pheromones. Apparently male urine is best. I could enlist Shaun's help here, but with the sophisticated anti-leukaemia drugs he's taking, we might end up with giant, genetically-modified rodents. I decide to leave it to the professionals and search on the internet for local pest control companies. It doesn't take long to discover that my situation could be a great deal worse. One of the websites I visit has a testimonial from a woman who had funnel web and black widow spiders.

Some treat this is turning out to be. My romantic pastoral aspirations are turning into a rodent-infested nightmare. I select a pest control company and the next day two helpful gentlemen turn up. It's half term so I've had to fib and tell Molly that she must stay out of the garden as we have a nest of angry wasps. The rat-catchers poke about and nod knowingly. Within minutes they've got the situation sussed. Our garden is at the edge of some woods and that's where the rats have come from, tempted by the contents of my well-nourished compost bin. Whilst I've been careful not to feed it with cooked food, I *have* been adding egg shells which I now discover is ill-advised. Also, Molly has been doing lots of baking, and recently some of her bread experiments have found their way into the bin.

The experts put poison at the entrance to some rat holes in the garden and place further poison inside three black plastic boxes. All in all, this is money well spent if I'm to avoid more nasty surprises, and more importantly to prevent Molly from leaving home, prematurely. A parting piece of advice is that we should get rid of the contents of the compost bin as they will be contaminated with rat urine. Shaun still has low immunity and the last thing we need is a dose of leptospirosis.

Regretfully, I bag up all my beautiful, part-digested compost and dispose of it. I've got no option but to start all over again.

NINE

The Naming of Treats

My problematic compost and David Attenborough's back catalogue are both ongoing projects that will take a while to complete. But as well as these, I'm now ready to make a start on several other slow-burn items from my list.

Having had my revelatory thoughts on the pointlessness of seeking completeness, I've been wondering what this means for these three latest treats. There are four series of Mad Men to date, six Jane Austen novels, and at least twelve sections of the North Downs Way. Do I have to do them all?

There are definite advantages to completing some things. For a start, they may only reveal their benefits when I persevere at them. But is there a point at which it's sensible to quit? My friend Esther raised this when I was telling her about my list.

'But you can change it as you go through, can't you?' she said, pragmatically.

'No,' I said firmly, feeling panicky at the very thought of altering it. For years I had no way of holding on to the things I longed to do. It's only been by listing them that I've started to feel they're possible.

However, although these three new treats are episodic, they do nonetheless, have defined boundaries. I think the best thing is to approach them with the intention of finishing them, but to keep an open mind and see what happens. Whichever way it goes, I'll learn something about the content, and myself.

I ask Shaun if he wants to watch the first episode of Mad Men with me, but he isn't keen. I've been disappointed that he doesn't want to share any of these experiences. I think he finds the idea of them irritating, possibly even threatening. The word 'treat' has become inadequate to describe what they're doing for me. I've tried to think of a more apposite word but can't come up with anything that sounds right. 'Goals' is too worthy, 'challenges' sounds exhausting, and 'experiences' is both dull and passive.

There is a definite problem, though, in that 'treat' conjures up the image of something lightweight and fluffy. It's true that some of them have a light froth on the surface, but as they become real they grow roots that anchor my life and stop me from being washed around. They're not about self-indulgence. They're helping me recover and to stay passably sane. In the absence of anything better, I'll have to stick with 'treat'. Perhaps from now on when I say the word, I should toss my head and roll my eyes to suggest post-modern irony.

SHARING TREATS

Before I came up with the idea for my own list, I'd encouraged Shaun to think about things he might want to do, and he identified two. One was walking the pilgrim's route, the Camino de Santiago in Spain. He'd planned to do a section of it last year, but then he got his hip tumour so he rescheduled it for September. That time whooping cough intervened and so it's still on his wish list. His other 'treat' was doing aerobatics. We'd arranged for him to do this just before his transplant, but it was January and the weather was so bad that it got cancelled. The disappointment was magnified by not knowing if he would get another chance. This year in celebration of his recovery I booked him an aerobatic flying session for his birthday.

The airfield was deep in the Oxfordshire countryside so we stayed the night before in a romantic village pub. The next morning we drove to the flying centre and I watched whilst Shaun and a couple of fellow novices were fitted with their special clothing and given an introduction to the aircraft and its controls. Then we sat around whilst the instructor looked at the sky and wondered if the clouds would lift. He pursed his lips a lot, and eventually he nodded. From then on things happened quickly. Shaun was the first to go up. I kissed him and wished him good luck, and he lumbered off in his flying suit and boots.

The car was parked at the edge of the airfield and I watched from there. Shaun was by now in the plane as it sat on the ground making a lot of noise. After about five minutes it moved slowly along the runway, gathered speed and took off, climbing into the distance until it was a speck no bigger than a housefly. I watched and watched. Thirty minutes passed and there was nothing to see. Then suddenly without warning the plane appeared from behind and taxied along the airstrip. It stopped nearby and I went to meet Shaun as he clambered out, looking both upbeat and queasy.

'Did you see?' he said, excitedly. "I took the controls. I was doing aerobatics. I asked the instructor if we could do them nearby so you could see.'

It's not the first time recently that I've been unintentionally looking in the wrong direction.

TREAT #9

I settle down to watch Mad Men, keen to find out why it crops up in conversation so much. It's like Brideshead all over again. I feel left out and annoyed by not understanding these cultural references. Who are these Mad Men? Why are they mad? And what do they do?

Fortunately it's easy to engage with. The characters are strong, the story is interesting and I quickly unravel the conundrum. The eponymous Mad Men get their name from working in a Madison Avenue advertising agency. I particularly love the 1960s sticky-out dresses and Betty Draper's gorgeous satin lingerie. There are fifty-two episodes, so there's plenty to keep me amused for many months to come.

Soon after starting Mad Men, I add Jane Austen to the mix. I've always wished that I'd done English literature for A-level instead of science and ever since then I've been trying to make up for lost opportunities.

I start with Pride and Prejudice and enjoy it very much. This is a peaceful, relaxing treat. Not life-changing, but rewarding. I read carefully, as I don't want to miss the wit. If Mrs Bennet fails in her attempts to get her daughters married off they will have to face the indignity of dependence on wealthier relatives. But this route to independence frequently involves compromise. We see Charlotte Lucas marry a fool in order to get a comfortable home and to escape the responsibilities of caring for her brothers. Elizabeth's match with Mr Darcy is much more satisfying. We, the readers, know that she married for love. I know that I did too.

My third new treat is to walk the North Downs Way. On long walks you can keep putting one foot in front of the other and for a while you're relieved of having to think about anything else. You know more or less what's going to happen next, all whilst absorbing a constantly changing landscape and wondering what precisely is round that bend that you can see in the distance. If on the other hand you *do* want to think about life's knotty problems, then there's no better situation in which to do it.

I intend to walk it in sections, as and when I can find the time. It runs from Farnham to Dover and covers 156 miles. A lot of it coincides with the ancient Pilgrims' Way, the route from Winchester to Thomas Becket's shrine at Canterbury Cathedral.

Molly comes with me and we do three sections over the

course of a few months. It's a good chance to spend a proper chunk of time with her. She never has any problem chatting away about this, that and everything in between, but there are a few steep hills where she goes quiet and just has to concentrate on climbing. I simply enjoy escaping from everyday life and taking in the open chalk downs, ancient broadleaf woodlands and tranquil lanes. Some areas are boggy after heavy rain and I'm glad that we have sturdy walking boots. Whenever we pass one of the many stunning houses with amazing views, I hope that the people who live in them are happy and appreciate their good fortune.

A bonus of doing this treat in stages is the challenge of solving the travel logistics. The starts and ends are rarely on a public transport route, so we take the car to the start and then have to fathom our way back with a mixture of buses, trains and extra walks tagged onto the end of the day. One fortunate feature of this walk is that it's well signed. So long as I watch out for the signposts with an acorn on them, then I can avoid directional mishaps. We do miss the turnings a couple of times and have to retrace our steps, but overall these first three stages take us the 34 miles from Farnham to Merstham with escapism, pleasant chat and sweet exhaustion.

TEN

WHY THE QUAKER BUILT A SYNAGOGUE

On my birthday in early February, Molly gave me a card. When I opened it, a slip of paper fell out. It read: 'Mum's very own univercity of life voucher. This voucher is for a day out that I have planned for the Friday or Wednesday of half-term. You will be taken by me to several different places that I hope you will like. Bring a warm coat.'

I've been looking forward to this, though Molly has been mysterious and won't tell me where we're going. She says she can afford to pay for most of it, but would appreciate a bit of help with the train fare. I glean from various clues that we're going to London. Her 'univercity' spelling blip has turned out to be an appropriate and endearing pun.

TREAT #12

The Friday of half-term arrives and we set off mid-morning. Molly is in charge and looks smug. After years of corralling children, it feels odd to trot along obediently.

As the train nears London Bridge, Molly finally reveals where we're going. She consulted my list and we're off to do a guided walk called 'The Old Jewish Quarter'. This journey through the history of London's Jewish community captured my imagination when I read about it several years ago. I felt sure that it would feature interesting and moving stories of migrant communities facing the challenges of adapting their skills, re-inventing themselves and carrying on with their customs in alien surroundings.

I've done a number of these guided walks before, sometimes with Molly, and other times with friends. The guides are impressive and present an eclectic range of engaging anecdotes spanning many centuries. One cold January afternoon in Little Venice I learned about the history of the Regent's Canal and enjoyed peering nosily through houseboat windows. On another walk I explored upmarket Notting Hill. My favourite walk so far, though, has been 'Old Hampstead Village' on a Sunday morning, with its panoramic views over London and streets so steep they have handrails.

Our walk today starts from Tower Hill underground station and we're a bit early thanks to Molly's excellent planning. We wander round the back of the station under various arches looking for somewhere to have a coffee. I mutter, 'Why is there never a Starbucks when you need one?' and without missing a beat, Molly says triumphantly, 'There's one,' thereby proving what we all know; Starbucks is well on its way to world domination.

Twenty minutes later we arrive back at the Tube station, and spot a man standing alone and holding up a leaflet. We smile expectantly, but when I mention the Jewish walk he looks sad and points to a large, animated crowd. It feels callous to walk away, but I have to remind myself that (a) his walk on the History of Tea is probably fascinating but it's not on my list, and (b) Molly is in charge today.

At first I can't see our guide; there's just a mass of tourists with backpacks and American accents. Eventually, though, we spot a tiny woman who is busy answering questions. Molly gets out her purse and pays for me. She goes free as she's under fifteen.

There are a few words of introduction and then we set off. Our guide sets the scene by explaining that after a massacre in Rouen, many Jews escaped to England at the invitation of William the Conqueror. This clearly helped them in many ways but one sticking point was their difficulty in getting employment. For most trades in those days you needed to belong to a London Guild and Jews were excluded as in order to become a member you had to swear a Christian oath. Fortunately they found a niche with money lending. This was something that Christians weren't allowed to do and the services that the Jews provided, oiled the growth of trade in medieval London. Many Jews became wealthy because of it. Their privileged position also earned them the protection of the king.

However, these benefits were counterbalanced by suspicion and jealousy from other groups and by 1189 when Richard I came to the throne, things were so bad that he banned Jews from attending his coronation. Some wealthy Jews offered gifts at the gates of Westminster Abbey, but they were stoned by a hostile mob. The anger escalated and a false rumour flew round that the new king had decreed that all Jews should be killed. Jewish homes and businesses in the City were set alight. Many Jews were slaughtered and the others fled.

At this point our guide throws out a snippet of information that I must remember to tell Shaun. He's fascinated by the origins of words and many a family meal has been interrupted whilst he checks some detail or other in his etymological dictionary. As night approached in the Middle Ages, a bell would ring in the City of London. This was the signal for people to put their fires out, and for the city gates to be locked. The buildings were made of timber so this seems like a sensible health and safety initiative. The Norman instruction for putting out fires was 'couvre-feu' and gradually this metamorphosed into the modern word 'curfew'.

With this etymological diversion noted, we return to the story of the Jews and our guide recounts that after the terrible events of 1189, things went from bad to worse. By 1290, the English Crown was in debt and Edward 1 attempted to solve the problem by banishing all Jews from England, and seizing their property. Many were hanged or imprisoned and most of the survivors fled to France or Germany. Those who remained were ordered to convert to Catholicism, but actually many continued to practise their Jewish faith and traditions in secret.

Jewish communities around the world had suffered cruelty and oppression for hundreds of years, but this particular act of aggression gave England the unpleasant distinction of being the first European country to expel its Jews.

Over three hundred and fifty years passed with England's Jews living in secret and then things took an unexpected turn for the better. By 1656, under Oliver Cromwell's rule, the Puritans were increasingly impatient to witness the second coming of the Messiah. At this time, large numbers of Jews were based in Amsterdam, having been exiled there from Spain and Portugal, and one of their leaders began negotiations with Cromwell. He argued that Jews could bring significant financial benefits to England and pointed out the scriptural edict that the second coming will only take place when Jews inhabit all four corners of the Earth. 'There's a distinct shortage of Jews in England,' he observed cannily, and this was enough to convince Cromwell who then encouraged their return.

The highlight of our walk comes when we reach a synagogue that was built for this very community. We're walking down a busy modern street when suddenly our guide dives off to the right, and there in a small courtyard is Bevis Marks, the oldest synagogue in England. It's tucked away because when it was built the law prohibited Jews from having their buildings on public thoroughfares. Today, this is a benefit as it's in a remarkably peaceful spot. I'm surprised to see how plain it is on the outside. We learn that Bevis Marks was built by a Quaker named Joseph Avis. Jews were still unable to be members of guilds and livery companies, so they had to get non-Jews to do the work for them.

We pay a small fee and are ushered inside. My first impression is of space and light. This is partly because the windows are plain glass. It was commonly used during this period as increasingly people were able to read the scriptures, but needed daylight to see them. With a guide to demystify it all, there's a lot to enjoy. She points out the twelve pillars that support the ladies' balcony; these represent the twelve tribes of Israel. We count the large candlesticks and find there are ten; one for each of the Commandments. Then she points out a huge hanging brass candelabra. This was a gift from the 'mother' synagogue in Amsterdam. It weighs at least a ton and is reputed to have stopped the roof being blown off during the Blitz. Another six replicas were made, and together they represent the days of the week.

Our next stop is Spitalfields, or 'hospital fields' as it was known in the twelfth century when there was a large infirmary there. It's near to the docks and newly-arrived Jews often settled here. We see evidence of poverty when we stop outside a brick building. It's been converted into expensive flats, but was once a soup kitchen, and still states baldly on its exterior 'For the Jewish Poor, 1902'. Many Jews made money and were able to escape up the so-called 'North-West Passage' to leafy, salubrious districts like Stamford Hill, Golders Green, Hendon and Finchley. I escaped a poor upbringing, too, and our recent financial insecurities have made me fear my own equivalent of returning to the soup kitchen. This is irrational as we're nowhere near being penniless, but the dread of returning to my roots is deep-seated.

Our last stop propels us forward into the middle of the twentieth century, and yet more hardship. Outside Liverpool Street station is a large statue: a memorial to the Kindertransport. Nearly ten thousand Jewish children were rescued from Nazi Europe in the nine months prior to the start of the Second World War. They came by boat to Harwich and then travelled on by train to this station where they were allocated foster parents. The statue portrays a group of children with suitcases and just a few possessions. One small child clutches her teddy bear close. Many of the children never went home as there was no family left when the war was over. I feel raw as I look at my lovely daughter standing next to me. The solemnity of the moment is somewhat diminished, however, by a man in a suit who is sitting on the statue eating his sandwiches. For a few seconds he looks discomfited as we surround him. Then he carries on stolidly munching away at his lunch.

This brings the walk to an end and the guide bids us farewell. She's done a great job. We've been entertained, informed and moved. The rest of the day is delightful too. We hop on the Tube and Molly takes me to the Museum of Advertising and Branding, in Notting Hill. Then much later, after dark, we go to see The Woman in Black at the cinema. It makes us scream.

PROPS

On the way home I ponder the things I've learned today about London's Jews, and faith in general. We've only scratched the surface of their story but it's been enlightening and stimulating; inspiring too, to hear the cruelties that people endure in defence of their beliefs. For my own part, I don't really know what my faith is, and wish I did. I haven't yet found a way to reconcile my belief in God with a church that is man-made and has so many limitations. I've certainly prayed when faced with challenges but am never sure if I'm 'doing it right'.

In my search for ways to cope during difficult times, I've put my faith in various rituals. My friend, Tilly, is responsible for one of these. On my fiftieth birthday she gave me a Chinese wishing jar. Shaun was in hospital having his transplant, so there was much to wish for. She instructed me carefully. Whenever I wanted to make a wish I should write it on a piece of paper, scrumple it up and place it in the jar. I've done this many times since then. Family and friends have all been unwitting beneficiaries and I've made wishes for myself too. A few months ago I noticed that it was getting full so asked Tilly what to do.

'Is it alright to take old wishes out when I put new ones in?'

'Oh yes,' she said, authoritatively.

I've been doing this and it's been enlightening to revisit my old wishes. They fall into three groups. There are those that came right, for which I say a big 'Thank you'. Whether

I'm thanking fate, the wishing jar, or God, I'm not sure. Then there are those that were not granted. What interests me about these is that they're generally no longer relevant. The wished-for outcome turned out differently, and usually for the better. It's back to that practice of letting life unfold. Then there's the third group, which is a curious one; those bits of paper that bemuse me. They carry wishes that must have been important once, but which clearly don't count for much now as I can't remember what they mean.

This week I made a wish that Shaun would find contentment. Nothing seems to please him anymore. He's been through terrible times and survived them. But he won't talk about it. I don't know how he's feeling. I don't how to help him.

I'm in a funny state of mind about other things, too, at the moment. I'm hugely grateful for the improvements in Shaun's health and our finances, yet still dread the next bit of bad luck, and wonder if I'd have the strength to cope. This causes most trouble in the middle of the night. When I wake up to go to the bathroom I put my feet on the floor and go through a few seconds of disorientation while I try to remember which bit of my life I'm in. It's like forgetting which chapter I've reached in a book. I go through a quick check; am I in a good bit or a hard bit? It's been such a relief recently, to remember that right now, the book is fairly steady.

My Chinese jar, a bit of Buddhism, an occasional nod to Feng Shui, and an interest in Quakerism; all these props have got me through, so far. I also place an unfeasible amount of faith in wishing whilst stirring the Christmas pudding, catching falling leaves, touching wood, crossing my fingers, and saluting single magpies.

I've fruitlessly racked my brain to try and remember if I broke a mirror in 2004. That's when our period of tricky fortune began. Fortunately I'm sure of one thing. Neither Shaun nor I dropped our wedding rings during our marriage ceremony. That would have doomed us from the start.

It's very late when we get home and I close the curtains firmly to shut out the dark, and all memories of The Woman in Black. It's our own form of curfew. I ask Shaun if he knows the origin of the word and without even having to say, "I'll check my etymological dictionary,' he tells me.

ELEVEN

A Birthday Present That's Twenty Years Late

My cousin Rita, and I grew up in different parts of the country and didn't get to know one another until I was a teenager. We've been very close since then, and a measure of the trust I put in her is that she was with Shaun and me when both Emma and Henry were born. She's wise, funny, energetic and inspirational and is godmother to all of our children.

Rita is seven years older than me and in June this year she will be sixty. It takes only limited maths to deduce that twenty years ago she was preparing to celebrate her fortieth birthday. For this special anniversary her husband, Eric, invited Shaun and me to join them for lunch on the Orient Express as it puffed its way romantically around the Kent countryside. We had a memorable and happy day, and during lunch, I gave Rita her card and presents. There were a few small gifts to open, but the main one was the promise of a day together at The Sanctuary, the ladies-only spa in Covent Garden.

Much as I enjoyed the birthday celebrations, I wasn't feeling well and shortly afterwards discovered that I was pregnant for the third time. Deep stomach-churning nausea put paid to any spa visits for a while, and I promised Rita that she'd get her present the following year. However, exhaustion and the complications of managing small children got in the way, and then Rita spent a number of years caring for her parents, whilst juggling her work as a teacher. This difficult period for her, was followed by tricky times for us when Shaun was ill and our finances fragile. But my broken promise preyed on my mind and the final straw came recently when I realised that in just a few months, my promise will have been hollow for twenty years.

I text Rita to remind her about our longstanding date. And it doesn't take long to realise that here is an opportunity to combine two things I want to do. I can fulfil my belated promise and also have a wrap treatment.

I've long been intrigued by the idea of being swaddled tightly whilst covered in Dead Sea mud, algae, peanut butter or even chocolate. The clinics that offer these treatments claim that they help in eliminating toxins and losing a few inches. I'm not particularly concerned about these results, but do think that the treatments sound bizarre and fun. Silky skin is a bonus, too. I suppose I could try an at-home version with a large roll of clingfilm, a jar of chocolate spread and some assistance from Shaun, but some things are best left to the professionals.

Rita and I agree a date for next week, so I ring the Sanctuary and book us in. I'm having something called a cocooning body wrap and Rita has opted for the hot lava shell massage.

Treat #13

It's Monday morning. How lovely to be having a treat instead of going to work. The train is quiet and while I do the crossword, I hum under my breath. I've had T. Rex's 'Ride a White Swan' stuck in my head for at least two weeks and it's driving me mad. This isn't helped by the fact that I don't know the words, so there's' a lot of 'uh huh huh uh huh huh huh'. Everyone has their own earworm, and I read recently that neurotic people suffer the worst. I've got it really bad right now. 'Uh huh huh uh huh huh huh', and so it goes on.

There's no sign of Rita when I arrive at The Sanctuary, so I go to reception and book us in. A few minutes pass and there's still no sign of her. Some people are always early, others are always late. She's definitely in the former category.

The receptionist suddenly puts two and two together and tells me that my 'friend' is waiting for me in the Jasmine Lounge. I glide—the spa atmosphere is already working its magic—upstairs. On the first floor I find Rita reading a magazine and looking very comfortable. She's been here longer than me so is positively oozing serenity.

The helpful receptionist hands out thick, white robes and offers to give us a tour once we've changed. We disappear into the changing room and somehow it takes us half an hour to get undressed and work out how to operate the lockers. That and a lot of chat. Usually when we meet, it's much briefer so we have to talk very fast. Today is different. We have eight hours in which to catch up.

Eventually we're ready and the receptionist shows us round. It feels like we've stepped back in time and have ended up in a Roman bath house on ladies-only day. For the next forty minutes, we relax in the koi carp lounge; then it's time to waft off to the dining room for lunch. I order chicken, which comes with dainty vegetables, and Rita has bream with roasted salsify.

Our package includes various treatments and after lunch it's the 'infra-red experience'. This is a dry sauna where you sit with one grill-like device in front of you, and another behind. It's perfectly pleasant but I do feel a bit like a pork chop. Then we go our separate ways. Rita's off for her hot lava stone massage and I'm very excited about my cocooning body wrap.

I sit alone in the treatment reception area reading a magazine, but it takes a little while for anyone to come and claim me. A therapist bustles along and peers at the computer screen.

'Are you Gloria?' she asks efficiently. I'm not. It turns out that Gloria is waiting on the wrong floor. She's rounded up and trips off happily for her treatment. I carry on reading my magazine.

Another therapist appears. 'Is it Sophie?' she says brightly. No it's not and no one seems able to find her.

Elizabeth arrives. Lucky her. She's whisked off immediately. I'm just forcing myself to remember that everything is booked and that it's not going to go wrong, when another therapist arrives. 'Is it Lynn?' she says. Suddenly I feel popular too.

We go into a small room which has dimmed lights and a big treatment table in the centre. I'm rubbed with warm sugar scrub, then hot oils, and finally I'm covered in a 'rich body butter'. The therapist folds large plastic sheets over me and presses a switch. Slowly, the bed rises up as it fills with water. The effect is of floating but without the inconvenience of getting wet. The lights go out. I'm all alone.

'Spa music' plays softly. My thoughts drift and I wonder whether anyone actually composes this or if it's computer-generated. It's like a water feature that keeps trickling along. It does what it's supposed to do though, and very quickly I relax and empty my mind. I've no idea how long this bit lasts. All I can say is that I enjoy the novelty of mind-emptiness very much and when the therapist says, 'Your treatment is over,' I'm sorry that it has to end. I get dressed slowly and uncharacteristically serenely, and float down the stairs to meet Rita in the koi carp lounge.

She thoroughly enjoyed her treatment too and we settle down on a big sofa that's so long we can sit side by side with our legs out in front of us. It's perfect for chatting, and we enjoy our complimentary pink prosecco. Then it's time for the final treatment. The helpful receptionist threw this in as a freebie when I mentioned Rita's birthday. We feel a bit guilty in the circumstances, but it's too complicated to explain that this is February, her birthday is in June, and she was forty nearly twenty years ago. So we just say 'Thank you,' and accept cheerfully. It's called a sleep retreat. We lie on beds in a peaceful candlelit room. They vibrate gently and a soothing voice talks to us through headphones. Birds twitter as we lie in an imaginary hammock and visualise a beautiful garden.

My thoughts meander and I reflect on cousinhood. Rita and I are cousins because our mothers were sisters. I also have a cousin on my father's side whom I didn't know until, as an adult, we discovered one another in curious circumstances.

Although my father had three sisters, there was a rift in the family long before I came along and they were never mentioned. My parents originated from London but by the time I was born they were living in Devon, and far-removed from their relations.

All my friends had grandparents, aunts, uncles and cousins living nearby and I felt that my family circle was impoverished by comparison. Then one evening I got home from school to find my parents drinking tea and chatting with a stranger. She had a relaxed American drawl and turned out to be Aunt Eve, my father's youngest sister who had gone to Nebraska as a GI bride. She'd lived there for many years with an alcoholic husband and her three children. But when her husband died, she returned to her English roots and resolved to look up her brother. After some initial reserve, my mother decided that this sister-in-law was alright after all. She even went so far as to say that she liked her. Over the years I saw warm but eccentric Aunt Eve on and off, especially after I moved to London to go to university. She'd occasionally mention my cousin Maggie, the daughter of another sister, Lucy, who had by then died. Maggie was about ten years older than me and had settled in South London with her partner, Philip. Eve often said that she'd arrange a meeting but then she decided to go back to America and we lost contact.

Time passed whilst Shaun and I lived in various parts of South London. We started off in Putney, then we moved to Wandsworth, and finally we settled in Balham. Our house was a typical Edwardian terrace. There are thousands and thousands of similar homes in South London, the gardens of adjacent streets backing onto one another like mirror images. Our kitchen window looked out over the backs of other houses, which were remarkably uniform, apart from one. This had a stylish loft conversion and was two doors to the left of the house immediately behind ours. Shaun and I agreed that if we ever extended our house we would copy what these people had done.

One evening we were invited for dinner with some friends who lived a couple of streets away. Two other local couples were invited as well; one we knew and the other we didn't. We were all making pleasant conversation when I realised that our new acquaintances were called Maggie and Philip. The inevitable question flashed across my mind, and then I couldn't get rid of it. This was a very tricky situation. You can't say to someone you've just met, 'I think you might be my cousin,' especially when other people are there. You risk being branded a fantasist who specialises in collecting new family members. I wasn't prepared to risk my local reputation so I knew I had to tread cautiously.

I racked my brains and tried to think of all the things I knew about my cousin Maggie, but came up with only a few vague, disconnected memories. I tried asking 'dinner-party Maggie' where she grew up... what she did... whether her father was an engineer... whether he was still alive... whether she had any siblings... where they lived...whether any of them were involved in farming...whether she had any family connections with Somerset... and all kinds of other questions. My knowledge of my cousin's background was so hazy, however, that none of them resolved the issue. Also my interviewee seemed naturally inclined to diffidence and was a little wary of this intrusive dinner guest who bombarded her with peculiar questions. Shaun had no idea about the torment I was suffering.

We moved into the dining room. I tried to keep up some light conversational probing but inside I was becoming hysterical. I couldn't let this opportunity pass without finding out if my hunch was correct. Then just as we'd started the main course there was a lull in the conversation and I thought of the killer question.

I took a deep breath and asked, 'Maggie, do you have an aunt called Eve who lives in America?'

'Yes, I do,' she replied cautiously, looking stunned.

'Then you're my cousin,' I blurted with relief.

It was an extraordinary evening. We discovered that despite me growing up in Devon and Maggie being raised in Kent, we had for some time been living almost back to back in South London. Their house turned out to be the one with the stylish loft conversion.

The next day we introduced all the children to one another.

Their daughters Rebekah and Catherine were at the same school as our children, but a couple of years ahead. Philip has said many times that the biggest miracle was not that we found one another, but that we all got on so well, once we did.

The sleep retreat comes to an end and very soon it's time to get dressed and return to the outside world. Rita says generously that today has been worth waiting twenty years for. When I wake up the next morning I'm amazed at how deeply I've slept. I feel unusually refreshed and astonishingly serene. A good night's sleep, babies-bottom skin, and life-enhancing relationships; these are all reasons to be cheerful. And then there are the miracles. Some people find fairies at the bottom of their garden. Very few find cousins.

TREATS COMPLETED THIS WINTER	TREATS IN PROGRESS
Zara	Compost
Truffles	Mad Men
Greenwich Market	Life on Earth
Jewish walk	North Downs Way
Wrap	Jane Austen

SPRING 2012

TWELVE

Plenty of Sunlight but not a lot of sunshine

I've got used to Henry being away. I've missed him, though, and resolve to go up to Liverpool so that we can spend a few days together. I organise a three-night stay in a small hotel overlooking Sefton Park. This stretch of Victorian greenery comes complete with a romantic glass palm house, lake and bandstand.

Everything is settled and then out of the blue, there's an unexpected bonus. Will has been teaching English in Estonia since the autumn, and announces that he's going to be visiting Liverpool for a week with some of his students; by sheer serendipity it will coincide with my stay.

The week of my visit arrives, but unfortunately it gets off to a bad start. I have a terrible cold. Elephantine sneezes and a sore throat combine to make me feel rotten. I can't see through my streaming eyes to read, let alone drive 260 miles, so I delay my journey by a day. But when I do finally reach Liverpool, it's well worth waiting for. My room is tiny but has everything I need, and it's only a ten minute walk away from Henry's hall of residence.

We arrange to meet at six at my hotel and Henry is very prompt. He always amazes me with his sartorial experiments and today's ensemble is no exception. It includes a turquoise paisley bandana tied around his head, Keith Richards-style, and a long sheepskin coat.

We walk companionably to a small Italian restaurant where Will is already waiting. We swap news and hear about his experiences in Tallinn. As one of the few native English speakers in his school he's often called upon to provide information. One Russian teacher avidly studies her Lonely Planet Guide to the UK and whenever she's puzzled she consults Will.

'Is it true,' she asked him recently, 'that in Britain, you sometimes call Marks and Spencer, Marks and Sparks?'

Retail is not Will's specialist subject but he considered the matter for a moment, and then nodded assertively. 'Yes—I think we do,' he said.

'Incredible!' the teacher replied happily, and set off to teach her class of Russian teenagers about the idiosyncrasies of British life.

The next morning it's a relief to wake up feeling better. My cold has shifted so I celebrate with a walk and breakfast in Sefton Park. There are swathes of daffodils all around the lake and it looks beautiful. The winter has felt long with rain outside the window and marital chilliness inside. I sit outside the little café munching my toasted bacon and tomato sandwich and sipping from a large mug of tea. I can't say it's sunny, though, so I keep my coat firmly on.

In fact I can't say I've ever seen sunshine in Liverpool. My first visit was in the summer of 2003 when we spent a family weekend here on our way back from Scotland. The day we drove home, we left torrential rain in Liverpool, only to find the South of England baking in the hottest day ever recorded. Since then, I've visited a number of times, whilst Will was at university, and it's always been wet. On one occasion the downpour began as I passed the 'Welcome to Liverpool' sign. Henry and Will assure me that it doesn't rain all the time, but when I checked the yearly rainfall figures I found that Liverpool's are indeed significantly higher than those for London. Anyway, the sogginess doesn't dent my affection for the place. I love it. When I look at the waterfront I become dreamily romantic, imagining people standing there with all their worldly possessions, full of hope, and just about to set sail for a new life overseas. Between 1830 and 1930 more than nine million emigrants joined ships here, bound for either the USA, Canada or Australia. It took thirty-five days to reach North America, and anything between ten and seventeen weeks to get to Australia.

Henry is in a lecture all morning and Will is busy with his students until lunchtime. This gives me an opportunity to go to Port Sunlight. I'm keen on Victorian social history and a visit to this model workers' village was one of the first treats I put on my list.

Breakfast over, I get the train to Liverpool Central. From there, I pick up another one to Port Sunlight station and when I get off the train it feels very familiar. I can't think why at first, and then I realise. It reminds me of Bekonscot Model Village in Beaconsfield, a favourite when the children were young. Like Bekonscot, Port Sunlight is a village that's tidy, manicured, and from another era. However, although it's called a model village, in this case it doesn't mean miniature, and people have lived here for over a hundred years. In fact it's still inhabited. Despite this, it's very, very quiet. There's hardly anyone around apart from a well-behaved party of schoolchildren busily filling in worksheets. They have that slightly bent-over earnest look that children get when they carry backpacks.

I make for the museum as this seems a good place to start. It's showing an entertaining short film about the history of the village and the fascinating story of the man who created it.

William Hesketh Lever was born in 1851. As a young man, he was employed in his father's grocery business in Bolton where one of his tasks was to cut up foot-long bars of soap into small saleable blocks. This was horrible stuff that was made by boiling animal fat and skimming off the gritty solids that floated to the surface. It smelt foul and rapidly went rancid. William was sure that this could be improved and got together with his brother James to form the Lever Brothers company in Warrington. There, they manufactured soap that was perfumed and produced a lather. There were other soaps on the market, but one of the innovations that marked out Sunlight Soap was its brightly-coloured cardboard packaging. William had a natural instinct for advertising and employed a team of salesmen whose job was to persuade shopkeepers to stock Sunlight Soap. Some even did door-to-door selling, visiting housewives in their homes and urging them to buy this miracle product that would make their busy lives easier and their laundry smell fresh. His methods paid off and the business grew rapidly. Before long it was manufacturing tons of soap each week and exporting it all around the British Empire.

As demand increased, the need for bigger premises became urgent and the brothers chose a site on marshland outside Birkenhead. Construction work began in 1888 and although it looked an unpromising environment it gave William just the platform he needed from which to carry out some of his radical ideas. Unusually for the time, he recognised that there could be no large profits without the support of his employees. He wanted to give some of the money back to them and came up with the idea of building a village where they could live healthily and happily. Not only did he recognise that tired, impoverished people are unlikely to be willing, industrious workers but he genuinely cared about their welfare, too.

The design of the village was orchestrated by William with meticulous care and he hired thirty architects to provide a mix of styles. They were instructed that the houses must be pleasing to look at and comfortable to live in. Space, light and a garden were to be fundamental features. Each home was to have a parlour, kitchen, hot and cold running water, and exceptionally for the time, a bathroom complete with a plumbed-in bath. At a time when slum areas typically had 150 homes per acre, Port Sunlight boasted just 13.5. And it wasn't just the bricks and mortar that concerned William. His philosophy encompassed an entire lifestyle that was packed with community and cultural activities. Amongst the many organisations on offer in the village were book clubs, a scientific society, a silver band, theatre, men's and women's football clubs, a gymnastics club, a library and an anti-cigarette league. Port Sunlight residents enjoyed summer picnics, fancy dress balls, dances, concerts in the bandstand, and swimming in the outdoor pool. There were green spaces where the children could play, and a school where, unusually, boys and girls were educated together. All in all, the conditions for workers were way ahead of their time. They got a week's paid holiday, membership of a pension scheme, subsidised entertainments, and free healthcare in the cottage hospital, years before there was a National Health Service. Surprisingly, there was one privilege that workers were not granted. A discount on soap.

The museum paints an idyllic view of the village, but I'm moved to wonder about the inevitable selectiveness of history. Skilled curation must present us with constant surprises. Either because people in the past were remarkably similar to us in their habits or attitudes, despite their different environment. Or the more common route to audience satisfaction is to recount how they were different from us in unexpected ways. If we were to pay our money and hear about people who are just like ourselves, it would be dull. But picking out the surprising bits often leads to an idealised view of the past. There are pictures here in the museum that show cheery residents beaming self-consciously at the camera, as they enjoy their modern homes and community entertainments. I wonder about the hidden miseries of depression and hollow marriages that must be there in the background. They were with us then, still are, and always will be.

The museum also recounts that William had some unusual habits. One of the oddest was his insistence on sleeping in the open air. In each of his homes he had a platform created in his bedroom, where he slept with his wife Elizabeth. Although the couple were sheltered to some extent by a canopy, they were exposed to rain, wind and even snow. William was also keen on cold baths, and liked to work at a specially-designed tall desk that enabled him to stand up.

Art was one of William's major interests and, a businessman to his core, this initially grew out of his search for pictures that could be used in soap adverts. But very quickly he developed an eclectic taste that didn't revolve around suds, and he used his immense wealth to build up a world-class collection. This is now housed in the village, in the Lady Lever Art Gallery. It opened in 1922 just after the death of his wife, Elizabeth, to whom he was happily married for forty years, despite their uncomfortable sleeping arrangements.

The gallery is astounding with room after room of treasures. I'm particularly drawn to a collection of furniture that's embellished with exquisite marquetry. Then there are paintings by Constable, Gainsborough, Turner, and a number of Pre-Raphaelites. In another room are display units crammed full of Roman figurines and Ancient Greek urns. Of less value, I imagine, but still very enjoyable, is a collection of early twentieth-century architectural photography. One of the photographers, Bedford Lemere, rather endearingly listed 'cheering people up' as one of his hobbies.

It would take several days to do proper justice to everything that is here, and of necessity my visit is brief as I've arranged to spend the afternoon in Liverpool with the boys. The main thing that strikes me, though, is that all these incredible riches came from one product: soap.

Despite a few reservations about historical selectiveness, this visit has absorbed and moved me with details of real people and their everyday lives. The broad brushstrokes of political and economic history don't engross me. It's always the relationships that I want to hear about. It's the same in my own life. My husband, my children, my extended family, and my friends. They're the most important things. This has helped in coping with our reduced circumstances and many of my relationships have blossomed during this time, as I've drawn on the love and support of family and friends.

This hasn't helped Shaun in the same way, though, and

baring his vulnerabilities to other people has been painful. I tell him that we have the most important things in life, but this doesn't seem to offer any comfort. I heard recently that it's easy to understand people like ourselves. The clever bit is understanding those who are different. I don't feel very clever at the moment.

Still feeling like I've landed in a miniature village, I remember various days out with the children. We had many enjoyable trips. It's easy to remember these in sepia-tinted museum hues, but there were some disastrous ones, too, when we all argued and came home grumpy. Such is family life. Much as I loved having young children, there were times when I was exhausted and it was very hard work. Logically, I should be glad that this phase is in the past but nonetheless love sprinkles an aching poignancy over these memories, confusing me so that I have to make an effort to remind myself that life is about making the most of 'now'.

At the time when Port Sunlight was built, many families had ten or more offspring. I found four children a challenge but then today most people expect to pack a lot into their lives and I think nothing, for example, of driving seventy miles each way to have lunch with my sister. Our standard of living has increased beyond anything that the Victorians could have imagined, but life is not necessarily simpler. There never seems to be a time when all of our labour-saving devices are fully functioning. Right now the ice-maker in the fridge has stopped working and one of the low-voltage light bulbs in the kitchen is dead. I keep putting off dealing with it because it's awkward to change. Then there's the microwave that works erratically, and the dashboard display in the car which flickers on and off. There's a wonky lampshade in the sitting room, and I could go on and on. The more we have, the more there is to look after and fret about.

Contrasted with the harshness of Victorian conditions when infant mortality was high, and life expectancy short, it seems ungrateful to even intimate that life is hard for us. However, I can't help but think that modern life is very stressful too, but in a different way. There's so much pressure to earn money and to keep up a high standard of living. In our family this has fallen mostly on Shaun's shoulders. One of my favourite possessions is a plaque on our kitchen wall that just says, 'Simplify'. It reminds me that I do have a choice.

I hop on the train back to Liverpool, and Will and Henry meet me at the station. We have a coffee at the new Liverpool Museum and as we're sitting there, Will hands me a package. It's a belated Mother's Day present; an old framed photo of Liverpool's waterfront.

'I know how you like to imagine all those people setting off for their new lives,' says Will. 'I thought you might like it.'

I study the photo carefully. It shows a stretch of the Mersey, some warehouses, a couple of ships, and the famous Three Graces. It's a lovely and evocative image and will be a welcome addition to our bedroom walls, which are still rather bare. I study it even more closely. The sky looks a little overcast. Am I surprised? Of course I'm not. Sunshine in Liverpool? Not in my experience.

THIRTEEN

A Cuckoo on the List

When I was making my list I found that some of the items took on a life of their own and insisted on being included. I wasn't sure at the time why they appealed, but I listened and gave them a chance. Now one of the things I'm enjoying is exploring why these and all the other wishes are there. The obvious reason is because they interest me but when I burrow deeper I can often find out more. There's usually something in past experiences or things I've missed out on that makes them attractive. And all of this helps me to address those pressing mid-life questions about who I am. However, there's one treat that stumps me.

'*See Derren Brown live*' is on my list but I'm not altogether sure how it got there. I'm aware that he's an illusionist. I also know that he appears on television, doing astonishing things, but I've never seen any of his programmes and I wouldn't recognise him if I passed him in the street. This treat is a bit of a risk. I don't know if he'll be my cup of tea, though when I made my list I must have thought it would be interesting to find out more about him. Either that or it's a trick and he got me to put it there.

Anyway all that matters now is that he's on the list. Some treats can wait and there's no urgency about them. Notwithstanding catastrophes I can be pretty certain that cities will still be there, whether I choose to visit them this year, or in five years' time. The books I want to read can be dipped in and out of, whenever I want. But it's different when the treat relies on a real person. He may decide to stop doing live shows and then what would I do? I discover that he's currently on tour with a show called Svengali and decide I'd better seize my chance. All the forthcoming performances are miles from home. In the end I choose Southampton, where he's performing for a week.

It'll be a 200-mile round trip, but it's closer than Llandudno or Belfast.

Shaun's still recuperating from shingles when I book, and isn't enthusiastic about a late night. Emma and Molly want to come, though, so I get three tickets for the Tuesday evening.

A Spot of Mid-Week Mindreading

It's Tuesday and we're going to see Derren Brown tonight. I'm travelling down by car with Molly and Emma is taking the train after finishing work in London. The day gets off to a bad start, though, as I wake up with a pain in my right hip. Shaun is away for a few days and I think I must have slept sprawled across the bed in a funny position. Either that or I'm coming out in sympathy with him as he's been having problems with his hip, too. It's well over a year since he had radiotherapy for his tumour but the physical effects have only become noticeable in the last few months. Almost a year to the day after he started the treatment, his skin became tight and shiny, and began to look burned. It's puzzling that it took so long to come to the surface. Odd, too, to think of it slowly working its way through all the layers of his body. The emotional effects take longer to emerge.

I hobble through the day and then collect Molly from school. We arrive in Southampton with a couple of hours to spare and set off to find somewhere to eat. But on the way, I'm innocently crossing the road when something rather strange happens. Half-way across I feel a jerk on my foot and then there's a loud crunching sound from under my left shoe. I'm wearing plain black pumps and when I reach the pavement I take the offending one off. I'm baffled to see a large piece of metal embedded in the sole. It's quite thick and strong, and is bent into a perfect right angle. Molly and I look at it with bewilderment. We stand on the pavement and do a kind of tug of war. She holds onto the shoe and I hop about, pulling on the metal. It's hard to know whether it's integral to the shoe and has somehow popped out and spontaneously bent itself through ninety degrees, or whether something in the road has attached itself to me. I wonder out loud whether it might be a bit of cat's eye. Molly looks distressed and horrified. 'Not a real cat's eye,' I reassure her. Then, as she's still looking at me suspiciously I have to explain what 'cat's eye' means in the world of roads and tarmac.

We get back to the business of tugging, but the metal bar won't budge no matter how hard we try. I have to put my shoe back on and make the best of the situation. Just when, aged fifty-three, I think I must surely have come across all the absurd situations that life can present, here's another I'd not thought of. I limp and crunch through the city centre with one shoe perfectly normal and the other like a half-hearted running spike. What with that and my dodgy hip, I'm sure I don't look quite right.

After eating we go to the station to meet Emma. Her train is on time and she's one of the first to emerge from the platform, Most of the other travellers are commuter-jaded but she looks perky and ready for a night out. We have a hurried catch-up whilst getting ourselves to the theatre as quickly as possible.

I can't go at my usual speed, but I do my best whilst lurching along and rolling from side to side, and eventually Emma asks what's wrong. Molly and I explain and look at her hopefully; optimistic that she might be able to cast some light on the mystery of the mutated pump. She's something of an expert having worked for several years in a shoe shop when she was at university. She examines my unhappy footwear with the air of a doctor examining a patient. There's a lot of prodding and lip-pursing. Finally, she diagnoses that the metal bar is part of the shoe's structure, but she's got no idea why it has emerged and bent itself into a right angle.

We arrive at the theatre, and it's packed. Our seats are right at the top, in the balcony. We go up, and up, and up. These were the only ones available by the time I booked, and I'm rather pleased about this. I imagine we're less likely to get roped into audience participation.

There are quite a few announcements before the show begins. I get the feeling that everyone is paying much more attention than they would normally. When we're told to turn our mobiles off rather than just putting them on silent, I'm certain that everyone obeys. After all, you don't want to be singled out for attention by a man who has the power to make you wet the bed for the rest of your life.

There's a bit of music, then there is the man we've all come to see. He looks a small figure on stage, but very quickly has the audience in the palm of his hand. There's complete silence with not even the usual rustle of sweet wrappings. One of the key things that makes him a good live performer is his confidence. The audience can relax and feel comfortable. At times there's suspense when a trick appears to have gone wrong, but he always makes it turn out right in the end.

I did some reading before the show and was surprised to find that he makes no claims to have paranormal skills. In fact, completely the opposite. Everything can be explained, he says, by 'magic, suggestion, psychology, misdirection and showmanship'. His methods include neuro-linguistic programming and expert analysis of body language. Then there's what he's best known for: hypnosis. He demonstrates this on a member of the audience, and then does something to them which should hurt a great deal. The victim doesn't even flinch. This does seem astonishing, but I can relate to it as I was once hypnotised myself, albeit under very different circumstances.

It happened when I was expecting Henry. We'd had a home

birth with Emma and it was a much more positive experience than when Will was born in hospital. We wanted the same this time around and booked the independent midwife who'd helped us through Emma's long birth. She monitored me throughout the pregnancy and by the due date everything was ready. We'd erected the cot, organised clothes and nappies, Rita was ready to come and stay, and a friend was on standby to look after Will and Emma. I'd even cleaned the oven and made all the other excessive nesting preparations that afflict pregnant women. Unfortunately, despite the great welcome that awaited him, Henry didn't want to come out. I was keen to avoid being induced unless it was necessary, so the due date came and went, and then another week passed, and another, and another. All this time our midwife was making regular checks and reassuring us that Henry was healthy. He was expected on February 12th but twenty-two days later there was no sign of any action. Shaun had taken a week of his two-week planned leave, and Rita had already been staying for a couple of days.

On March 6th, we adults had lunch and then sat looking at one another. I felt that Shaun and Rita were waiting for me to perform, but unfortunately I couldn't make it happen to order. I said idly, 'Do you know, I'm so fed up with this that I'd even consider being hypnotised.' That was enough. Shaun grabbed the Yellow Pages and before I knew it, he'd made contact with a local hypnotherapist who was also a State Registered Nurse. When Shaun explained the situation she said, 'That sounds an interesting way to spend a Saturday afternoon,' and agreed to come over.

In less than an hour she arrived. She was elderly and carried a large bag. Although it would be an exaggeration to call it a carpet bag, it *was* a close approximation. All in all, she was the nearest thing to Mary Poppins that I'd ever met. She was efficient too, and quickly got down to work. I waited for her to say, 'Spit spot.' First of all, I was instructed to focus on a point on the ceiling whilst she talked soothingly. It was very relaxing. I was fully conscious and aware of what was happening all the time, but the point at which I knew I was hypnotised was when I had a contraction. Although it was uncomfortable and I wanted to relieve the pain by rubbing, I couldn't move my hands. They were fixed. It was a most peculiar feeling. After she'd gone, Shaun and Rita looked at me, long and hard. There was still no sign of Henry, though, so we carried on trying to pass the time.

That night I finally did go into labour. Whether it was the hypnosis that started it, we'll never know. I suppose Henry had to come out eventually, but I was definitely calmer than in previous labours. Despite this I was far from agreeable. At one point Shaun was holding my hand when I had a strong contraction and got very cross indeed.

'If you don't move your hand,' I said irrationally, 'I'm going to bite it—very hard.'

'It's alright,' he replied, 'I've got another one.'

It occurs to me with Derren Brown that he could save himself a whole lot of trouble. I'm sure if he wanted to, he could hypnotise the entire audience within the first few minutes and make us believe we'd seen a riveting show. Then we could all go home happy, and he could have an early night. However, that doesn't happen and instead I have a thoroughly enjoyable evening with my girls and some excellent entertainment. We return contentedly to the car and set off on the journey home, stopping half-way to fuel my alertness with some caffeine. It's late when we get to bed and I'm still not sure how this treat ended up on my list.

TREAT #7 (CONTINUED)

I've just finished watching my second David Attenborough series and this time it's the reptiles and amphibians that take centre stage. Life in Cold Blood comes in five episodes. Like Life of Birds it's magnificent and enjoyable but once again my absorption is imperfect and only a handful of snippets lodge in my memory.

One of these concerns the essential difference between a frog and a toad. This is something that I've always wondered about. Now I know. Both are, in fact, members of the frog family, but the animals we generally call frogs have moist skin whereas toads are dry and often a bit warty.

Then there are the anacondas, the heaviest of the snakes. I thought that all reptiles lay eggs, but I'm clearly wrong. These don't. Instead they give birth to up to forty live young at a time, which swim off into the water fully formed.

There's one reptilian tale, though, that stays with me, above all others. It's about a python. We, the viewers, see speeded up footage showing how it lies quietly for months on end, barely moving, with just a pilot light metabolism. Then with no apparent warning it decides it's time to eat, senses an antelope nearby and strikes out. It wraps the unlucky animal in its coils and then over the course of several hours swallows it head first with its feet sticking out. It goes down more easily that way and the snake's flexible jaws stretch wide open to accommodate its large meal. There's little space left for air to go in and out, though, so in order to avoid suffocation the python leaves the top of its windpipe hanging out of its mouth, like a piece of flexible tubing. Once the antelope is finally encased within its body, the python's physiology begins to change. During the next few days its liver doubles in size and its heart increases by forty per cent. It takes about four weeks for the python to digest its meal; hair, horns, hooves, everything. Then it goes back to sleep again till its next mealtime many months later.

I love this story so much that I tell it to various people I meet. Then at a dinner party with new acquaintances there's a discomfiting lull in the conversation. This makes me nervous so I jump in recklessly and share my python obsession. I've just finished the account and people seem to be digesting it, when I get a reaction from across the table. A German guest looks at me curiously and says, 'You have told that story before.' Since I've only met her twice I take the hint that I need some new interests.

FOURTEEN

ON MY OWN

It's the Easter holidays and Shaun and Molly have gone to Germany for a few days to stay with friends. It's rare to have a whole weekend to myself. Although Emma and Henry are around, they've got their own plans, and won't be needing any input from me.

I wake early on Saturday morning and go for a walk around the local park. What should have been a peaceful meander, though, ends up being unexpectedly energetic. A surprising number of runners are out. They keep thundering past, and I have to do a lot of hopping from side to side to keep out of their way. It only seems a few weeks since the lake was frozen and the ducks were skating on it. Now the daffodils are out and there's wedding cake blossom in the trees. Before long there will be ducklings, and the diligent little moorhens will start busying themselves with their broods.

Back at home I enjoy the novelty of a slow breakfast. Porridge with a sprinkling of cinnamon. I push a teaspoon of set honey deep into the bowl. It liquefies in the thick heat. A delicious pool of sweet intensity.

Then I get started on my plans for the day: painting the kitchen. Transforming it from an uninspiring magnolia to a pretty duck egg blue, whilst listening to Radio 4, is satisfying. While I paint I wonder what to do with my gift of free time tomorrow.

One option is to have a day in London. I've got a book with fifty walks in it, all of them enticing with their insights into the history and culture of small areas of London. I like the idea of wandering around at my own pace, reading as I go, and stopping to find out more if the fancy takes me. Doing *one* of these walks is on my list, but I think I might manage to fit in a couple of them tomorrow. Exploring the secret passages of St James's, Piccadilly sounds perfect for the morning, and then in the afternoon a slightly longer walk from Bayswater to Belgravia.

As I'm putting the second coat on the kitchen walls, I listen to Weekend Woman's Hour and there's an engrossing item on people's need for time alone. A much greater number of people report that they would like 'more time on their own', than say they want 'more time with people'. This reassures me that it's normal to crave periods of solitude. For years I've felt guilty about this as Shaun hasn't seemed to need it. He's preferred to be with people all the time. He has his own sculling boat but doesn't enjoy going out in it, as this means being alone. For him, teamwork is what makes any activity enjoyable. I enjoy the self-contained nature of swimming and walking. This difference has led to tension in the past. But since his illness he's different. He spends more time alone. For me, the balance has now gone too far in the opposite direction and I miss the periods of togetherness.

A MILLION CANNIBALISTIC SPIDERS - 1ST APRIL 2012

TREAT #16

It's a beautiful day and London is a very relaxing place to be on a Sunday. The city is populated by tourists who wander around clutching guidebooks and Tube maps. Nearly everyone you see is out to enjoy themselves.

My walk starts at Piccadilly Circus and very soon sends me through St James's Church and out into Jermyn Street. From there it's a short walk to Blue Ball Yard with its pretty mews houses. This is a view of London that you only get on foot, and I had no idea they were there. There are several enticing little hotels in the area, too, and I daydream about bringing Shaun here in a couple of months and surprising him with a birthday lunch.

The book directs me along the edge of Green Park and then tells me to take a short cut through to St James's Palace. It then provides me with some timely information. Although I'm standing outside the only royal palace in London that's closed to the public, it is possible to attend services at its Chapel Royal on Sundays between October and Easter. Today is Palm Sunday and the service is due to begin in about twenty minutes. Two policemen stand on guard in the archway that leads into the palace courtyard. I ask hesitantly if I'm in the right place for the service, and like magic they nod and wave me through. It's as if I've uttered a secret password.

I go through the archway, and the Chapel Royal is on the left. There's a plaque on the wall and when I read it, I shiver. This is somewhere very special. Charles I received the sacrament here on the morning of his execution in 1649. Several hundred years later, Queen Victoria married her beloved Prince Albert here, and half a century after that, it was the setting for the marriage of her grandson, the future George V. In 1997 Princess Diana's coffin was placed before the altar the night before her funeral, so that friends and family could visit privately. I'm a little in awe, but as I enter, a charming sidesman beams and greets me as if I were a regular. The aisle is lined with boxed pews. He opens the door of one and shows me where to sit. Helpfully, he also warns me about a small step, but it's too late. I've already tripped. For the next hour I watch as other visitors do the same.

It's a beautiful chapel, and surprisingly small, with seating for only a hundred. It was built in the reign of Henry VIII and the ornate ceiling with its intricate coats of arms was painted by Holbein. Behind the altar is a huge stained glass window bearing the date 2005. It's a representation of the Commonwealth as a tree, with member nations as leaves on its branches. I spot the Solomon Islands, Nigeria, Vanuatu and Singapore. It looks very cheerful as the sun streams through its pale yellow glass. Best of all, it has one of my favourite quotations; 'All shall be well and all manner of thing shall be well'. Dame Julian of Norwich claimed that God had spoken them to her. She lived in the fourteenth century and had unusual and radical beliefs. She was also the first woman to write a book in the English language. Her philosophy was based on the ideas that God loves everyone and that sin is important because it helps people to learn about themselves.

The service begins and as my book promises there are sixteen choristers: six adult men and ten boys, dressed in rich scarlet and gold coats. The children are from the City of London School, and are called Queen's Scholars because the Queen pays two-thirds of their fees. Originally the term 'Chapel Royal' applied to the clergy who would accompany the sovereign on travels. In the medieval period this often meant going to war. Today it refers to this chapel, but also to the people who serve the spiritual needs of the monarch. In a few days, the Chapel Royal, in the form of clergy and choir, will accompany the Queen at York Minster when she distributes the Maundy money. The Queen has thirty-six chaplains who are members of the Royal Ecclesiastical Household and could, at any time, be called away from their normal duties to minister to, and support her. Today's sermon is delivered by one of them; Canon Easter, who is very appropriately named for the time of year.

When it's time to go up and receive communion, I wish I was better dressed. I came prepared for a day walking around London, so am wearing comfortable shoes and slightly tatty tracksuit bottoms. Everyone else is impeccably dressed. The ladies are mostly wearing brightly coloured jackets, smart skirts and large jewellery. The gentlemen are all in suits. I try to be inconspicuous but inevitably trip over the step again.

The service ends and I shake hands with the Canon as I leave. I'm so pleased I came. Not only is the building beautiful, but it's known as the 'cradle of English church music'. Purcell, Handel and Tallis have all spent time here.

Back in the real world, the book guides me as I dip in and out of various yards and passages; I find all kinds of old and surprising buildings including the London Library. This was founded in 1841, and today has more than one million books stored on fifteen miles of shelving. Anyone can join for an annual fee and the library will post books anywhere within the UK or Europe.

Nearing the end of my walk I turn back into Jermyn Street and spot a glossy black cocker spaniel trotting along jauntily with a large stick in its mouth. It's clearly extremely obedient as it's not on a lead. As befits the area, its two accompanying gentlemen are exceptionally well-dressed. This trio look for all the world as though they've just had a pre-lunch stroll in a Cotswold village, rather than a bit of stick-throwing in Green Park.

I've finished the first of my walks and now I'm ready for the next one so I take the Tube from Piccadilly Circus to Bayswater. In Kensington Gardens people are soaking up the Spring sunshine whilst variously skateboarding, skipping, running, riding scooters, playing football, walking dogs, cycling, and throwing Frisbees. All this activity makes me hungry so I buy an organic sausage in a roll from a small stall. It comes with onion relish on the side and hits the spot completely as I sit on a bench and watch what's going on around me.

One of the joys of being a tourist is that you can stare quite unashamedly. Everyone expects you to look gormless so there's no harm in fulfilling their expectations. I first experienced the pleasure of undemanding anonymity in Stockholm about ten years ago. Shaun was at a business meeting and I was exploring on my own when I suddenly came across a large crowd of people, lining the street. I'd no idea what was going on, but I joined them and waited optimistically. Within about ten minutes, a parade of dressy mounted soldiers came along, followed by a couple of open carriages. Inside, were the King and Queen of Sweden and, rather more surprisingly, the Emperor and Empress of Japan.

Today is a novelty because for once I have no constraints on my time. For years, there has constantly been some member of the family needing me to do something for them. Sometimes they've all wanted things at the same time. I recall one occasion when all four children formed a queue as they waited to speak to me. One wanted me to sign a form and write a cheque; another started crying and wanted a hug. I can't remember what the other two needed, but I do know that when Will's issue had been dealt with, he went straight to the back of the queue and lined up again. Being a mother has affected most of what I've done for well over twenty years. My sister has four children, too, and it's been the same for her. She once turned up at a hospital appointment and was mortified to be shown a letter that she'd written to the consultant and signed, 'love Mum'.

Lunch over, I leave Kensington Gardens and pass the grandiose Albert Memorial with its enormous gilded statue of the Prince under a towering Gothic canopy. Opposite, is the Albert Hall. Victoria really did have a magnificent obsession and was determined that her husband would never be forgotten. Passing round the back of the Hall, I find yet another memorial to him; a huge statue. I feel a bit haunted by Albert today. He keeps cropping up. First of all, matrimonially, at the Chapel Royal, and now again and again and again in devotional memorials.

As I walk past the Royal College of Music, piano notes drift out. Someone is practising scales. Then a few minutes later I'm in the midst of the Victorian museums that were built using the proceeds of the Great Exhibition. I'm in no hurry, so decide to stop off at the Victoria and Albert (there he is again) Museum. Once inside I spot something intriguing. In a side room, there's a bright yellow robe, displayed in a glass case. The information tells me that it's made from the silk of golden orb weaver spiders. They're found in the mountains of Madagascar and their silk is naturally golden in colour. It's stronger than that produced by silkworms, but is very difficult to obtain in quantity because the spiders are cannibalistic and therefore difficult to farm. The silk for this particular robe was obtained using an ancient method. Local people caught the spiders in the wild each morning and harnessed them to a hand-operated machine that harvested their silk. At the end of each day they were set free again. It took the silk from over a million of these spiders to make the cloth for this robe.

Back outside again I walk towards Knightsbridge, and the book guides me through various little streets, squares and mews yards. Many of the houses are painted in pastel colours. This area, just behind the hectic Brompton Road is as pretty and peaceful as the heart of Wiltshire. Eventually, my circuitous route takes me round the back of Harrods and brings me out on Sloane Street, where I pass the Icelandic Embassy. I heard on the radio yesterday that the population of Iceland is only just over 300,000. That's about the size of Cardiff. For such a small country it's had a pretty big impact over the last few years. First there were the tremors that resulted from their banking collapse, and then there was the ash cloud from the volcano with the unpronounceable name that caused thousands of flights to be grounded. I can write Eyjafjallajökull, but I can't say it, even after reading the BBC pronuniciation unit's guidance which tells me it is pronounced 'AY-uh-fyat-luh-YOE-kuutl-uh'. There are plenty of other embassies to see too. Those I've passed today include Serbia, Germany, Finland, Trinidad and Tobago, and Equatorial Guinea. By the time I reach the end of my walk at Knightsbridge underground station, I feel like I've been on a world tour.

A couple of hours later, I'm lying in the bath at home. Pick of the Week is on the radio and I'm barely listening as I doze and soak my sore feet. It's just background noise. Then I start to take an interest and hear that they're discussing a shortage of donkeys. Apparently, more and more churches want to have them at their Palm Sunday services, and there just aren't enough to go round. In response to this crisis, the Church of England is exploring alternative options, including llamas. The owners of the Ashdown Forest Llama Park give an earnest interview and report that they've had an exceptionally busy week supplying their llamas to local churches. As I lie in the water I reflect that there were no donkeys at the Chapel Royal, and certainly not any llamas.

My feet are beginning to feel better and I linger in the bath a bit longer, relishing the warmth and pondering idly. The first two walks in my book were certainly very enjoyable. I'd definitely like to do some more and as there are another forty-eight to choose from, that should keep me busy for a while. Then another thought pops into my head. Palm Sunday... today's date...no wonder there were no llamas.

FIFTEEN

Watery Mishaps

About ten years ago we had a barge holiday. For a week, we travelled sedately along the Worcester and Birmingham Canal, the Severn and the Avon. It was satisfying to drift under bridges and see traffic jams on land as we meandered peacefully along with very little to impede our progress. It was all going splendidly—then we got to Stratford and it all went wrong.

We moored in a large basin in the centre of town. The first bit was fine and we enjoyed a pleasant lunch on board. But when we tried to get going, the barge refused to respond to reason. We went backwards and forwards, bumping into everything in our way. People shouted at us. That was bad enough, but our shame was magnified by the tourists who stood on the bridge, watching as though we were some kind of traditional English entertainment. There were dozens and dozens of them, and as they pointed their cameras at us, our humiliation was complete.

This has stuck indelibly in my mind, but another strong memory from that holiday was of gliding past the Royal Shakespeare Theatre. Seen from the water it looked very enticing and I thought how I would like to take the children to a performance there. Since then I've been to many other theatres but as I've never managed to return to Stratford this is why 'Take one of the children to the Royal Shakespeare Theatre', had to be on my list.

This is one of the easiest treats to arrange so I go online and book to take Molly to a Saturday matinee performance of Twelfth Night.

We make an early start and travel by train from Marylebone. This is a pleasure in itself, as it's small, charming and inextricably associated with Monopoly. Then when we eventually reach Stratford and get to the theatre, it's a relief to find that although our seats are amongst the cheapest, the view is good, and we don't have the ubiquitous 'man with a big head' who often sits in front of me.

The performance sparkles and it's rewarding to see that Molly is enjoying it. Although I don't know Twelfth Night well, Shakespeare's influence on the English language is so profound that a number of phrases sidle in like familiar friends: 'If music be the food of love, play on'; 'cakes and ale'; 'midsummer madness'; 'westward ho!', and 'some are born great, some achieve greatness and some have greatness thrust upon them'. But those that make the most impression are new to me. My spine tingles when Viola says:

> O time, thou must untangle this, not I
> It is too hard a knot for me t'untie

These simple words, expressed with such elegance, resonate with my experiences over recent years. When we were in the midst of complicated problems it felt like we were trapped in a tangle of knitting wool. As we tried to negotiate the formidable knots we each had a phrase that we'd return to again and again. When I got scared Shaun would comfort me by saying, 'It's like guiding a ship, we just have to steer a steady course.' When he was in despair, I'd tell him that we just had to 'keep putting one foot in front of the other'. Fortunately there has never been a time when we've been at rock bottom together. One of us has always been able to stay afloat and hold out their hand to stop the other one from drowning.

Shaun was right, and Shakespeare was right too: steer a steady course and time does untangle the knots. But it requires a great deal of patience and this has not come easily to me. There was a time when the knots only seemed to get tighter. Shaun was trying so hard to get work but all kinds of obstacles got in the way. Contracts fell through, he didn't get considered for jobs because he was over-qualified, and clients' plans changed. Then out of the blue at the end of last year, an old contact got in touch, and within a few days Shaun had the kind of work he'd been struggling to find for years. It's well-paid and in a company where he's valued, and able to use his talents. It fell into place so easily. It was like pulling the tails of a bow and watching it untie. We don't know how long the job will last, but for now I'm grateful. It's a gift—and a knot that time untied.

SIBLINGS

A number of treats are progressing quite nicely at the moment and I'm pleased to be back on track with my compost. The bin is filling up, there's no sign of any rats and I've finally owned up to Molly about what happened. I've had to do this so she knows not to put eggshells or cooked food in with the carrot peelings and apple cores. She was horrified to find out about our unwelcome visitors at first but has come to terms with it surprisingly quickly.

We've also done another stage of the North Downs Way. This was on a slightly chilly Spring day. The walk remains in my memory as impressionistic dabs of damp, dappled woodland and open grassy hillsides, patched in shades of green and brown. But as so often with the treats, it's the unexpected backstories that stick with me.

This time it was something that happened the night before. Molly and I had done the first stages together, tramping along for hours, alternately exhilarated by the graceful descents and desperate for the jagged ascents to end. We took quite a long break while the weather was bad, but with a hint of sunshine one Saturday we decided to resume the next day. Emma heard us discussing it and said she'd like to come too. I was delighted that she wanted to join us and without hesitation I told her that, of course, she would be very welcome.

Shortly afterwards I'm in my bedroom when Molly appears looking upset and complaining that these walks are *her* time with me and she doesn't think it's fair if Emma comes too. I'm a bit surprised. I can see Molly's point. She had an expectation that this walk and any future ones were going to be just her and me. But on the other hand I don't want to hurt Emma's feelings. I go and ask Shaun what he thinks but for once he doesn't have an answer and he seems preoccupied. I feel a huge weight on me. Maybe it's best to call the whole thing off.

Then an image of Rita pops into my head. She's always fair and I respect her opinions. But one thing puzzles me: she says that she always knows her own mind and never has any problem making decisions. I could do with a bit of this certainty. With four strong-minded children chipping in, I've spent a great deal of time and energy trying to keep them all happy. In taking everyone else's opinions into account, I've oscillated so much, that I've sometimes lost sight of my own views. I'm not sure how I've let this happen. My working life in social science research required me to consider hypotheses and to draw rational conclusions based on evidence that I gathered. Family life has corroded my reasoning powers. For some time now my decisions have been distorted by the loudest shout, saddest face, and canniest twist of the knife of maternal guilt.

Right—I've made my mind up. Things are going to be different from now on. I think hard about what's important in this situation. I don't want to disappoint Molly, but on the other hand I don't want to reject Emma. Then I realise that all I need is to identify the key things that matter to me, and stick to them. Fundamental principles. Core values.

I think I've found one. 'Never tell a member of my family that I don't want them there unless there's a very good reason'. Sometimes

Shaun and I need time on our own and have to tell the children to go away. I don't have a problem with that. But this current situation does *not* count as a good reason. Later, in the privacy of my bedroom I tell Molly. 'Emma is coming with us tomorrow.' She's cross and argues, whispering fiercely and urgently. I explain once again that my decision is made and that is the end of the matter. She goes out, slamming the door noisily, on her way.

TREAT #11 (CONTINUED)

The next day my two daughters and I start out from Westerham Hill, with Molly still a bit grumpy. 13¾ miles later we reach Wrotham at the end of a very satisfying journey.

On the way we stopped on a hilly slope near Chevening for our picnic lunch and there Emma was upset and confided that she'd had a difficult week. She and her boyfriend have been in a relationship for two years but now she wants to end it. Neither Molly nor I had any idea she was going through this. We sat close together on our picnic rug in the thin sunshine.

There used to be a great deal of sharp sibling elbowing to get my attention or Shaun's, but these days it's relatively rare. Sharing uncertain times has made our four children protective of one another and their competitiveness has receded. There was a particularly powerful demonstration of this one teatime near Christmas. Shaun's hip tumour had been diagnosed a few weeks previously, and although Henry and Molly were both at home, we'd not wanted to tell any of the children until they could all hear the news together. Emma and Will were both in Yorkshire and arrived back for Christmas on the same afternoon, full of good cheer and glad to be home. We sat around our familiar kitchen table, with the big red teapot and a plate of spicy Christmas biscuits. There was the usual noisy chat and teasing but for once I couldn't join in. I sat on the outside, watching a film of my family life and knowing what was going to happen next.

Shaun started to speak and they immediately went quiet. Calmly, he explained about his hip pain, the tumour, the radiotherapy he was due to start soon, and the further infusions of cells he would need from his donor. The mood tipped and froze. What was warm so recently was displaced by the cold, almost metallic fear that we all recognised so well. The children's faces were blank with shock. Then their features tightened with pain and before I could do any holding and comforting I saw them fly to one another. The moment the gravity hit the eldest two, their concern was for their younger brother and sister. Molly clung to Emma who enfolded her protectively whilst they sobbed almost silently. The boys, too, were entwined in a hug and then we all joined together. Shaun stayed remarkably composed for someone who was at the eye of the storm—but the rest of us wept.

It means a great deal to me that our children have each other. One of my greatest wishes is that they should continue to support one another and I like to think that they will do this even when I'm no longer around. I'm sure they will, as they have their own strong relationships independent of me, but I'm so used to organising family events that I can't resist making a few post-mortal arrangements. I've told them that I would like my ashes to be put in an attractive jar which will then spend three months a year with each of them. That way I can, from beyond the grave, ensure that there will be regular get-togethers as various pairs will have to meet to hand me over. I've even come up with a plan to vary the order of my visits so that different combinations of children get to see one another. Overall, I think this is a splendid initiative but I do have two niggling reservations. The first is that my children might resent this and remember their mother as a control freak. The second is that Will might absent-mindedly leave me on a bus somewhere in the depths of Eastern Europe.

SIXTEEN

NOSTALGIA

TREAT #9 (CONTINUED)

I've been steadily working my way through the fifty-two episodes of Mad Men but have a blip in the third series. I settle down to watch Disc 3 and am puzzled. It looks familiar. The character who was sacked is back again. He seems to have been re-instated with no explanation. After some confusion, and inserting and ejecting several discs to compare them, I discover that I've been given two copies of Disc One and no Disc Three. This is curious as I bought a brand new set online and it arrived wrapped in cellophane. Then I remember Cousin Maggie telling me how she and a friend worked in a pie factory one summer vacation. They would liven up their tedious routine by occasionally slipping an apple pie into a steak and kidney pie box. Maybe my Mad Men problem was also the result of student boredom. I email the retailer, who replies and is also mystified, but agrees to send me a new Disc Three.

I'm enjoying Mad Men very much. Aside from great acting and interesting storylines it presses my nostalgia button very effectively. Although I was a child in the early sixties, so much of what I see strikes chords and sends me off on some satisfying memory tourism.

I was reading about nostalgia recently and discovered that it was originally classed as a medical condition. The term was first used in 1688 by Johannes Hofer, a medical student who observed a strange condition amongst Swiss mercenaries fighting in France and Italy. They frequently became ill with symptoms such as fever, indigestion, fainting and a deep longing for the mountains of their homeland. Hofer wanted to give it a label and it was nearly named 'philopatridomania' but in the end he settled on 'nostalgia', which was derived from two Greek words 'nostos' (homecoming), and 'algos' (ache). The explanation for the affliction suffered by these soldiers was that their brains and ear drums had been damaged by the constant clanging of cowbells in the Swiss mountains. They were banned from singing their traditional songs in case it reminded them of home and anyone caught breaking the rules faced harsh punishment.

My life so far has been remarkably free of cowbells but I'm still easy prey for Sixties nostalgia. Yet those times were not happy ones for me. My parents lived apart until I was eleven, but when they did spend time together they were at war. In their world it was acceptable to do anything, say anything and throw anything. And they didn't hold back because I was there. I was 'just a child' and my feelings didn't matter.

Money was often the trigger for arguments. Sometimes my father wouldn't send what he'd promised and then my mother would panic. I learned not to ask for things but I also knew that when she had money she would be generous. She was always happy to share what she had and talked warmly of her own father who'd radiated bonhomie and indulged her when she was young. The contrasts with my father were unfavourable and frequent. His background was different. He came from a poor East End family and didn't see the point in spending money unless he had to.

My parents grew up in London and met at a dance when she was twenty-four and he was twenty-nine. He was tall and slim with a strong resemblance to the film star, Clark Gable. Within a few months my mother had become pregnant so despite having little in common, they married. My brother was born in the war and two years later my sister arrived.

During their early years together, my parents ran a pub in North London. My mother was a good cook and built up a reputation for what she called 'businessmen's lunches', with the standard English fare that was popular then. Years later, she reminisced to me of dishes like shepherd's pie, steak and kidney pudding, stewed lamb with caper sauce, steamed syrup sponge, and blackberry and apple pie. My father ran the bar and drank too much.

This is not a recipe for success and sure enough things did not go well. In the mid-fifties they went their separate ways and my father returned to his original trade as a welder. But despite their fundamental incompatibility there was clearly some bond between them and after a while he persuaded her to try a reconciliation. He was working in Devon and promised her a new life there, including buying a house. She was impoverished and living in a caravan with my brother and sister, so, with few other options and a great many reservations, she agreed. They set up home in a rented house by the river in Dartmouth. My mother was keen to get into the property market, and at that time my father was earning reasonable money. But their differences couldn't be resolved. Despite his earlier promises he saw no point in committing money where he didn't need to, and by the time she was unexpectedly pregnant with me, he had settled the family in a council house on a big estate at the top of a windswept hill. It was badly built and my mother fought to keep it bright and cheerful, doing constant battle with the leaky windows and the powdery mould that painted the bathroom black. By the time I was two my father had been made redundant and went away to work in Wiltshire, leaving his family stranded and appearing unannounced every few months or so throughout my early childhood.

He died when I was twenty-eight, and my mother died ten years later. Although she ended up living in Devon for the rest of her life, she always missed the liveliness of London, with its mix of people, and anonymity. She talked of it longingly. One of the things she hated about small town life was 'everyone wanting to know your business', as she put it. For her, a friendly enquiry was viewed as nosiness. It was only after she died that I began to understand why she was so sensitive.

My sister is twelve years older than me and we're very close. I thought we'd talked about most things to do with our family but when we were clearing out our mother's house, we had a conversation that took me by surprise. I'd always been aware of a long scar down my mother's left cheek. She used to dab powder over it and when she smiled, this line melded into her face like a straight vertical wrinkle. It never crossed my mind to question why it was there. I thought she'd been born with it—but of course she wasn't. People aren't born with long scars down their face; nor are they born with a distorted broken nose. She had that too; another feature I never questioned. I learned from my sister that before I was born, my mother fell in love and had an affair. This happened during one of many separations from my father, but he found out and attacked her. As a result he went to prison for three months for assault. In some ways it was a shock, but in other ways it explained things that my mother had alluded to but never made explicit. I'm sad that she carried this burden, quietly, for so many years, feeling ashamed rather than wronged.

Much in my childhood was covered with the dust of disharmony but there were good things too: escape through reading voraciously...long walks in the peaceful lanes with nodding hedges of red and white campions and meadowsweet... the subtle perfume of primroses in the Spring...fishing for tiddlers with my stiff nylon net as I slipped about on the stone steps that led to the boats, the air full of fishiness and seaweed...being encouraged at my small primary school and loving learning, particularly history, facts about the world, and anything to do with books...the roots of many treats are tangled up in these memories.

My upbringing was no worse than many others, and a lot better than some, but I wanted more out of life and eventually university provided a means of escape. I went to London and created my own version of what my mother missed so much. I lived in a hall of residence in the King's Road at the height of punk and adored everything about being there. I got cheap theatre tickets and went anywhere and everywhere that I could. Museums, galleries, concerts, and parties; it was all so exciting after small town life. Unfortunately in my wish to get away I'd not chosen my course well and whilst I loved the social life at university, I hated the nursing degree I was doing. I came to dread the blocks of time on the wards. I was young and unprepared for the immensity of the pain that people were suffering and the terrible betrayals that their bodies could inflict on them. And I loathed the smells. Overcooked food, disinfectant, sharp human odours and imminent death. By the summer, I couldn't face the idea of another three years, and left. I lived with friends, worked for a while and then went back to university to study speech and language therapy. Half-way through my first year, I met Shaun and from then on things got better and better.

Perhaps a key aspect of nostalgia is one that I haven't thought of until now. It's about a longing for the things we've left behind, but it can also be a way of confirming that things are different and better and that we've made progress in our lives. Mad Men is full of behaviour that is undesirable to modern eyes. Racism, sexism, homophobia, disregard for the environment; they're all there. We've come a long way since then. I look at my own life and see that I have too.

Humour

Treat #10 (Continued)

I've been enjoying some more Jane Austen recently and have finished both 'Emma' and 'Sense and Sensibility'. Although my world is very different from hers, the comedy still glints today. Like previous generations I find her wicked wit, sly and satisfying.

Nothing surprising there, but this has set me thinking about humour more generally. Why do we have a sense of humour? What makes things funny? I do a bit of reading and discover that there's been a great deal of research into this subject. There are academic societies, conferences and journals all dedicated to its study. I've never thought about it much. I've just taken for granted that a sense of humour is important to me in choosing my partner and friends. Up until now, if anyone had asked me why humour is so vital, then I would have said, 'Because it's enjoyable.' But of course, that's only scratching the surface. Like saying we eat because the food tastes good. The pleasure we get from humour is no more than a reward for using it; the stroke that makes us want to repeat the experience and find new ones. The reasons why it's important are altogether different.

One benefit of humour is that it helps you get to know someone and develop a shared understanding with them. Jane Austen introduces us to characters who are variously snobbish, sycophantic, boring, puffed up with pride, and just plain silly. But it's not these characters we develop a bond with. They're too full of their own foolishness for us to want that. Instead it's her, the writer who draws us close. The clues are subtle, but as readers, we pick up what she thinks and are in on the comedy. Jane is an unfailingly polite and proper observer, but the choices she makes about what to recount, reveal her sharp understanding, whilst we, the readers, bask in the reflected wisdom of getting the joke.

If humour bonds people together, then it's clearly an important ingredient in marriage, too. Jane leaves her readers in little doubt that Elizabeth Bennet and Mr Darcy will flirt and tease one another, whilst living happily ever after. Emma and Mr Knightley, too, will delight in laughing together, though it might take Emma a while to understand her husband's affectionate ribbing.

Incongruity lies at the root of much humour. Seeing something that's out of place strikes most people as funny.

The dog that seems to say, 'sausages', the elderly couple whose conversation is a series of non sequiturs, and the lorry driver whose sat nav took him from Glasgow to Plymouth via Spain. There's an evolutionary view of humour which says that being alert to incongruity helps in staying grounded and gives an adaptive advantage. Being able to detect when things aren't quite as they should be, is useful as it means we're in touch with reality and therefore less likely to make bad decisions.

I was amused to read that the Prince Regent sent an envoy to Jane to tell her that he would 'allow her the honour' of dedicating Emma to him. The prince was an unpopular, overstuffed, philandering gambler, and it's likely that Jane was underwhelmed at his demand. For demand it clearly was. Nonetheless she obeyed the monarch-in-waiting and her dedication was suitably obsequious with 'respectfully dedicated', three mentions of His Royal Highness, and reference to herself as a 'dutiful and obedient humble servant'. Despite the fine words, I imagine her writing this with raised eyebrows and a wry smile.

I share jokes with Jane across the ocean of two hundred years, but recently I've been struggling to share one with Shaun across the width of the dinner table. He's stopped teasing, and at family meals he's there physically but sits apart emotionally, seeming unable to join in with light-hearted chat. Without the shared bond of humour, I'm finding it hard to know what's in his head. I think we've had so many intense issues to negotiate that we've forgotten how to have fun. He above all is the one who has made me laugh most throughout the past thirty years with countless jokes shared together in the unique intimacy of marriage.

He's been away a lot recently with his new job, and it feels like we've had few opportunities to put some fun back into our life. But now there's a chance to have a weekend away together. Will is living in Estonia, and is keen for Shaun, Molly and me to visit.

This will be the first of my treats to involve a flight and was the last to be added to my list. It came about because Will completed a TEFL course last summer and then started to apply for jobs, teaching English abroad. He sent off about sixty applications to countries as diverse as Mexico and Kazakhstan. There was an exciting week when he got replies from many of them, but in the end, he and a language school in Tallinn seemed destined for one another.

When I mention to friends that Will is working in Estonia, the reaction is nearly always the same. Polite interest and a blank look. Most people have heard of it, but know very little. Emma found the same when she went to visit Will in February. She rang her bank to let them know she'd be abroad for a few days.

'I'm going away for the weekend,' she said.

'Lovely—' said the customer service assistant. 'Where are you going?'

'Estonia,' replied Emma confidently.

There was a long silence. 'Which country is that in?' asked the assistant.

'It *is* a country,' said Emma, patiently.

Another silence, even longer this time. 'We're having trouble finding that,' said the assistant. Fortunately the pilot knew where to find Estonia, and Emma had an interesting, if rather cold, weekend. The temperature was -25C.

We've learned a lot about Estonia in the past few months, as Will has become very fond of it. He warns us not to call it 'Tiny Estonia' as this is a journalistic cliché and by European standards it's not actually that little. Although it's smaller than the other Baltic states, Latvia and Lithuania, it's bigger than Switzerland, the Netherlands and Denmark. However, there's no denying that the population *is* tiny at about 1.3 million.

I book flights for Shaun, Molly and me. We'll be going in a few weeks' time. This will be the first treat that I've done with Shaun and I'm looking forward to having some fun with him. Suddenly humour is a surprisingly serious subject.

SEVENTEEN

BIRDS

Although the nightingale usually gets the glory amongst British songbirds, my loyalties lie elsewhere. I love the blackbird. Its singing has been likened to a man whistling dreamily as he leans against a wall with his hands in his pockets. Over the years, I've come to associate this sound with contented garden pottering. Weeding, deadheading, planting up summer containers, and frequent breaks for a mug of earth-spattered tea and contemplation. On lucky days this takes place against a fluting, mellow backdrop. The company of a blackbird makes me happy. I want to be able to recognise other songs, but like all my treats, I put this on the list without any idea of how it would materialise.

TREAT #18

Then I hear Simon Barnes on the radio. He's talking about his book 'Birdwatching with Your Eyes Closed' so I buy it, download the accompanying podcast of birdsongs, and begin to work my way through. The author is wonderfully reassuring. When I listen to birdsong in the garden or park, it sounds like a glorious cacophony, but he insists that with practice, it will become possible to pick out individual members of the ornithological orchestra. 'After all,' he writes encouragingly, 'everyone can already identify quite a few.' We all know what cuckoos say. Ducks quack, crows caw, and Desert Island Discs is preceded every week by the cries of herring gulls. If I can already distinguish a trumpet from a double bass, there's no reason why that auditory refinement can't be applied to birdsong too.

There's no doubt that it's difficult, though, and I struggle with even the first chapter. This is about robins. I learn that their soft insect-eating beaks produce a thin, soft song. They're usually the first to get up in the morning and the last to stop singing at night. They're also one of the only birds that can be heard singing during the winter. I take in all this information, and then listen to the podcast. Unfortunately instead of achieving clarity, I'm more confused. It sounds like a blackbird to me. I try to put my fledgling knowledge to use on my walk round the park and get frustrated. Is it a robin? Is it a blackbird? Even worse, is it neither?

What I do hear quite clearly, though, is a bird that sounds like a saw. It's distinctive and squeaky. I always hear it at the same point on my walk. This 'squeaky saw' bird unwittingly provides my breakthrough moment. When I get to the chapter on the great tit, I read that they say, 'Teacher, Teacher' and that this sounds a bit like a leaky pump. I begin to wonder. Could one woman's squeaky saw, be another's leaky pump? The podcast confirms my hunch. I can now say proudly, 'That's a great tit' and be pretty confident I'm right. The same thing happens when I read about the chaffinch, whose song is likened to a fast bowler's run-up and delivery. When heard it's unmistakeable. And then there's the greenfinch. I hear one slide down the scale, and say, 'Zwee' just like it's supposed to. This is really exciting.

Our bedroom is on the ground floor of the house, overlooking the garden, and I often watch the bird table from there with Shaun. We've seen a nuthatch feeding in its distinctive upside-down pose, a handful of times, and this year a pair of bullfinches have regularly sat side by side on a feeder, swinging pensively backwards and forwards. The male has an intensely pink bib. Up until now, I've assumed that the only birds in the vicinity are the ones I see. I'm beginning to realise, though, that there are others like the greenfinch that I may not see, but *can* hear.

There are a great number of ancient trees behind our garden and these provide an ideal habitat for a variety of birds as I discovered one Sunday morning last autumn. Molly and I set out for a walk and were perplexed to see dozens of men wearing woolly hats, and walking around with tripods on their shoulders. We soon discovered that they were twitchers. Our estate had become the temporary resting place of a black poll warbler. This is a North American bird, so must have been blown off-course during its migration. They're extremely rare in Britain and word spread rapidly throughout the twitching community. All day long these men walked up, down and around the local roads, in pairs and small groups that seemed to ignore one another. It *was* all men too. Friends came for lunch that day, and as we sat at the dining room table, we looked out onto a row of tripods lined up outside the window, all focused on the trees behind our house. I'm not used to paparazzi, so it was a novel experience. Molly, ever the entrepreneur, was keen to set up a coffee stall, but my main concern was that our cat would find the bird. I worried about having to stuff it and prop it in a tree.

The podcast and book have got me started on my identification, but I need more support. A guided dawn chorus walk would be just the thing and it's the perfect time of year for it too. An internet search reveals that there are several in my area but none on dates I can make. I widen the search a bit further and find a walk at Painshill Park, an eighteenth-century landscape park in Cobham. It will require a very early start as it's about forty miles away but I go ahead and book for the walk and the breakfast that follows. That leaves me about four weeks to carry on reading and listening so that I'm not completely ignorant on the walk.

THE LITTLE OLD MAN WHO LIVES UNDER THE LAKE

TREAT #19

Our flight to Tallinn is an early one, so Shaun, Molly and I stay the night before in a budget hotel near Luton airport. Since

Shaun became ill we've had to learn to take things steadily. Setting off from home before dawn is worth avoiding if we can.

I sleep through most of the flight and wake up just as we pass over a large lake on the outskirts of Tallinn. Soon after, we're in a taxi heading for the centre of town. The rain is pouring down but despite this, it looks charming. The whole of the Old Town area is a World Heritage Site, and this is where we're staying.

It's been a long journey and we're pleased to arrive at our apartment which is clean and spacious and has everything we need. Outside, the roads are narrow and cobbled and we're opposite Oleviste kirik, (St Olaf's Church). It's so close that it fills the entire view from our bedroom window. In the sixteenth century it was the tallest building in the world.

Like all good travellers we read the instructions in the apartment very carefully. They tell us that according to Estonian law, we must 'keep silence from 11pm to 7am'.

Molly looks worried. 'Does that mean no talking?'

She's such an incessant chatterbox that Shaun and I are tempted to say, 'Yes.'

We've arranged to meet Will in the main square at 8 o'clock, after he's finished teaching, and although there are crowds there, we spot him right away. He takes us to a lively Estonian restaurant where we tuck ourselves away in an alcove and exchange news. Over drinks, we study the menu and unanimously decide to avoid 'peppered lard'. Instead we share some delicious sprats which come accompanied by tiny, crisp squares of rye bread. These are followed by pork with beetroot sauce, which is also very good.

Later, as we wander through the cobbled Old Town, Will recounts an Estonian legend. It's about a little old man who lives under Lake Ülemiste, the large stretch of water that we saw from the air this morning. Every year he knocks at the city gates and asks the same question: 'Is the city finished yet?' According to the legend, if the answer were to be 'Yes,' he would flood it. The canny citizens of Tallinn are determined to avoid this disaster so have to ensure there is always an incomplete building that they can point to. Provided the disagreeable little man sees this, he'll go back to sleep for another year. Currently the SEB Swedish Bank building fulfils the important function of 'unfinishedness'. Although it was technically completed in 1997, there is still some scaffolding at the top.

Will drops us at our apartment and we settle down for the night. It's quiet outside and we sleep well. 'The silence' has been observed. In the morning Will comes back to collect us and we climb up a small hill to an area called Toompea, where all the embassies and Government buildings are located. Our first stop is the Dome Church. This is the Estonian cathedral and it's white, both inside and outside. Family crests dot the walls and glazed pews jut out like theatre boxes.

A short distance away is the Alexander Nevsky Russian Orthodox Cathedral which is a very different kind of church. We step inside cautiously as there's a mass in progress and we can hear chanting. It could not be more of a contrast to the cool Scandinavian simplicity of the Estonian cathedral. Every surface is richly decorated and glossed with gold leaf. Outside the cathedral are four babushkas. They hold begging bowls and have weatherworn faces and headscarves tied under their chins. Immediately behind is the Estonian parliament building and I agree with Will that it's impossible not to warm to a country whose political headquarters are based in a building resembling a pink and white birthday cake.

The hill raises us high above the city and offers far-reaching views. We can see the docks and half a dozen gleaming cruise ships. In the distance is the modern part of the city with its tall hotels and office towers. Beyond that are grey concrete Communist-era blocks of flats. They're very different from the Old Town, where we stand looking down on red-roofed buildings painted in pale shades of beige, green, blue and yellow.

A little later, during lunch back at our apartment we discuss how to spend the afternoon. One suggestion is the Museum of Occupations. Molly assumes this is to do with careers. The truth, however, is nothing cheerful like the ins and outs of what an ergonomist does, or how an orthotist is different from an orthoptist. Estonia's history is dark and it has been invaded and occupied so many times that a whole museum is devoted to these traumatic events.

Another possibility is the KGB Museum which is also dedicated to telling the truth about terrible times. Eventually, though, we decide to go to the Estonian History Museum and reach it by walking along the beach at the edge of the city. The first thing we see when we get there is a sign; 'The Estonian state is not something its citizens can take for granted'. And as we work our way through the rooms it becomes increasingly clear what that means. This small nation has been occupied by the Poles, Danes, Swedes, Germans, and Russian Tsars. Even the name of its capital city translates as 'Danish town'. A brief, glorious period began in 1920 when it gained its independence, the economy grew strong and the citizens were optimistic. Then in 1939 the Soviets crossed the border and it all went wrong again.

This first year of Soviet occupation was called the Year of Suffering. In one night ten thousand people were deported to Siberia. One third were children. The Nazis made a stab at Estonia too and had some success before the Russians re-invaded from St Petersburg in 1944. Estonians were forcibly conscripted into the two armies and those who resisted were shot. There were many cases of brothers, or fathers and sons, fighting one another. By 1945 the conflicts were over and the Russians took formal control, dragging the small country into the Soviet Union. In the museum we see some satirical posters, drawn by Estonian students. The text underneath states starkly, 'They lost their lives'.

About 70,000 Estonians tried to escape to the West at this time. Many travelled in fishing boats and were drowned. Others were killed by Soviet planes. One key reason for wanting to get away was that Stalin had started the process of Russification.

Over several decades, tens of thousands of Soviets were sent to take over Estonian homes, farms and businesses. The little country of Estonia no longer existed and by the 1960s, forty per cent of the population was Russian.

However, Estonians are patient, dignified people and they found ways to resist. An astonishing number of young men and women took to the woods and lived in underground hideouts. There were thirty thousand of them. They called themselves the Forest Brothers and their mission was to ambush Russians and fight for freedom. They believed that the West would rescue their country from its plight, but this never happened and the last of the Forest Brothers was captured in 1978.

The other great wave of resistance came, surprisingly, through singing. Although Estonia is a tiny country, it has one of the largest collections of folk songs in the world. Ever since the nineteenth century, the people have celebrated their musical heritage with huge folk festivals where they wear their national costumes and sing traditional songs. In 1947 everyone wondered what would happen, but the Soviets did allow the festival to take place, intending it to be a display of support for the communist regime. However, the clever Estonians subtly undermined this propaganda. They sang 'Land of my fathers, land that I love', in their own language. Somehow this slipped past the censors, and the song became the symbol of Estonian nationalism. Throughout this era, deportations to Siberia continued, it was forbidden to celebrate Christmas, and the blue, black and white Estonian flag was banned. People were not even allowed to wear these colours in combination, in case it aroused nationalistic fervour.

Severe oppression continued for many years but following 'glasnost' under Gorbachev and peaceful demonstrations throughout the late 1980s, Estonia became independent again. Today the country is beginning to flourish and is often called 'E-stonia' because of its advanced digital development. Skype is an Estonian company, and everyone's health and education records are digitised. Things are going well for the citizens of Tallinn but they're wise to ensure that the city is never completed. They've had to endure much hardship and can do without trouble from the little old man.

We fly back to Luton Airport on Sunday evening, arriving late. But instead of going straight home we drive round the M25 to Stansted Airport. Shaun is heading off early tomorrow morning to spend a week walking part of the Camino de Santiago, the pilgrimage route in Spain. He's staying in an airport hotel so Molly and I drop him there. He gets out of the car and pulls out the rucksack which he packed before we left for Tallinn. I kiss him goodbye and say that I hope it's a wonderful experience. I know how much this trip means to him. It's something he's wanted to do for several years, and at one time it seemed that he might not live long enough. He hoists his rucksack onto his back and adjusts it with a few efficient shrugs. Then he sets off purposefully through the gloom of the car park towards the bright lights of the hotel reception. He doesn't look back.

EIGHTEEN

BACK AGAIN

It's a week later and I'm back at Stansted Airport on another dark Sunday evening. This time I'm collecting Shaun. He's phoned several times whilst he's been away and has sent me regular texts. From a distance I've been able to share in some of his experiences. He's seen beautiful flowers, heard a skylark, and for a section of the walk he joined up with a French choir, singing as he tramped along with them. In one hotel he was bitten by bed bugs and had to sleep on the floor.

I spot him coming through arrivals before he sees me. He looks happy. I'm glad that it has done him some good.

THURSDAY

After Shaun got back from the Camino he went away for a couple of days because of work. But he got back last night and this is the first morning for a while that neither of us has an early start and we've been able to wake up together. I make two cups of tea and bring them back to bed. Peppermint for him, weak builder's for me.

A bit later, after Molly has left for school, we sit at the kitchen table eating our porridge together as we have done so many times before. He likes cinnamon on his. I'm more self-indulgent and enjoy a spot of maple syrup as well. When we've finished, I load the dishwasher and as we're both working from home this morning, I suggest a quick walk around the park before we start. We often do this and call it our 'walk to work'. It feeds the soul better than simply climbing the stairs to the spare bedroom that doubles as a study for me, and going the short distance across the garden to the wooden office that is Shaun's working space.

There's a steep hill to climb on our way to the park and I hold onto my husband's arm. It's satisfying that this is no longer because he's weak and needs support, but instead it's for affection. In the park I point out the 'squeaky saw' song of a great tit. We remark on the united little Canada geese families. They each have two parents who constantly keep their long necks extended looking out for danger whilst their chicks peck about on the grass, fluffy and carefree.

Twenty minutes later we've completed our circuit round the pond and are back home. While the kettle's boiling, I straighten our red and white checked duvet cover and plump the pillows ready for another night. I put four tablespoons of Arabica coffee in the cafetière, just as usual and then I pour two mugs of coffee and take Shaun's to the bathroom where he's applying the various ointments that are helping his hip to heal from the radiotherapy burns. I take my coffee upstairs and settle down to do some work. It's about nine thirty.

At about ten thirty I hear Shaun coming up the stairs. He knocks on the door and asks if I want a cup of tea. He looks really unhappy. He tells me that he's made an appointment to see his counsellor this afternoon.

'I hoped the Camino would help,' I say.

His face looks entirely blank. He doesn't know how to answer. Then some words appear in my brain. They pass across it, as if in rehearsal. I feel like I'm teetering on the edge of a cliff. I'm not sure if I'm going to say these words or not. Then suddenly they're out and the air in the room is full of their strange unfamiliarity.

'I don't make you happy, do I?'

Something profound happens to Shaun's face. A number of emotions pass rapidly across it. Somewhere in amongst them I think I recognise relief. Like I've acknowledged something he's wanted me to say for a while. 'No,' he says.

Then come the words that surprise me more than any of the millions of words I've ever spoken in my fifty-three years. I hear myself saying clearly and calmly: 'Then I think our marriage is over.'

As I speak these alien words it's like they've invaded and taken me over. These aren't things I say. I married for better for worse, for richer for poorer, in sickness and in health. But these words didn't simmer out of my rational thinking self. They've boiled over from my unconscious emotions which have known for some time that Shaun has become disengaged from me and they've worried how my consciousness would cope. Now the truth is out.

Once out I know immediately that there's no taking these words back. No saying that I didn't really mean it. I look at Shaun but already he seems unfamiliar. I can't quite take him in. In the split second since the words were given to him, he's erected a fence. He's standing in the doorway. He's central to my vision, but at the periphery I linger on the detail of the architrave. It's solid and familiar. The shiny gloss of the white paint which has built up in layers over the years. There are a few places where the wood is dented, and others where it's been chipped into small bare splinters. Then there's the light brown mark where the oil of an unsealed knot is seeping through.

Shaun gestures to the small boxy sofa and we sit there together, not touching, his legs stretched out, mine bent up to try to contain the churning. I can't take this in. The words I didn't even know I was going to say, have hijacked me. Within a few minutes of them escaping we're planning our separation. How to tell the children. How things will be from now on. He's happy for me to stay in the house.

Like the familiarity of the chipped architrave, I absorb the solid, blocky arms of the sofa, and the matt brown suede-effect upholstery. These are things I understand. In amongst all the strange words I hear Shaun saying that for him our marriage has been 'broken' for the past nine years. I don't think I believe him, but if it *is* true then I wish that he'd mentioned it before we started our long and weary trudge through the tough times.

His good prognosis and well-paid job were for me the haven at the end of the slog, but for him it seems they're a passport to another life.

We talk for half an hour or so, but despite there being so much to say, there's nothing much to say. Like the diagnosis of a terminal disease there's no option for negotiation. He's going to London for a meeting and then he's going on to see his counsellor. I offer to drive him to the station but he declines politely as though I were a stranger offering him a lift.

After he's left, looking purposeful and energised, I can't think what to do. I walk up and down the stairs several times, then I ring my friend, Sue. More strange words. It's the first time I've ever had to say, 'Shaun and I have decided to separate.' She's a dear friend who has followed our ups and downs attentively over the years.

'I'm on my way, right now,' she says.

Forty minutes pass. I walk up and down the stairs a lot. Then there she is on the doorstep.

Friday

Yesterday was one of those days that 'just has to be got through'. Like labour or a vomiting bug. But the difference is that today there's no warm baby to fall in love with. No relief that the nausea and cramps have passed. No soothing sips of flat lemonade or restorative little triangles of dry toast.

In many ways I'm functioning normally. I cooked a meal for Emma and Molly last night—they don't know about the earthquake yet. I unloaded the dishwasher and had a bath before I went to bed. I haven't even cried properly. But I know that things aren't right because already I can't remember great chunks of what has happened since yesterday lunchtime. It's become a collection of images with gaps in between. The bits that I can remember are:

- Sitting at my round, granite kitchen table opposite Sue and feeling guilty that this is the second time she's been through this in the last few days. The husband of one of her other friends walked out this week with no warning after thirty years of marriage. But also feeling that Sue's very good at warm, calm empathy and that this is *why* she's been called on twice this week.

- Ringing my sister, who answers her mobile in her usual breezy way. She's in the middle of a game of bridge with friends. I take a deep breath and spill out the 'Shaun and I have decided to separate' words, very fast. 'You're joking,' she says.

- Tussling with the peculiarity of it all and trying to squeeze alien feelings into a rigid compartment in my brain where they can be contained. I need to appear normal to the girls. At least for the time being.

- Meeting Frances at a village pub a few miles away. Sitting side by side on a big sofa at right angles to the fire. Hoping that she, a friend who knows me so well, can help me make sense of it all. She tells me that she'd seen for ages that I wasn't happy and that it was like I was slowly disappearing.

- Shaun texting me to say he's walking home from the station in the rain.

- Remembering that it was the fifteenth anniversary of my mother's death.

- Shaun texting me again to say that he's had a call from the nursing home in Suffolk where his 92-year old mother has been in a semi-comatose state for four years. They think that she's fading so he's driving up to see her straightaway.

Now it's Friday. I wake up to a text from Shaun to say that he got there a couple of hours before she died. They weren't close but she was still his mother, so I compose a reply to say I'm sorry and that it's good he was there. I put a couple of kisses at the end as I always do. Then I remove them as they're probably not appropriate. Then I put them back again because it looks sad without them. Then I take them off again and send it.

Shaun replies to say that he will come to the house at six so that we can tell the girls our news. Molly has an inset day today and Emma is working at home. The day passes with as many distractions as I can come up with. I take Molly swimming. Up and down the pool mindlessly. Then I buy her some blue nail polish and paint her toenails. We have a walk around the park. Twice round the pond. Then at six on the dot, as agreed, Shaun arrives and we are once again at the kitchen table with our children as their father delivers some shock news. It takes me back to the afternoon eighteen months ago when he told them about his relapse. Again the table is at the centre of it all, hard and shiny. Their faces focus on him. He has all their attention.

One difference is that this time he's standing up.

'You may have realised,' he says calmly, 'that Mum and I haven't been happy for some time. So we've decided to have a trial separation.' I sit on the fringes observing what's happening. I don't feel part of this.

Emma's eyes fly to Molly, instantly monitoring how she is reacting. They hug and sob. For the first time since yesterday morning the tears come for me too. Shaun looks awkward but offers no comfort. In the circumstances I suppose there's no reason why I should expect it. But it's a shock. The fence he erected so quickly yesterday has now grown protective thorns. He's cold; he's behaving as though I've done something wrong. I have a sense that he's disappointed in me; that he is the adult in a regrettable situation.

He continues to take charge and explains that he'll be staying in a hotel for a few days until he can sort out somewhere to live locally. He'll make sure that he spends plenty of time with the girls. Another cut into our marriage as I realise that plans in future will not include me. I've always been at the centre of family gatherings. It feels very odd to think of them going on without me. I won't be welcome. Later I expect it will begin to hurt but for now it just seems a very curious idea

There are decisions to be made. We have to work out how to tell the boys. It's going to be a big shock for them. There's probably no option but to tell Will on the phone as he's so far away, but Henry is in Liverpool so one of us could go and tell him in person. We agree that I will go up first thing tomorrow and that Shaun will spend the weekend here with the girls. I say that I will set off at eight. He says he will arrive here shortly after so that the girls aren't left on their own. There's a sense of this being like a military operation.

I contribute my own addendum to the strategic plan and request that we have no direct contact for ten days. He looks surprised so I explain that I need some space to get my thoughts straight. My head feels full. He agrees and then he brings the meeting to a close.

'Please don't go,' Emma, Molly and I say as if orchestrated.

Then he goes. The table is still there. Solid on its metal legs. The round black granite surface flecked with silver. We look at one another. There's no script to follow. We take our confusion into the sitting room and sit in a circle on the floor.

NINETEEN

I didn't sleep well last night. Or to be entirely accurate, I didn't sleep until about 3am. It's hard to wake up and I'm fifteen minutes late leaving for Liverpool. As I drive out of our cul-de-sac I see Shaun's car in the rear view mirror. He's been waiting in a parking area out of sight of the house. I watch his red car glide smoothly into our driveway. The parental handover has been seamless and silent.

The journey takes several hours longer than it should due to a diversion off the M40. I don't mind as it delays the task that I'm dreading. I follow the road signs mindlessly. A couple of times I switch on the radio but discover that peace is preferable. Every now and again I surprise myself by saying something out loud— 'How did it happen?'—'What's going on?'—'I don't know what to feel'—'This is horrible.' My brain is filled with chaotic thoughts that spill out incontinently. I'm glad to be on my own.

With the delays and a short restless break, it's three o'clock by the time I arrive at Henry's hall of residence. I pull into a parking space and call him on my mobile. 'Hi Mum,' he says cheerfully.

'Are you in your room?' I ask. It's a relief when he says that he is. If he'd been out, I'm not sure where I'd have gone to do the inevitable agitated pacing up and down.

'I'm in the car park downstairs,' I say. 'Can you come and let me in?'

'You can't be,' he says, confused. Here's someone else who thinks I'm pulling their leg. First my sister. Now Henry. I'm slightly offended that they both think I'd make such feeble jokes.

As I convince Henry that I really am outside, I hear his

pleasure at an unexpected visit—and then fear. Within a minute he appears at the heavy door, fumbling with the entry mechanism. His face is taut and pale. It's clear that he thinks I've come to tell him that his father is dead.

I say quickly, 'It's not Dad.' But I can't deliver the blow on the stairs. We get up to his room and I take in the detritus of a normal student Saturday afternoon. I can see the remains of his lunch. His guitar is propped against his desk. There are books open. He's part-way through an essay.

We sit cross-legged on the bed. I take yet another deep breath and tell him the news. He is devastated. I hate having to hurt him like this. It goes against all my instincts as his mother.

We sit facing one another for several hours as I try to give him an explanation of something I don't understand myself. Eventually we've talked, hugged, cried and gone over the same things so many times that I think we need a change of scene. I suggest having something to eat and going to see a film. Henry says that we can get the student bus from outside and that this will take us into the city centre. We choose a little French bistro where Henry has duck and I have salmon. It's not the fault of the food but our mood makes it a joyless affair. The only pleasure comes from the closeness I feel to my son in our shared bloody state.

We go up the road to the wonderful FACT, an art house cinema that I've been to several times with Will. We sit on a comfortable sofa and watch 'Salmon Fishing in the Yemen'. It's a surprisingly effective distraction. At the end we walk through the exuberance of a Liverpool Saturday night and wait at the bus stop. When we get on the bus I have a brief unexpected moment of sheer happiness. It's so different from my normal experience to be on a bus with a crowd of students, on my way home after a night out. Three words pop into my head—free, untethered, unstable.

When we get back to Henry's room we try to make a plan for what to do next. Does Henry want me to go home first thing tomorrow? Or does he want me to spend some of the day with him? He doesn't know. So we agree that I'll find somewhere to stay and will meet him tomorrow outside the café in Sefton Park.

There's a room free at the small hotel where I stayed on my last visit and it's a blessing to fall asleep quickly. In the morning we meet outside the café and order bacon sandwiches and coffee. Henry's still not sure what he wants, so we talk through some options. I suggest a few places we could go for a day out. This feels strange. An outing that would normally be for pleasure is going to become just a way of getting through another day. But we have to do something. We can't sit and stare at one another. I suggest to Henry that I give him ten minutes to think about what he wants while I go and make a few phone calls. I talk to Molly. She sounds OK but is worried about Henry. She asks what we did yesterday.

'We went to see Salmon Fishing in the Yemen,' I say.

'What was it about?' she asks.

'Salmon Fishing in the Yemen,' I say.

'I know,' she says. 'What was it about?'

'Salmon Fishing in the Yemen.' I say again. My brain feels simply too numb to come up with a better explanation.

When I get back, Henry says that he'd like to go to Knowsley Safari Park with me. This is just outside Liverpool, so that's what we do. The monkeys climb all over the car as we drive round very slowly. They make faces at us and pull off a bit of the car trim.

At about two we go back to Henry's room and spend an hour or so swapping YouTube clips. I show him the wondrous eccentricity of Kate Bush performing Wuthering Heights, and he introduces me to the raw bluesiness of Howlin' Wolf singin' Smoke Stack Lightning. Then I have to leave him.

There are no holdups on the way home and I'm back by eight. The military strategy has worked and there's no sign of Shaun. The girls are both there. They're trying to be positive but we're all lost. The evening passes until we're tired enough to face our beds. I learn that:

- Shaun drove Molly to a tennis tournament yesterday. They were in the car for several hours but the subject of the separation wasn't mentioned.

- Shaun is looking forward to gathering together a collection of all the music that he likes and putting it on his phone. I puzzle over why he couldn't do this whilst married to me.

- Shaun plans to come and spend Wednesday evening with the girls. I need to arrange to be out.

I have an image of a tornado sweeping through the house and sucking out the glue that bonds our family together. Those of us that remain after the devastation are clinging to anything that is solid. But there are sensitivities to be negotiated; there are unexpected sharp words in places where before there was safety and trust. We discuss what to do tomorrow. It's a Bank Holiday. Together we come up with a plan to go to Tenterden and possibly have a trip on the steam railway. None of us sounds very enthusiastic but we all recognise the need to get out and do something.

Thursday Again

A week has passed since the bomb exploded. Everything is destabilised. I'm prey to tropical storms, with frequent sobbing downpours. These give temporary relief but the clouds are always above, their shadows oppressive.

The girls are suffering too. I worry as I see their concern for me. Bringing cups of tea. Offering to cook dinner. This is the wrong way round. I should be protecting them but I have so little energy. One gesture of care I *can* make is to take the phone into the garage where I talk to friends and cry in private.

We had our day out on Monday. We sat on a steam train. None of us really wanting to be there. Then we shopped for food. We made a chicken curry that none of us really wanted to eat.

On Tuesday I told Will. This was the most difficult phone call I've ever had to make. I messed it up. He was devastated like Henry and there was no way to comfort him. I want to fly out to see him, but I can't. I'm needed here, too. I'm stretched thin and holes are appearing.

I had a few days of compassionate leave from my job, but I'm back now, trying to keep a bit of my work-related brain safe from incursions. Life has to go on even when life as I know it has stopped. In amongst the rain there are thunderstorms. Moments of fury when I rage to friends about what has happened. And I had a scalding row with the girls this week. We all screamed at one another. It relieved some tension—for a while.

Now today it's Thursday again. I've told many of the people who have to know but have avoided telling cousins Maggie and Philip. Shaun and I met them together and our families have become close. Their girls have grown up with our children, and they think that we are stable, steady parents like theirs are. There's something about telling them that I'm particularly dreading. An admission that our separation is real. I ring Maggie and say, 'Shaun and I have decided to separate.' I've now said this many times. I no longer say it fast but instead struggle to get it out between the tears which lock my mouth into shapes where there is no space for words.

ANOTHER THURSDAY

I don't like any part of the week at the moment but Thursdays seem particularly bad. That was the day of partition, so each one marks out the time I've spent in this new part of my life. The one where I don't want to be.

Last night Shaun came to see the girls again. I took

sanctuary at a friend's house and when I got back I found an envelope propped against my computer. Inside was a note in the clear, measured handwriting that's so familiar. In business-like terms it informed me that these two weeks apart have convinced Shaun that our marriage is over.

I slept fitfully and woke up this morning with feelings so huge that my body doesn't feel big enough to contain them. In amongst the chaos is:

- Sadness that it should end like this after all we've battled through together.

- Bleakness that the man who has been my best friend isn't there when I'm in pain.

- Frustration that we cannot work together to make things better again.

- Fear that my family and all we have created is falling apart. That the children will be damaged and hurt.

- Anger that my opinions don't count.

- Humiliation that he seems happier without me.

- Exhaustion and feelings of being overwhelmed. Of not being strong enough to care for Molly…support the other children… work …and negotiate a divorce.

- Confusion that he is so cold.

I hold it together until both girls have left the house; Emma for work in London, Molly for school. Then everything seems so quiet and empty. There've been many times over the past twenty years, when I've longed for a bit of peace and quiet, but not this sort.

I can't work; I'm not sure how to get through the next five minutes, let alone the whole day. I walk up and down the stairs a bit. Then I ring Rita. Fortunately she's not working. 'Hello, darling,' she says soothingly and explains that she's making cakes for a funeral. She can hear that I'm desperate and suggests I spend the day with her.

It's such a relief to get into the car. To have a sense of purpose—at least for the next hour or so, I know where I'm going. I have Radio 4 on as I drive to Essex. I've no idea what Melvyn Bragg is talking about, as the conversations in my head dominate. But there's a certain comfort in having him there—familiar, calm and nasal.

There's no queue at the Dartford Tunnel and I arrive at Rita's house twenty minutes later. The kitchen surfaces are full of cakes, smelling buttery and fragrant. I perch on a stool. We chat, I soak a lot of tissues, and Rita makes the cakes look beautiful. I explain that I'm willing to help, but if I do she will have to tell people that her 'young cousin' helped with the decoration. My efforts would resemble those of an enthusiastic seven-year old. Rita wisely and tactfully declines my offer. As the day goes on the weeping gets less. Somehow she has managed to glue me together to face another day, and I'm home by the time Molly returns from school. I might look a little worse for wear, but it's bearable.

I think I'm in shock but the only thing I can do is try to cling to some normality; keep putting one foot in front of the other. I decide that I'll go ahead with the dawn chorus walk I arranged several weeks ago. It's booked for the day after tomorrow.

TWENTY

The Birds Sing On

My alarm goes off at 3.30 am and ten minutes later I'm in the car and on my way to Surrey. Again, it's good to have a sense of purpose; to know what I'll be doing for the next forty miles. Not surprisingly, the roads are fairly quiet, but there's still a lot more traffic than I expected. I wonder where everyone is going. We can't all be headed for a dawn chorus adventure.

I arrive at Painshill Park a bit early and, as instructed in the information pack, go to the delivery entrance. There are double metal gates there but only one side is open. I'm not sure what to do as it looks too narrow to drive through. After several minutes of pondering I decide it *must* be wide enough and edge forwards. Unfortunately, I immediately get wedged and have to go backwards and forwards a lot, all the time accompanied by a horrible scraping sound as the side panel of my car acquires a long, deep scratch. I do manage to emerge on the other side at last but feel idiotic and hope that no-one saw my mishap. My first instinct is to cry. I think how cross Shaun will be and then I remember. There's a silver lining in amongst the thunderclouds. The state of my car is now entirely my own concern: I can drive a dented car if I want to.

The road winds through attractive trees and I park just outside the café. Inside are two young women. We sit and wait together. Suddenly, the door opens and a man appears. He looks at us thoughtfully for a moment. 'Are you here for the dawn chorus walk?' We look bleary and a bit surprised to be asked this. It's 4.55am. I think we can safely assume that's the reason we're sitting here.

The man turns out to be Steve, our guide for the walk. Several other people arrive and after coffee and croissants, we set off. It's fascinating to have the company of an enthusiast, and the next three hours are pure entertainment. The 'issue' is never far from my mind but at least I get a break from the crying.

The expert nuggets come thick and fast. I learn that birds can have different dialects, so a Norfolk dunnock, for example, might sound different from a Northumberland one. Even more confusingly, birds sometimes copy one another. Steve says he recently heard a great tit doing an imitation of a marsh tit.

When we get to the lake a common sandpiper swoops fast and low across the water, making a mournful 'pipit' sound. Then we reach a copse of pine trees. Steve says this is just the sort of habitat where we're likely to hear goldcrests and coal tits. Sure enough we do. Later with some guidance I learn to recognise the call of the chiffchaff which sounds just like its name. The magpie also says its name, but it's clever and can say it in Latin; 'pica pica.'

On the way back we see a large black bird strutting about. Someone asks, 'Is it a crow or a rook?'

Steve quotes an old saying. 'A crow on its own is a crow. A rook on its own is a crow.'

I have to think about this, but it's pleasing when I get it, and it leads on to a discussion about crow intelligence. Steve says that they can count to seven. I ask how this has been tested, and he says it's done by putting people into a bird-watching hide. It's only when they've all come out that the watchful crow will treat it as empty. Then there are the Japanese crows who have solved the problem of how to crack nuts open. They drop them onto the road so that cars crush them. The problem, then, is that they have to weave in and out of dangerous traffic to retrieve their treats. The cleverest of all are those who drop their nuts from above a pedestrian crossing. The nutshells are crushed and when the traffic comes to a halt, the crows dart down to feed in safety.

I confess to my fellow bird-listeners that I'm having trouble distinguishing robins from blackbirds, and ask for their advice. Although this is Chapter One in my bird book, no-one in the group makes me feel stupid. They tell me that the robin has a huge range of songs, but it's easy to recognise because it sings a little phrase, then stops for a few seconds, before starting again with a new one.

It's amusing to walk along with Steve, as every now and again he shouts out the name of a bird he's heard. He says this is quite an affliction, and whilst entirely appropriate in this setting, it can at times be embarrassing, especially for his wife. I have a similar affliction at the moment. However, it's a different word that keeps escaping spontaneously from my lips; something less to do with birds and more related to husbands.

I'm thoroughly satisfied with my morning but the journey home is hard. I've enjoyed several hours of relative relief but a grey, heavy cloak wraps around me as I leave the Park. Then when I arrive at the house I'm not quite ready to go in. I get out of the car and stop for a moment. There's a very noisy bird somewhere nearby. It sings a merry little phrase. Then it waits. Then it sings another, but different verse. Is it a blackbird? Is it a robin? For the first time I can answer that question with confidence.

TREATS COMPLETED THIS SPRING	TREATS IN PROGRESS
Derren Brown	Compost
Port Sunlight	Mad Men
London walk	Life on Earth
Stratford	North Downs Way
Tallinn	Jane Austen
Birdsong	

SUMMER 2012

TWENTY-ONE

PADDLING

Forget anything good that I've ever done in my life. There's only one thing that matters right now. I am a woman who is unable to make her husband happy. This fact floods into every corner of my life and I have to concentrate harder and harder to hold my head up. I don't really care on my own account. Drowning might be a peaceful release, but the children need me to keep paddling, to keep afloat for them.

It's exhausting.

999 CALLS

Things are changing at a surprising pace. It's as though the decision to separate released a mechanism that held us together. Once the catch was lifted we sprang apart with great force.

In these first few weeks Shaun has become different: energised; business-like in his contact with me, a shift from glasses to contact lenses. And now he's going to Atlanta for a week to see an old colleague who might be able to get him some work.

I want to be different too. I want to do something that lifts me out of this pit and the only thing I can think of at the moment is to have my hair restyled. I've had a fringe for as long as I can remember. Perhaps it's time for a change. Sam, my hairdresser, responds to my plea and comes to the house. She's delighted to have a challenge and within an hour or so, I've got a shorter, perkier style, and a warmer colour. I'm pleased—and wonder what Shaun will think.

There's something else I could do while I'm thinking about my image. 'Learn to do eye make-up better', is on my list, and this seems the ideal time to do it. Several times over the years, I've bought products from persuasive sales assistants, but after initial enthusiasm those products have lain in my drawer, unused. Most have eventually disappeared into my daughters' make-up bags.

I'm not sure how to approach this treat. I could buy a book—I could look for make-up demonstrations on YouTube—I could ask a friend to help. Then I have a better idea. Years ago I had my 'colours done' and ever since then I've bought lipsticks by post from the same company. For the past seventeen years I've had friendly exchanges by letter, and latterly by email, with a woman called Fiona in North London. I send an email explaining the situation and she replies quickly. I sense that she's well used to helping women boost their damaged self-esteem and face the world. She's sure she can help, and as well as giving me a lesson, she'll do a general update on my make-up. She offers me an appointment within a few days. Life is odd in all kinds of ways at the moment, but it's reassuring to know that emergency hairdressers and emergency make-up consultants are on hand to help me through.

NEW MASCARA

Yesterday I received a letter from Rita: a handwritten list of 142 ideas for things to do when I need cheering up. They remind me that I could dance, cuddle a teddy, contact old friends, buy new underwear, and refuse to feel guilty.

I couldn't face breakfast before I set off for my make-up lesson in London, but am now feeling empty. I buy a coffee at the station stall, and also a packet of peanuts to keep the rumbling at bay. I'm trying to avoid sugar at the moment as it makes me feel worse. I know I need to look after my health but I can't sleep and I've lost my appetite. I'm also coughing a lot. My GP thinks it's caused by acid reflux. This makes sense. For several years I've been aware of literally swallowing worries.

At times I've caught myself mid-gulp as I've tried to stop panic welling up and overwhelming me.

For some reason today I notice all kinds of things I've never seen before. The world really does seem to have changed in the past few weeks. One way that I've changed is that I'm no longer wearing my wedding ring or the diamond ring that Shaun gave me. I feel peculiarly naked. Every time I catch sight of my bare left hand or go to fiddle absent-mindedly with my rings, I get a desolate lurch. But there's also another feeling germinating in amongst the sadness: liberation.

The train arrives at London Bridge and I set off up the Northern Line to Chalk Farm station. Fiona lives a short walk away in Primrose Hill. It's a pleasant area, but what stands out is the amount of building renovation that's going on. Every second house has a skip outside.

I see a poster for a forthcoming event. Derek Jacobi is shortly going to be in conversation with Dame Joan Bakewell at Primrose Hill Community Library. How *very* North London.

TREAT #20

It's really good to meet Fiona after all these years of letters and emails and she immediately puts me at my ease. She takes me through all the different stages of skincare and make-up, starting with the basics, like cleanser and toner, which I do not possess but promise to use every day from now on. Then we do foundation and other bits and pieces of make-up. It's fun to experiment with colours and I choose a different shade of lipstick for a change. The most interesting bit, though, is the eye make-up. I try mauve, grey and deep purple rather than the browns I've used before. I also see how the faintest use of eye pencil can be effective. The session lasts over two hours. I'm pleased with the results and the biggest bonus is that I've forgotten about 'the issue' for a while.

The mascara has made my eyelashes lush but I'm not sure if

this is a good thing or not. In Polynesia it's a sign of affection to chew your partner's eyelashes; prestige is attached to short eyelashes as it means someone loves you. Regrettably, I might have to accept having long eyelashes for some while.

By the time I leave, it's early afternoon and I haven't had any lunch so Fiona directs me towards the high street. I expect to end up in a mundane coffee shop with an overchilled sandwich. But instead I end up somewhere quite different. The first café I see is Russian. I'm about to move on when I think, 'Why not?' Before I know it, I'm sitting inside and ordering lunch.

It feels exotic. The walls and ceiling are rich crimson, and shelves line the walls, full of golden samovars and colourful Russian nesting dolls. There are shiny mirrors, stained glass and dark wood furniture. I study the menu, pondering whether to have borscht, Russian salad, blinis, or salt beef. Eventually I settle for goat's cheese on rye bread. This proves to be utterly delicious and quite unlike the toasted goat's cheese I've had in France. The discs of cheese are grilled to a slight crunchiness on the outside, and are creamy-soft inside. They rest on a mixture of salad leaves, roasted peppers and aubergines, and slightly vinegary strips of carrot. The thing that makes it wonderful, though, is the bread. It's faintly sweet, with a hint of caraway. The combination of these flavours with the cheese is exciting and memorable. It's the first time in days that I've been able to summon any enthusiasm for food.

I also order Russian tea. An optional accompaniment is cherry syrup, so in the spirit of exploring the unknown, I choose that. The waitress brings a sturdy but elegant silver teapot, with a dish of sliced lemon and a small cup of red liquid. I pour the tea and add the syrup. It's rather pleasant, despite a slight medicinal taste.

I leave feeling stimulated and quite cheerful. It's odd how grief comes and goes. I can go to bed feeling reasonably happy and then wake up desolate at 4am. I wish I knew how to control it. I think, though, that there's no option but to wade through it like in the children's book: We're Going on a Bearhunt. 'Can't go under it—can't go over it—got to go through it.'

I buy a copy of the Big Issue and read it on the way home. There's an interesting article on coping with trauma that seems relevant to how I'm feeling right now. A professor of psychiatry writes that personal resilience is partly dictated by genetics and upbringing, but also by how easily people relate to others. If you're offered support and an understanding shoulder to cry on, you're likely to recover much more quickly. It's helpful if you're good at resolving problems and have strong beliefs. You must also be able to 'test your environment' accurately. No underplaying or overdramatising.

I'll remember that. The truth for me at present is that it's devastating and painful. That's the 'not underplaying' bit. As for avoiding the overdramatising, then I believe there may be things to look forward to, but I can't see what they are yet, and have to be patient. It's early days, but the world looks very slightly different through my newly mascaraed lashes.

TWENTY-TWO

Shaun is negotiating to rent a flat nearby so he can see the children easily. Until that's all sorted out, we're keeping up the arrangement where he comes to the house when he wants to see them, and I go away.

He's back from America and wants to spend Saturday with Molly. I organise a busy day, drawing on the generosity of friends. Breakfast in a café with Anne, lunch with Ros, tea with Stella, and then—I've got a standing invitation—spending the night in Melanie's spare room.

After tea and buttered toast with Anne, I drive to Ros's house. She went through a divorce a few years ago and I take comfort in seeing that she survived it. There are times at the moment when it's hard to believe I will do that too.

We're sitting in the sunshine, chatting and catching up on news when there's a flash of serendipity. I mention my list and when Ros asks what's on it, I mention that I want to 'Go to the races', Ros looks surprised. 'I've got free tickets for Lingfield Races tonight,' she says. 'Come with me and I'll teach you to gamble.' This really is a bit of luck. It's the one day in the year when the racecourse opens its doors to local residents, free of charge. 'Then you may as well stay the night,' says Ros, 'though you will be sharing with the chicks.' I'm not quite sure what this means but decide to cross that bridge when I come to it. I text Melanie and say I don't need her spare bedroom tonight, then drive off to see Stella, arranging to be back by 5.30.

Stella has been a good friend since we had our youngest babies in the same week. When they were little we'd sometimes take it in turns to look after them so that we each got a bit of child-free time. On one occasion I had both babies at my house when a neighbour rang with words that made my heart sink;

'Your goats are in my garden.' This neighbour lived about a quarter of a mile away and this presented me with a complex logistical problem. It took me a while to consider my options.

I could drive up there, but I had two babies and only one car seat. Also would two nonconformist goats fit in the back of the car? Probably not.

I could run up the road and bring the goats home, but that would mean leaving the babies alone. Definitely irresponsible.

I could wait until Stella got back but that might result in an irate neighbour and a desecrated garden.

The only option in the end was to walk up the lane with a long piece of rope, and the babies in the double buggy. I parked them outside the neighbour's house and spent ten minutes chasing the goats around the garden. They had a habit of standing very still and looking at me through their wild, elliptical eyes, all the while chewing pensively on holly leaves. When I was within a snatch of grabbing them they'd be off and then the whole rigmarole would start again. Eventually I got them both attached to my rope and the five of us made a strange little party as we zigzagged our way back home.

I'm not sure I ever confessed to Stella about the adventures I'd put her baby daughter through that morning. However, it's good to see her today. She's full of wisdom and support. In her work as a complementary therapist she treats clients facing all kinds of challenging situations. We talk about the mysteries of how serious illness can change people. I know that the loving, family-centred husband I had when he was diagnosed with leukaemia is not the same man who is now so dissatisfied with his lot. I've known and loved him for thirty years but can no longer predict his responses. Did nearly dying make him reconsider his priorities? Did the heavy-duty drugs change his personality? Have all the various pressures made him want to escape? Have I changed and become unlovable? Did I fail him in some way? Am I inextricably associated with the bad times?

By the end of the afternoon, after tea, cake and speculation, I'm back at Ros's house. Fortunately, I put a summer dress on this morning so am suitably dressed for our outing and it's only a short drive to the busy racecourse car park. The first thing that strikes me is the mix of people. There are serious racing types in tweed jackets, but there's a great deal of bling too; girls in very short skirts, with extravagant hats and orange legs. I spot some amazing tattoos, but the big surprise for me is that this is a family occasion. There are dozens of toddlers in buggies, out with their parents in the evening summer sunshine.

We get a racing card which gives details of the races, horses, jockeys and trainers. I've always been curious about race meetings and this treat is about demystifying the experience. We go to the ring where the horses parade round, giving punters a chance to study them before placing their bets.

'Number 4 is lame,' says Ros, knowledgeably. I'm impressed. I'm not able to compete on technicalities, but can see for myself that number 7 is naughty. It rears up and throws the jockey off. He hobbles out of the enclosure, and this is all before the race has even started. Men stand around in the ring, some wearing trilbies, others in Panamas.

'What are you supposed to look for?' I ask. Ros confesses that she's not altogether sure, but it's something to do with the flexibility and muscularity of the horse's rear legs.

We make our way down to the course where there's a row of bookies, all shouting for business. One stands out from the rest. He's large and his jacket is the definition of 'loud' with broad blue, yellow and grey stripes. I choose one of the quieter stalls and place a bet of £2 on number 7. The ticket shows me that I will pocket £68 if he wins. One bookie is shouting, 'No minimum stake,' so Ros puts £1 on number 2 and will get £1.60 if she's successful. This caution turns out to be wise. Her horse wins, whilst mine comes in seventh out of eight.

We go through the form-studying again and this time we both lose our bets. It *is* exciting, though. We stand by the track and stare at the huge screen that's mounted in front of us. I'm a little disappointed that the commentator doesn't do that clever, superfast talking that I remember from television horseracing when I was a child. Instead he's rather measured and I can understand everything he says. I suppose this makes for a better communicative experience, but it's not as thrilling. I watch the horses on the screen and then peer into the distance where I can see the real thing. They look like specks at first, then suddenly they come careering round the bend and gallop into sight with colossal power like they've burst through the TV screen. There's a brief noisy moment when everyone jumps up and down, shouts and waves.

We decide to investigate the Tote next. It sounds mysterious and is in its own special building. I say confidently to the woman behind the desk, '£5 to win on number 3.' She nods and gives me a ticket. I obviously said the right thing, and feel smug. So much of life is about feeling either in or out of things. I learn later that the Tote is just a different bookmaker. It was set up in 1928 under the guidance of Winston Churchill as a state-controlled alternative to the less salubrious bookmakers who were then in business. In 2011 it was privatised and sold to Betfred.

My rashness has done me no good as yet again my horse loses. By this stage I'm £9 down on the evening but Ros, who has had another win, is doing much better. She's only 40p in deficit.

All this excitement has made us hungry so we head off to join the long queue for fish and chips. I can't have potatoes because they give me migraines and fish does seem rather dull and lonely on its own. Then I spot a large jar of pickled eggs. 'Fish and a pickled egg,' I say to the young assistant. She's rather refined and wrinkles her nose at my choice.

'Sorry it's not the Savoy,' says Ros a few minutes later, as we settle down on high stools.

'It's better than the Savoy,' I say, biting into my pickled egg. 'Much more fun.'

We study the form for the next race and I resolve to be more considered in my gambling. The racing card gives each horse in the race a star rating. This takes into account the position of the jockeys and trainers in the championship table, as well as the horses' records over different courses and distances. Up to now I've just been going for names that I like. That's probably why I've not had much success, although Strawberry Duck *is* a lovely name. This time I go for Hill Street as he has a five-star rating. One of the entries in this race has odds of 200:1. I wonder what kind of hopeless horse this is. I'm tempted, but instead stick with reason and place £2 on Hill Street.

This proves a successful strategy as when the horses come thundering past, a few minutes later, Hill Street is right at the front. I go to collect my winnings. I'm due to receive £3; my original stake plus a pound. I explain to the bookie that this is my first ever win and as he hands me my £1 in winnings, he reminds me to spend it wisely.

The racing comes to an end and people start milling towards the exit. To our left a sleek black helicopter takes off. It's the epitome of sophistication, and the sight of it takes me back to my fiftieth birthday.

There was no opportunity for celebrations as Shaun was hospitalised and in isolation having just had his transplant. I wanted to see him on my birthday, though, so we planned that I would collect Molly from school a bit early and drive to London where I'd leave her with cousins Maggie and Philip. Then I would visit Shaun. Unfortunately, the day before my birthday there was a heavy fall of snow which closed all the local schools, blocked the roads and stopped the trains. I rang Shaun to tell him it was unlikely I'd be able to get to London. He sounded disappointed.

Half an hour later he rang back and said, 'You *are* coming to London tomorrow; I've organised a helicopter.'

'Don't be ridiculous,' I said.

'No, I mean it,' he replied. 'Be ready. A taxi will collect you and Molly at 9 in the morning.'

And so it did. Molly was wearing her smart red coat and holding a chic overnight bag. She looked every inch the sophisticate, whilst I had my toothbrush and tomorrow's knickers stuffed into a shopping basket.

The taxi driver edged his way skilfully through the snow, skidding several times on the ice. Eventually we arrived at Headcorn Aerodrome. We stood in the waiting area for just a few moments and when a helicopter landed, the staff said, 'That one's for you.' The rotor blades whizzed dramatically as the co-pilot dashed across the tarmac to pick up our bags, and lead us back. He settled us in our seats and then he and the pilot introduced themselves and kitted us out with headphones so we could talk to them. They were charm itself and made us feel very special.

The whole of the South East was covered in a thick duvet of snow. The motorways were shut and very little was happening anywhere. I'd assumed they were taking us to Battersea Heliport, within walking distance of Maggie and Philip's house. Unfortunately, our pilots informed us that for the first time in twenty-five years, Battersea Heliport was closed by snow, so they were taking us to High Wycombe. I was a bit taken aback; that was as far away from where we wanted to reach, as home. However, they reassured us that a taxi had been booked to take us on to South London, so I decided to sit back and enjoy the adventure. I chatted to the pilots for the first twenty minutes or so, as they pointed out landmarks. Then I started to feel sick and went quiet. After forty-five minutes in the air we landed at High Wycombe aerodrome and the co-pilot escorted us to the waiting taxi. He stowed our bags in the boot and gave us some travel sweets for the next stage of our journey.

We had lunch with our cousins and then I set off to visit Shaun, coming down to earth with a bump after my glamorous morning. Public transport was patchy and after slithering along icy streets I had to take three buses and two underground trains to reach the hospital. Shaun was looking pale and weak, but very pleased with himself and longing to hear about my adventures. I'm still not sure how he managed to organise all of that from an isolation room with just his laptop and mobile phone. Nor am I sure how he managed to pay for it in our straitened circumstances. He said that he used an overdue payment from a client. Looking back now I remember that for much of our marriage I loved his refusal to do things in a conventional way and to always look for a clever solution. This became less appealing and more of a worry when we were constrained by problems and family responsibilities.

Spending the Night with Chicks

We get back to Ros's house and the sofa-bed is all made up. It's a simple gesture but I appreciate it very much. It looks so welcoming; a haven when much outside feels daunting and threatening.

She wasn't joking about the chicks, either. Her daughter recently bought some fertile eggs from a website, and they arrived in polystyrene trays. An electric brooder kept them at mother-hen temperature for 21 days, and then they hatched. The resulting twelve little balls of fluff are now in an incubator at the end of my bed. They're asleep and look angelic, all huddled up together. When I climb in between the sheets I go straight off to sleep. I've enjoyed this treat but the best thing has been sharing the evening with an understanding friend.

At six in the morning I swim to the surface from my dreams, puzzled by the strange noises I can hear. 'Cheep, cheep, cheep.' Not the usual kind of dawn chorus, for sure.

Life is full of surprises.

TWENTY-THREE

Moving On

Another weekend, and I'm driving to Liverpool to bring Henry home for the summer. When I did this a month ago, on my way to tell him about the breakup, I was tear-free and on autopilot. Now I'm soggy. Noisy, too, with sobs and wails that surprise even me. The pain is almost unbearable. Distraction doesn't work. The radio just washes over me making no sense at all. Even Ella Fitzgerald has no success. I talk firmly to myself but I find it hard to concentrate on what I'm saying. Then I try forcing myself to smile. I read once that this persuades the brain that you're happy and releases endorphins. Every few minutes when the horrid feeling starts in the pit of my stomach I grin wildly. It feels incongruous and it's exhausting, but it does provide brief moments of relief.

I stay over in Henry's room and the next day we set off for home. His company makes the return journey easier. When we get back there's no sign of Shaun but he *has* left us some food: pasta with a spicy sausage sauce and a salad to go with it. He's clearly taken some trouble. This leaves me with muddled feelings. It's a gesture of kindness—but from someone who wants to distance himself.

It's been a month now since we separated and I feel I should be coping better. Each time I was in labour, I would repeatedly ask the midwives, 'How long will it last?' They'd smile to themselves in a most annoying way and say they didn't know. It's like that now. I want someone to give me an answer but instead of being minutes or hours, I know we're talking months. I'm determined it's not going to be years, though, as some people have suggested.

The split does mean that I'm free to try new things. I already have a different haircut and thicker eyelashes, but I want to do something more substantial. There are courses I could do, clubs I could join and various charities that I could get involved in.

While I'm browsing on the internet for a new life I spot that the local branch of the Samaritans is holding an information session on Tuesday this week. I decide to go along and find out whether I can become a volunteer.

When I get there I'm surprised to see so many people—it's quite a small room, and it's packed. We listen to a talk about the varied and challenging work, and then the speaker mentions the training dates: two Sundays and five weekday evenings. I add my name to the list and put the dates in my diary. I'm pleased that I've managed to hold myself together and do something constructive.

On Wednesday evening Shaun wants to stay in the house so I arrange to go to some friends. The next morning when I come home we have our first proper conversation since the split. We're alone in the house. He makes a pot of coffee and we sit at our familiar kitchen table to discuss the logistics of getting divorced. We agree that we want to avoid going to court if possible and I tell him that I plan to instruct my friend Melanie, to be my lawyer. He seems pleased that I've given this some thought. He looks pleased too when I tell him that I want to be a Samaritan; like it's good that I'm coping. Then he looks at me and says that he will 'work hard to restore our family fortunes.'

I reply sharply. 'That's not going to matter much now.' Perhaps I'm too sharp. He looks stunned; like I've slapped him. To me the words sound hollow. What's money when our family life is shattered? But for him what's important is the knowledge that he has provided for us.

He leaves and I settle down to try and do some work. Then I see out of the window that although he got into his car, he hasn't driven away. He comes back to the house. I'm sitting at my computer at the dining table. He's standing up. He's at right angles to me. Time stands still again. His face is set. I focus on the texture of his jacket: it's tweed, quite old, and little bits of thread stick out of it where they've been snagged. There are tiny black and grey specks of pilling that sit like ants on the surface. I want to pick at them and free them; to make the surface of the jacket smooth and new.

'I've got something to tell you,' he says. 'I will be seeing someone.' These words could mean many things. He could be planning to see a counsellor, a doctor, a dentist, or a candlestick maker. But I know immediately what they mean. I know too that I have to control my face and not let the faintest twitch give my feelings away.

'Did you know her before?' I ask.

'I've never been unfaithful to you,' he says.

He makes eye contact with me. He doesn't look away; he is showing that he's sincere. I smile rigidly and say that it's OK and I hope that he's happy.

After he goes my face collapses. The words come back to me. He chose them carefully; they were crafted—as if by a lawyer.

Later that night when Henry and the girls are asleep, I sit in the dark of the garage. It's 2am and I can hardly breathe. I'm holding the phone. I have to talk to someone. I dial a number. It's the Samaritans. A calm female voice answers. For the next forty minutes or so, I sob, and she listens.

The next morning I open my diary and cross out the training dates. I send an email saying that I'm not ready to volunteer yet.

MOVING OUT

I'm spending another weekend away, this time with Margot in Portsmouth. She's the mother of an old school friend and I've known her since I was twelve. We talk as equals now, two grown up women whose marriages have ended, although for her this is now in the distant past. But on another level we're not equals. She's motherly towards me and I'm grateful for her kindness. Her guest bedroom is cool, welcoming and white. It feels safe in a way that home no longer does.

In the morning she brings me a cup of tea, then prepares

a simple breakfast of croissants and marmalade from Seville oranges that she picked in Spain. She's French and despite having lived in England for years, she still has a light continental elegance. This suits my mood as even though I find it hard to eat at the moment, her food is unthreatening and I can pick at it. And she listens patiently. I go over and over the same events. Again and again. Like so many friends who knew us both, she is mystified.

I avoid returning home until Sunday evening as Shaun has been moving his things out. He has rented a flat about a mile away in the centre of town. This is an odd idea in itself. I only know homes that we've made together, and I can't imagine him making one without me. I left a message saying that I'm happy for him to take anything he wants apart from two things that I'm particularly attached to: my birdbath and the sign in the kitchen that says 'Simplify'.

When I get back, the house is oddly changed. There are random bare patches on the wall where he's taken pictures and his side of the wardrobe contains nothing but dust. One of the worst stabs comes when I see my childhood teddy on the bed, alone. For thirty years he and Shaun's bear leaned together. Molly sees my distress and hands me one of her bears. It's hard for her and Henry, and we're all having to learn new skills. Inscrutability is one. They helped Shaun to move but they know not to discuss it with me.

I'm not sad to see the back of some of Shaun's possessions, though. For years we carted around a large blue plastic crate filled to the brim with dozens of cables and connectors. I had no idea what they were all for. I don't think he knew either. From now on I plan to have just the cables I need, and they will all have a label on them. Simplify. This is what I want for my new life.

I can't complain that he's taken very much. He's been remarkably restrained, really. There's very little of the past thirty years that he seems to want. We're in such different places. I'm mourning the loss of my love. He's celebrating escape from his.

TWENTY-FOUR

Today has been the worst day. Not just the worst day of this particular patch of awfulness. It's been the worst day I've ever had.

The week has got progressively more difficult, each day sharper; cutting deeper. I can't control the questions that go round and round in my head. It's quiet in the house. Emma is away and Molly is on a school trip to Devon, so it's just me and Henry here.

I don't know where to put the pain. I know I need to contain it but it keeps spilling out. I'm leaking grief in my tears, my noisy sobs and outbursts, and my agitated movements. These leaks allow me to keep some level of control but I'm nearing my limit. I'm going to explode. I'm not sure what this means but I know the pressure is fighting with my sanity. I have to do something to stop this terrifying feeling.

There's only one thing I can think of. I ring my sister and tell her what I'm going to do. She advises against it. But I ignore her. I have to. I can't think of any other way to deal with this crisis.

The first thing to do is to ring Shaun and suggest we meet for coffee. He sounds surprised but agrees as there's a practical issue we need to discuss and this would be a good opportunity. I set off to walk into town and he comes to meet me half-way. We kiss politely on the cheeks. I keep the conversation light. It all feels very civilised and grown-up. But before long we're in the department store café and are facing one another across the table. I chose a quiet corner, deliberately. Then my prepared speech spills out.

'We've had thirty years together, and four children,' I say. 'We've got a lot to lose. I'm so unhappy I don't know what to do. I can't sleep. I can't eat. It hurts so much; I don't know how to get through the next few minutes. Please can we try again? I'll go to counselling with you. I'll do whatever we have to do to make it work.'

There's another of those moments when time stands still. But this time there's no mix of fleeting emotions on his face. There's just sheer horror. 'You've made me angry,' he says. 'You've brought me here to a public place and cornered me.'

Immediately I can see that it was a bad idea and apologise for being thoughtless and stupid. Of course it won't work. He's already started on his new life.

He can tell that I'm in a bad state, though, and says he'll walk me back to the house. He holds my arm. The sleeve of his jacket and my coat are in contact. That's all. There's no touching. No intimacy or comfort. I feel like a naughty child.

When we get home, we sit side by side on the sofa. I hold my head in my hands and close my eyes. I'm holding it together; concentrating on not letting the grief leak out. Then suddenly something changes. I can't do it any longer. The pressure is too great and I have to move.

I run to the kitchen and grab the knife that's lying on the worktop. It's my favourite. It's got a dull black handle with silver rivets, and a long, sharp blade. The edge is bevelled. There are tiny imperfections in the metal where regular use has worn it away. Thoughts flash quickly across my mind: images of fruit and vegetables I've chopped with it; family meals it's been part of, the meat I've cut. And now I'm standing here at the kitchen sink like this. I take it in my right hand and hold my left hand out. I look at my wrist. I wonder about my options and am not sure what to do next.

I'm only there for a second or two and then Shaun is next to me. 'What are you doing?' he roars. His voice comes from a very deep place. He's strong and grabs both of my arms, completely immobilising them. I'm not ready to be restrained yet, though. The pressure's not released. I can't do anything with my hands, but my feet are free. I kick him and we end up on the floor. His fingers close over the edge of the knife and there's blood. Then I punch out. My hand strikes his nose. That bleeds too.

More thoughts flash through my mind. I think of all the

times we've held one another. This will be the last time. Here on the kitchen floor with blood and crumbs.

Shaun starts shouting to Henry who is upstairs.

'Call an ambulance,' he bellows. 'She's trying to commit suicide.' Henry appears. He's in his snakes and ladders pyjamas. He looks young and very scared. Shaun tells him again that he has to dial 999.

'I'm not trying to commit suicide,' I say to Henry. 'I'm just really, really unhappy.' I say it again, but no-one's listening. I hear Henry talking to the emergency services call handler. My head is pounding and he sounds a long way away.

'Tell them she's got a knife,' says Shaun.

Eventually he releases his grip and picks up the knife from the floor. He puts it out of reach. 'They're sending an ambulance,' says Henry. 'They're sending the police too.'

I stagger to the other side of the kitchen and sit at the table. My head is back in my hands. It's a Friday morning. It's half past eleven. I hear sirens.

I am so ashamed.

TWENTY-FIVE

A GIFT

The sirens stop and the doorbell rings. There are distant whispers in the hall. Again I catch that note in Shaun's voice and feel like he's discussing a child. But this time, one who's not only naughty, but also dangerous. Then it grows dark in the kitchen. A policeman's presence fills the room like a cloud passing overhead on a thundery day. I stay at the table and brace myself. I'm expecting to be arrested or, if I'm lucky, sectioned and carted off to a psychiatric hospital. But instead he sits down and gets out his notebook. He looks at me kindly and asks me to explain what happened.

The ambulance men, too, are gentle when they arrive. Shaun sits on the stairs round the corner from the kitchen, so he doesn't have to see me. They dress his cut hand and fill in lots of forms. Several times they ask me what I want to do. But my brain is empty and I can't answer.

'I need some help,' I say eventually.

'We'll take you to hospital,' they say. 'You can see the Mental Health Crisis Team.' As we all troop out to the ambulance I pass Shaun who is still sitting on the stairs. I've never felt more alone.

'I'm so sorry,' I say. 'It was a stupid thing to do. I'm going to hospital. Will you come with me?'

'I've had enough of hospitals,' he replies coldly. 'Take Henry with you.'

We wait a long time in A&E, probably about three hours but I can't tell for sure. Some moments fill my attention, looming at me so that I'm forced to take notice. Others drift by. Then a consultant psychiatrist appears.

'I'm sorry you had to wait so long,' she says kindly. 'But when I saw your notes come in, I decided to see you myself.'

We go into her room and Henry comes too. She's compassionate. She listens, and I sob. She tells me I'm not mad, or violent or suicidal. She understands. I'm glad that Henry has come with me. I want him to hear these things.

As I sit there I know that I will never forget this doctor. When I left Shaun sitting on the stairs with his jaw set firm, I felt like I had wronged him. She takes a different view. Talking to her is helpful but there's not a great deal more that she can offer. She puts me on the list for counselling assessment and tells me to contact my GP on Monday morning to get some anti-depressants. Then that's it. Henry and I call a taxi and return to a house that feels unusually quiet; like it's in shock after witnessing dreadful things. The cushions in the sitting room are scattered across the room. There are splashes of blood on the kitchen floor and crimson drops on the stair carpet. And my two sharp knives have been removed.

At six I go to collect Molly from her school trip. Henry and I have agreed that we'll try to be as normal as possible. We don't want her to know what happened today. I make a curry and we all sit on the sofa together watching England play Sweden in their Euro 2012 match. Later, I chat to her while she's in bed and hear about the adventures she had in Devon. Then I put the light out and retreat to the privacy of my bedroom. I don't feel real—apart from the crying: it makes my face wet and my throat sore, and these sensations remind me that I *am* real.

The next morning a note drops through the door.

The following day there's another one. This time I see Shaun as he walks away. He's wearing jeans and a shirt with blue and pink stripes. I've never seen him wear it untucked before. It doesn't suit him. His back looks long, and it radiates anger and self-righteousness.

I learn a number of things from these notes:

- Shaun doesn't want to have anything to do with me for a very long time.

- He has arranged for us to communicate through an intermediary.

- He isn't going to take the matter any further on this occasion but reminds me that I have the care of a child.

- We will proceed to divorce as quickly as it can be arranged.

Then I understand. When I picked up the knife it became a weapon for Shaun too. I have handed him a gift: a reason to be angry and his justification for no longer wanting to be married to me.

On Saturday, the day after the knife day, I met up with Rita in London. I was still feeling ashamed but with the support of a strong coffee, I told her the story and confessed what I did. When I got to the bit in the coffee shop when Shaun said he was angry, she said, 'What?' She sounded incredulous. 'You were with him through all those difficult times in hospital. And when you asked for help—just once—he was angry?'

'But we're separated,' I say. 'He's already started his new life.'

'That doesn't matter,' says Rita. 'He could have said he was sorry you're in pain; that he knows, and you know, that it isn't going to work. He could have been kind.'

During the rest of this week I've confided what happened to a few trusted friends. In just a small number of discussions these women that I know so well have revealed secrets. I learned that when faced with pain:

- Beautiful B cut off chunks of her long dark hair and stabbed at her thighs with a screwdriver.

- Dependable D slashed at her legs with a Stanley knife. On two occasions.

- Generous G opened her bedside table drawer and swallowed every pill she found there. She woke up in hospital, and years later, still doesn't know how she got there.

Nicky was different. She didn't turn the pain in on herself. She was just plain angry— she threw bricks through the ground floor windows of her ex-partner's house. Good for her.

Sheila, too, showed some healthy rage. She cut the sleeves off all her ex-husband's jumpers.

These revelations all help me to feel less ashamed but the sadness and anger are still overwhelming. What am I going to do? Friends will listen while I rant and cry. They'll provide welcoming spare rooms where I can sleep and feel safe. But no-one can get me out of this pit of depression. I've got to do it myself.

On Monday I speak to my GP and decide to try coping without anti-depressants.

On Tuesday I have a telephone assessment with a psychologist and am now on the waiting list for some counselling. I'm not considered urgent so the wait is likely to be at least four weeks and probably longer.

On Wednesday I feel despairing again as I remember that I tried my best, but Shaun seems to be disappointed in me and to feel that I can't be trusted. I get a recommendation for a private counsellor from a friend.

On Thursday I have my first appointment. I like her. She listens calmly as I tell the story and manage not to cry very much. She tells me that I must protect myself from Shaun. When he throws arrows at me I should imagine that I'm wearing armour which deflects them.

On Friday I think about contacting old friends so I can remember who I was before I met Shaun.

On Saturday I look at my treats list.

PLANS

When I created my list, one of the things that excited me most was not knowing how the treats would become real. Each was a tale waiting to be written and I wondered a great deal about the words and pictures that would accompany them. Some are turning out to be short stories; others are heftier tomes. Together they're building into a library with genres spanning much of what life has to offer. There's travel, adventure, biography, chick lit, history, comedy, drama, cookery—these have all come to life without too much effort. But now I've reached a challenging section: the self-help shelves.

I need to force myself to get out, so I look down the list for something that's easy to arrange and easy to enjoy. It doesn't take long to decide which treat fits best. I want to go to a jazz club. This is something I've been curious about for ages. I like jazz, though I don't know a lot about it, and the idea of going somewhere special to listen to it, sounds exciting and exotic. Ronnie Scott's is the best-known, so I go online and find that there's a Ray Charles tribute coming up in just over a month. I don't know if I like him or not, but Henry is a fan, so I take a chance and book for us to go together. There are two performances. One's at 6pm and the other is at 10.30pm. My first thought is sensible: 'It'll have to be the early one or we'll miss the last train home.' Then I book for the late one.

I rack my brains for other things I could do. There are no treats that seem to fit the bill at the moment, but there *is* something that's not on the list. I want to do a writing retreat and there's one with the Arvon Foundation coming up in a few weeks. Five days in the Pennines.

I'm just thinking that I'm not up to spending that amount of time with a group of strangers and then I find I've dialled the number. The friendly person on the end of the phone tells me there's just one place left and this means I will have to be in the only shared room. This is a blow as I know I'll cry a lot. I need somewhere that I can retreat to and be private. Then I try to think positively. I might like the person I share with. And even if we don't get on, then it *is* only five nights. That should be bearable. I cross my fingers and book the last place.

My need to feel that I'm being proactive is not quenched

yet, though. I want to meet people going through similar experiences to me. I realise now that in the past when I heard someone was separating I thought I was being sympathetic and understanding but in fact I was just another 'smug married'. I knew that divorce was bad but I had no idea how bad or how all-consuming; how it knocks your confidence in your present and future, and makes you doubt what was real in your past. I search the internet for divorce groups and the nearest I can find is about twenty miles away. It runs six-week courses covering topics in the general domain of divorce. How to cope with your ex-spouse. How to help your children. How to forgive. I ring one of the volunteers. He sounds kind and tells me that the next course is due to start in September. I ask him to add my name to the list.

A GENEROUS OFFER

I'm still drawing on the strength of friends and relatives a great deal and this is a very important crutch. But it doesn't move me on. It's like taking a painkiller that provides relief for a while, but doesn't cure the headache. I text Frances, who has been a rock to me in many hard times.

'How do I find my inner strength?'

Her reply is characteristically wise and concise. 'Don't expect to walk when you've got a broken leg. You need the support of your friends.'

Nicky is a rock, too. We met shortly after Shaun and I moved to Sussex from London. A mutual friend invited us to dinner on a cold, rainy November evening. It was a Friday and Shaun was delayed on his commute home, so arrived late. I got there on time, though, and as I was getting out of the car I managed to shut my finger in the door. It was agony. Somehow I got into the house and was immediately introduced to Nicky and her handsome husband, David. I either had to laugh or cry, but was keen to make a good impression so the cheerful route was the best option and I kissed them unusually enthusiastically for a first meeting. They didn't seem to mind and over the years the two of them, Shaun and I have spent many happy times together.

Since the split, Nicky and I have had some long, pensive walks. She knows how depressed I've been and recently came up with a generous offer.

'Your garden's looking a bit sad,' she said. 'Let me help you to make it lovely.'

She's a talented painter with an artist's eye for colour and shape, and her garden is casually elegant. Like everything she does, she makes it look effortless but I know that in reality it takes a great deal of skill. I was touched by her kind thought and we fixed a date for my garden makeover.

Not only is this kind offer of practical use, but it also ties in with one of my treats. I've always loved old-fashioned, fragrant roses and planting some in my garden is on my list. They take me back to our first house in London, a three-bedroomed terrace in Balham. It was tucked away in a quiet little road and despite the urban location it had the feel of a cottage. The thing I loved most was that as you came into the hall you could see straight through the kitchen into the small garden. Previous owners had planted some blowsy, scarlet roses and when these were in bloom the window was like a beautiful painting. That house was my favourite of all the homes I've had and both Will and Emma were born whilst we lived there. Life seemed simple and there was plenty of love to go round.

TWENTY-SIX

GORGEOUS GERTRUDE

Nicky and I have agreed that we'll make an early start today. The garden really is a bit sad and it's going to take a lot of work to brighten it. But first of all, Molly and I have breakfast together. She comments on how relaxed the mornings are these days: we can just drift along with no-one complaining about the noise of the dishwasher being unloaded or getting furious about news stories on the radio. Her only regret is that there's no 'Poor Thing' column to read today, as it's Saturday. This is a fashion page in the newspaper which fascinates her. It takes six women and puts them in various 'stylish' outfits. Almost always, we look at these women and say that if we saw them in the street dressed like that we would feel very sorry for them. This is how it came to be called the 'Poor Thing' column.

TREAT #22

A short while later I'm bumping down the long potholed drive that leads to Nicky's house. It's heavily wooded on either side. In the Spring there's a sea of bluebells to the left and I was once excited to see an adder slither across in front of me.

I've heard that a small local nursery offers a wide range of plants at very reasonable prices, so we agree to start there. I have a budget and Nicky has a master plan. We're the only customers there and we wander around like foodies at a farmer's market. I'm aiming for a pastel palette of pinks, blues, purples and whites. We mull over geraniums, heuchera, petunias, cosmos, osteospermums and nicotiana. My trolley fills up, and then I spot the perfect rose; like deep pink tissue paper. She's called Gertrude Jekyll and I must have her in my garden. Her perfume is addictive.

The nursery-owner tots up all our purchases and we're amazed to find I've still got a big chunk of my budget left. A lot of the plants are past perfection, but will still have plenty of life when put into pots, so she's given us some hefty discounts. She's got some reasonably-priced lavender plants, too, and Nicky suggests we buy these and create a border to peep up behind a low brick wall outside my bedroom.

With the car loaded and Nicky barely visible behind a cloud of pink geraniums, I drive home very carefully. We've earned a coffee and one of Sainsbury's finest stem ginger biscuits. A bit later as we're unloading everything, Emma appears and tells us cheerfully, a propos of nothing, that 'racecar' reads the same backwards as forwards. She's full of odd information at the moment as she's working in a publishing company in London and reading all kinds of random things.

There are a few key plants that we didn't manage to find at the first nursery, so we set off to track them down. We've got Molly with us, and are dropping her off at the tennis club. We've just started out when a long text arrives. Molly reads it to us. It's from Rita. She was listening to the news on Radio 4 yesterday evening and was interested to hear a report about a prisoner who'd escaped by climbing over the prison wall using discarded knitting. As a keen knitter herself she could admire his craftsmanship. Images flashed through her mind. Perhaps he had done knitting classes in prison? Probably some of the other prisoners had got impatient with their efforts and had thrown them in the bin in frustration. The would-be jail-breaker must have secretly retrieved them, week after week, and spent many productive hours in his cell, stitching them all together until he had a knitting ladder long enough to effect his escape. These daydreams were dashed when her husband said patiently, 'No dear, discarded netting, not knitting.'

We drop Molly at the tennis club and have an hour to explore another couple of garden centres. The roses are my main focus as I'd like some more to keep Gorgeous Gertrude company. Nicky recommends Iceberg as a good climber to go on the back fence. It's white and described as having a mild honey fragrance. We find this, and then I fall for Falstaff. He's a blowsy maroon shrub rose with a pleasing perfume. Just what I'm looking for, and the colour will give depth to the new bed that we're creating. I also buy a salmon-pink rambler called Albertine, which can climb up the side fence and intertwine with some clematis.

My budget is now all spent and we go home for a simple lunch of Greek salad with warm rolls. It's a rare, sunny day so as soon as we finish eating we set to work. This summer has been the wettest on record and there's no knowing when the next showers will interrupt us. We dig and weed the overgrown bed, compost it liberally, and gradually fill it with our new purchases as well as sugar pink bizzy lizzies, purple cranesbill and alchemilla mollis from Nicky's garden. I would have just dotted things around, and they'd have looked underwhelming.

'We'll put them in groups of three,' says Nicky, and that's exactly the right thing to do. We also fill masses of pots, putting plenty into each one and softening the edges with plants that produce a cascading froth of blossom.

The only cloud is when Nicky falls over. We're moving a big blue pot together, knees bent to protect our backs and suddenly she topples over sideways. It all happens in slow motion and I see her face form into an expression of surprise. I'm surprised too. It seems odd. She's been having strange dizzy feelings recently and I'm worried about her.

By the end of the afternoon my garden is transformed. I drop Nicky back home and then give the plants a long drink. Gertrude and Falstaff look happy together in their new bed. As for me, I'm on a stony path but at least the garden is sunny and the roses smell sweet.

HOLIDAY NEGOTIATIONS

Shaun is still angry so we're having no direct contact. Messages have to be passed through his intermediary. This is probably a good thing as I would find it difficult to face him. We're in very different emotional states. He is focussed on his new life and I'm all over the place. There are many unsettling exchanges, though, as he's determined to get the divorce and financial settlement pushed through 'rapidly'. He wants to be free as soon as possible. But I struggle with the speed. It's still only two and a half months since we separated, and I'm nowhere near ready to start dealing with these overwhelming issues. He makes it clear that this is very inconvenient; that he thinks I'm being unreasonable and uncooperative.

Earlier in the year, before the split, we booked a two-week holiday at our friend's villa in the South of France. Since we can no longer go together, we've agreed that Shaun will take Henry and Molly and they'll be leaving whilst I'm away on my writing retreat. In the good days we had many happy family holidays: amongst them were a canal boat in the Midlands; a cottage near Loch Ness; camping in Austria; a villa in Corfu; a gite in the Loire Valley; a motorboat on Brittany's waterways, and skiing in Vermont. I'd always suggest going somewhere that we hadn't been before. I wanted our children to experience variety. I loved watching their faces as we rose high into the Alps on a ski-lift, as they sampled new foods, and as they learned to operate canal locks. Holidays were often harder work than being at home, though, and occasionally Shaun and I would look at one another and decide we'd had enough. We crept back early from a couple of holidays. But despite the mixed blessings they were always the part of the year I looked forward to most. A couple of precious weeks when I'd get Shaun and the children all to myself.

Sharing a Room

It's Monday morning and I set off for my writing retreat in Yorkshire. During the long drive I chat to myself and resolve to take up two new hobbies: things that might help me to cope better. The first is inspired by Bedford Lemere, the photographer I read about on my visit to Port Sunlight. He listed one of his hobbies as 'cheering people up'. I'd like to do that. I've had a lot of kindness shown to me recently and it would be therapeutic to give some back. The second of my new hobbies is swearing. I've always found it helpful in moments of frustration but have kept it to a minimum so as not to upset those around me. Now, with a lot of time to myself, I can indulge this new passion fully. I'm sure it will be beneficial.

The drive passes without any tears, which I take as a sign of progress. I feel quite cheerful. Perhaps I'm getting over it.

I reach Yorkshire with a couple of hours to spare and decide to explore Hebden Bridge. It looks like a nice enough place but it's recently had severe floods and there are sandbags stacked outside the shops. Many are closed and it's clear that the town is in trauma. I'd envisaged sitting in a peaceful teashop reading my newspaper but I can only find one that's open and it's a rather desultory experience. My cheerfulness dissolves into the dampness and I begin to worry that I won't cope with the retreat. I've come all this way, and I'm not ready for a challenge yet.

A couple of miles and many deep breaths later I arrive at the Arvon Foundation centre, an isolated house that once belonged to Ted Hughes. The first evening feels a bit odd, but the house is old, comfortable and rambling with lots of intriguing photographs of writers on the wall. I immerse myself in conversations with the rest of the group and when I feel lost I look at the pictures or study details in the textures of the cushions that are scattered around. The only really difficult moment comes when we sit in a circle and have to introduce ourselves. I struggle to avoid saying that my marriage has recently ended. This is the feature of myself that dominates above all others, and I long for it not to be. I can't avoid mentioning it, though. I say a bit about myself and then at the end mumble, 'Life's been a bit difficult recently.' I don't want to be the member of the group who is the 'Sad Woman from the South' but it turns out that other people here have had hard times, too.

The next day, Tuesday, I'm calm and enjoy some moments of genuine happiness. The views from the house are stunning: the windows are filled with sweeps of trees and hills that soar up to the sky and down to the gorge with the swollen river. The people all have interesting stories to tell, not least my roommate who turns out to be a thoughtful woman a few years older than me. We chat a bit but are careful to respect one another's space in our small, shared environment.

Wednesday morning is good; Wednesday afternoon is very bad indeed. During lunch I feel an overpowering need to cry bubbling up inside. I don't understand what has triggered it but I know I have to go somewhere and be alone. The mornings and evenings are structured but the afternoons are free, so I put on my purple wellies and red cagoul and decide to have a walk. It takes only one step into the privacy of the outdoors for the tears to begin. I don't have a plan but after trudging along for about a mile, blurred and wet, I reach the small stone village of Heptonstall, perched high up in the Pennines. There are some attractive houses but not a lot else. Then I spot the church and have a moment of hope. The door is half open and I step inside. There's no-one around so I sit in a chair at the back. The wood is golden with streaks of grime in it and I can hear someone bustling about in a side room. I long for a kind vicar to appear and offer me some emotional sustenance. But I know that this isn't going to happen—I'm going to have to make my own map and effect my own rescue. I try to say a prayer but as always I don't know how to do it. Not like Shaun, who is a Christian and spends a lot of time on his knees.

The grave of the poet Sylvia Plath, is in the churchyard so after a while of failing to make any spiritual headway I go to seek it out. I'm surprised to find an unassuming headstone surrounded by straggly grass. It says, 'Sylvia Plath Hughes' and I remember reading recently that there have been repeated attempts to chisel off her husband's surname. She has many fans who believe that Ted Hughes was responsible for her suicide. She was only thirty when she died. She put her head in a gas oven. Six years later so did Assia Wevill, the woman that Hughes left her for. She killed not only herself, but also Alexandra, the four-year old daughter she had with Hughes. I sit here for a while. The grass is damp.

Later, I'm in my room trying to hold myself together when my roommate, Maud, comes in. We chat politely about what we've been doing. I manage to disguise a few sobs as hiccups but then I lose control and start crying properly. She's kind and sits patiently on her bed whilst I intrude on her holiday. She listens and as I tell her why I feel so sad her mouth falls open.

'This is very strange,' she says. 'Your story is exactly what happened to my friend, Isla.'

My mouth falls open, too, as she tells me about this woman who was happily married for three decades and whose husband suffered from leukaemia for five years. Then he had a bone marrow transplant. She longed for him to get better but when he did she discovered that he'd changed out of all recognition. He found a new much younger love on the internet and left his wife to set up a very different kind of home, many miles away.

Shaun's new partner lives in America and he met her whilst walking the Camino. She is a cancer nurse and they plan to set up a charity together, to help the carers of those with blood cancer. In moments of dark irony I've wondered whether I could apply to them for a grant.

Yet again I speculate about what has happened. Was it the drugs, the transplant, the life experience, or something in me and this other woman, Isla, that changed? Maud says that she will put us in touch. We seem to have a lot in common.

The next day is better and during lunch I chat with another member of the group who has had a difficult couple of years—much worse than mine. Then I remember my resolution about cheering people up and ask if she would like to join me for a walk this afternoon. She looks a bit hesitant but agrees, so we wrap up well against the driving rain and set off across the fields. We chat about the retreat and share some stories about our lives. It's all very enjoyable and seems to be going well. Somehow, though, we lose our way through the woods and end up having to scramble down the side of a gorge which is slippery after the recent downpours. On the way back up, I go ahead and have to tread carefully in order not to lose my footing. Suddenly, I hear a cry of pain and see that my companion has fallen down the wooded slope. I slither down to join her and discover that she has ripped trousers, a gashed knee and grazed palms. She also says that her ankle is hurting. I'd like to suggest that she tries my other new hobby, swearing, but don't feel we know one another well enough for this.

I encourage her to stand up and somehow we get to the top of the hill. I help her over a wire fence as she winces and then she hobbles across one empty field, a second field which has cows in it, and then a third field. I'm wondering what on earth to do, as she's getting slower and slower and I don't have a clue where we are. Eventually it's clear that she can't go any further, so I leave her propped in the shelter of a stone wall and run to the nearest road. From there it's a couple of miles back to the house. I go as fast as I can and fortunately when I get there, spattered with mud, the centre manager is still on duty. I explain the emergency and she grabs some blankets and enlists help from one of the men in the house. Together we all hop into her Land Rover and set off with me desperately hoping that I can give accurate directions. For once I manage and when we reach my new friend she is very relieved to be rescued. We get her back to the house and she spends the rest of the evening dosed up on painkillers, with her foot raised and strapped to a bag of frozen mixed vegetables.

My first attempt at cheering people up has not been a great success.

TWENTY-SEVEN

A Squashed Butterfly

Despite my ill-fated new hobby, I enjoy the retreat very much and by the time it ends on Saturday morning I'm sorry to leave. The people have been inspirational and stepping outside my comfort zone has been a significant step in moving forward. I feel stronger.

Now I've got a long drive ahead of me. But for once there's no reason to rush home as the children are away with Shaun. In fact, I'm rather dreading returning to an empty house, especially as it's nearly two weeks until they get back. This seems a long time to fill on my own and it upsets me to imagine them all having a good time without me. There *is* something that I've planned as a distraction, though. I'm not far from the National Media Museum in Bradford, and as it's on my list I decide to make a detour and drop in there on my way back. I've a general, but rather untutored interest in film, TV and photography, so I'm hoping it will be a constructive way to postpone the unavoidable silent return home.

On my way into Bradford, I drive through a village called Shelf. This cheers me up a bit. It makes me think of other place names I've enjoyed over the years. There's been Boot, Sheet, Friendly, Scratchy Bottom, Pant, Thwing, and my all-time favourite: Splott.

TREAT #23

A tourist sign directs me to the National Media Museum and soon after, I'm sitting in the cafe, studying a leaflet and planning my visit. The photographic section is on the ground floor so this seems a good place to begin.

There's so much to see. My concentration has been very poor since the separation, but here I enjoy walking round slowly and taking in random pieces of information. One thing that amuses me is a newspaper item about the bounderish 'camera fiends' who once loitered in seaside resorts. A letter to the Weekly Times & Echo in 1893 reported that 'Several decent young men are forming a Vigilante Association for the purpose of thrashing the cads with cameras who go about at seaside places, taking snapshots of ladies emerging from the deep.'

Then there are the famous Cottingley fairy photos, taken in 1917 by 15-year old Elsie Wright and her 10-year old cousin, Frances Griffiths. Their camera is on display along with copies of the photos which show Frances with fairy-like creatures. The photos came to the attention of Sir Arthur Conan Doyle, who was an enthusiastic spiritualist and delighted to have some 'evidence'. He used them to illustrate an article about fairies that he wrote for the 1920 Christmas edition of The Strand Magazine. It wasn't until the 1980s that the two girls admitted they'd faked the photos using pictures cut from a children's story book. They said that having hoodwinked the brilliant creator of Sherlock Holmes, they thought it best to keep quiet.

Another exhibition case chronicles the brief 1930s fashion for small coloured cameras. These were marketed specifically at women and advertised as 'The Modern Camera for the Modern Girl'. I imagine this being said in breezy, clipped tones. They were available in five colours; bluebird (blue), cockatoo (green), sea gull, (grey), redbreast, (red) and Jenny Wren (brown).

I reach the end of the photographic displays and take the lift up to Gallery One. As I step out, I turn right confidently. There's just a meeting area and a drinks machine. This seems odd. There's not much to look at so I go up to Gallery Two. There I meet two eager, underutilised guides. I ask, 'Did I miss something?' They take me down the stairs, and to the left of the lift the whole of Gallery One awaits me. I wonder what else I've missed in life by turning the wrong way.

Most of this floor is taken up with an exhibition about ways to capture movement on film. There's a great deal of detail and definitely too much for me in my current distracted state so I go quickly past most of the displays. But there are a couple of exhibits that catch my interest. One is a photo of the Duke and Duchess of Windsor, taken in 1956. They're mid-jump, in the air, holding hands, with their shoes empty on the floor. The photographer, Philippe Halsman, claimed that when you ask a person to jump, their attention is mostly directed towards the act of jumping. Their mask falls and the real person appears. He called his philosophy 'Jumpology', and in 1959 he published 'Philippe Halsman's Jump Book' containing 178 photographs of celebrity jumpers, including Marilyn Monroe, Brigitte Bardot and Richard Nixon.

I get a wave of nostalgia when I spot a screen showing speeded-up footage of flowers coming into bloom. This kind of thing was very popular in the 1960s when I was at primary school. At least two or three times a year my classmates and I would troop into the assembly hall to watch a film. It was supposed to be a treat. The blinds would be closed, the projector would make preparatory whirring noises, and dark shadows would flicker across the white screen at the front of the room. We'd all sit on the floor getting splinters in our knickers and wondering excitedly what we were about to see. Some optimistic child would start a rumour that the school had procured The Sound of Music, or even a Disney film if we were really lucky. But it always turned out to be one of these flower films—possibly even the same one each time. There are other mystifying things that I remember from my schooldays. One that has perplexed me for forty years is the visitor who came to take assembly, and cut his tie up. He stood in front of us and chopped it into pieces. I can still picture that clearly, but his talk clearly failed to make any impression as I have absolutely no idea why he did it.

The next floor is devoted to television history and everywhere I go, I can hear the theme music to Dr Who, hissing and bubbling. I concentrate quite well here, but although I discover all kinds of interesting snippets I don't see any mention of my favourite TV curiosity: the Armchair Theatre play, 'Underground'. It was broadcast live in 1958 and continued through to the end despite being dealt a major blow part-way when one of the main actors suffered a fatal heart attack between two of his scenes. The director ordered the rest of the cast to improvise without him. The really odd thing was that his fictional character was due to die in the same way during the second half of the play.

At the far end of the floor is TV Heaven where visitors can select a programme to watch in a soundproofed booth. There are over a thousand to choose from, dating from the early 1950s. I browse through the catalogue, and eventually settle on the first episode of Butterflies: Carla Lane's wistful 1970s sitcom. It's about the stifling effect that marriage and family have on a woman's life. Wendy Craig plays Ria, whose husband is more interested in cataloguing his butterfly collection than in spending time with her. When suave, attentive Leonard comes into her life, she's tempted to have an affair and spends a great deal of time daydreaming about him. Her imagination gives her respite from drudgery but in the end she resists temptation.

The fashions look dated but it resonates with me in a way that it couldn't have done when I watched it years ago. Perhaps it *is* best to look for happiness in our imagination rather than being wrong-footed by the shortcomings of reality. Ultimately we're all on our own so we need to be self-sufficient emotionally. Ria's husband describes marriage, cynically: 'It's like a butterfly; you see it, you grab it, then it's all squashed in your hand.'

Ria longs to spread her wings and fly. I wonder whether *I've* been set free and given the gift of new wings? Only time will tell, but so long as no-one squashes me, I rather like the idea of being a butterfly.

I've been back home for nearly two weeks now and am surprised by my reaction to Henry and Molly being away with Shaun. There's been some poignancy that I'm missing out on the fun but not the heartache I'd dreaded. I've realised that during this time I can do what I want for the first time in a long while.

Molly and Henry have rung me daily. The calls have come more often when there's been news to share, such as Molly being stung by a jellyfish, or their jet-skiing adventure. I'm glad that they're having fun but it *has* been galling to miss out on the first holiday in seven years that is not dominated by Shaun's ill health.

Emma came down to spend one night with me, and we had a simple meal outside in my newly-planted garden, chatting way into the dark. Welcoming her to the house that is now just mine, made me feel strong and independent.

Another unexpected bonus of being on my own is that I'm learning to be quite slummy, though I haven't yet plummeted to the depths reached by the Naked Civil Servant, Quentin Crisp. He didn't do housework at all and claimed that 'After the first four years the dirt doesn't get any worse.' He was, incidentally, very wise to change his name from Denis Pratt. My simple pleasures are to ignore the washing-up that's piled in the sink and to leave my clothes scattered all over the bathroom floor. It's relaxing and liberating not to care about these things and makes me realise just how much energy I used to put into trying to be a good wife. Now I can write my name in the dust on the hall table. Happily there's room for the odd expletive, too. My swearing hobby is going quite well.

The other one continues to be considerably less successful. Last week I received an email from my unfortunate rambling companion telling me that in addition to the multiple injuries she sustained when walking with me, an x-ray has shown that her ankle is broken. I sent commiserations and a few days later got a second email giving me the unhappy news that she has now developed a deep vein thrombosis.

A Nice Sleep

Although I have periodic stirrings of excitement at an unknown future, there are still many moments of unadulterated grief and despair. I'm learning to be better prepared for these, though, and I've found a number of things that help: weekly appointments with my counsellor challenge my feelings of failure; friends are thoughtful, and texts are a lifeline giving instant messages of encouragement. I've also had some anonymous kind gestures. Several times, a neighbour has put my dustbin out for me, when I, made scatterbrained by grief, have forgotten to do so. I don't know who's done it, but I'm grateful that someone's looking out for me.

And then there's my drug habit. I'm now on so many different pills that I no longer know what they all do. Every time I'm recommended one that might alleviate some facet of the struggle, I've added it to my arsenal. Now I daren't stop any of them as I'm not sure exactly which ones are holding me together. Some are over-the-counter herbal remedies and others are prescribed by my GP who is supportive and reviews my situation every few weeks. Although I'm still resisting antidepressants, I *have* succumbed to sleeping tablets. But I only take them when I'm really desperate as whilst they give me some longed-for sleep they also give me a headache. I prefer to do without them if I can and spend many nights awake, mulling over and over recent events. These obsessive thoughts are a real nuisance. The 'issue' is the last thing I think of before I eventually drop off, and it hits me like a wet, heavy towel as soon as I wake up.

Another troublesome problem has been acid reflux. This is causing a deep, hacking cough that makes me sound like a Victorian consumptive. It's almost certainly stress-induced but my GP wants to rule out other diagnoses and so has referred me to the local hospital for an endoscopy. At the same time she advised me to take any medication I'm offered as 'some people find the procedure distressing.' So when I had the appointment this week and the hospital doctor gave me the option of having sedation which would make me feel 'a bit floaty,' I accepted with no hesitation. This was clearly a good move as before the examination even started I went straight off to sleep and don't remember anything about it. I woke up in the recovery room wondering how long I'd been there. Far from feeling that I'd had an unpleasant experience I was instead extremely grateful to have had a nice sleep. My friend Tilly was waiting to drive me home and said I was like a dormouse, dropping off between sentences. The endoscopy revealed a hernia and this coupled with the stress-induced excess acid is what has been causing my annoying cough. The doctor prescribed some pills to reduce the acid and I've now added these to my sizeable pharmacopoeia.

Mansfield Park 1

My brain is not working properly. Finally, after fifty-three years of soaking up quite a lot of useful information and a great deal of random rubbish, I think it's full. This is only a hunch, but there have been a number of indications recently that suggest I'm correct.

Last week I went through an entire day at work cheerfully believing it to be Friday, only to have the disconcerting discovery at five o'clock that it was, in fact, Thursday.

There are also great chunks of the last few months that I can't piece together. I've had a number of lost weekends. Where was I? What was I doing? Who was I with? I can't even use the excuse of having been in an alcoholic haze. I think so much of my brain is given over to processing change that there's not a lot of room left for anything else. It's like driving along on autopilot and suddenly realising that you don't recall anything of the last few miles.

This feeling is also affecting my ability to read. I started Mansfield Park recently, but unlike the previous three Jane Austen novels, which I enjoyed, this one left me unamused, unmoved, and uninterested. I managed the first thirty-five pages and since then it has stayed unopened on my bedside table. I've made no progress in watching David Attenborough, either, nor with my North Downs Way walk. But I do manage to keep feeding the compost heap.

FORMALITIES

There are some things that demand concentration, though, and cannot be avoided, however hard they seem. I've now composed myself enough to formally instruct a solicitor to act for me. This was a big step and made the separation feel real. Melanie is a friend who understands the background to this breakup and I trust her advice. Shaun is very keen to avoid us going to court because of the costs involved and the fact that we don't have a huge amount to argue over. I agree with this and say I'm willing to have a series of meetings to negotiate but only if he uses a local solicitor. He has instructed one who is based a hundred miles away. This means that whenever we meet, one of us will have to pay travel expenses for our solicitor, as well as three or four hours of travelling time at £200, or more, an hour. For once I insist. The family home is still based where I live. I think it's reasonable for the meetings to be here. Shaun is cross and says I'm being controlling.

I was discussing his reaction with Rita the other day and she reflected that when you live with someone, they know most things about you, including the bad bits that friends and colleagues don't usually see. These might be five or ten per cent of your personality, if you're a fairly reasonable, easy-going person. When life is just jogging along, they seem tolerable, but when you separate they can become the focus so that your partner sees you as one hundred per cent bad bits. There's also what my wise friend, Lynne, calls unconditional negative regard—whatever you say annoys the other person.

TWENTY-EIGHT

MORAL TURPITUDE

Earlier this year I had a small windfall when Shaun's mother left me a bequest in her will. As I wonder idly about all kinds of ways to spend it, I realise that I could weave several needs together and create something positive:

- I want to spend some special time with the children.

- I'm dreading my first separated wedding anniversary at the end of August.

- I want to go to New York. It's on my list because it's one of the world's great cities and I would hate to die without seeing it.

The perfect solution. Instead of having an unhappy day remembering our happy wedding, I will distract myself and fly to New York. Will is just about to start a new job in Latvia, and Emma has used up all her holiday for the year, so neither of them can come. Henry and Molly are delighted, though, and we spend an evening of excitement and frustration, researching budget hotels and trying to find cheap flights. We nearly end up with a 17-hour journey and a stopover in Iceland. Eventually, though, after quite a bit of swearing, we manage to make reservations for direct flights and a centrally-located hotel.

I also apply online for our ESTAs, the electronic travel permits that have replaced visas. I have to answer a number of questions and some of them strike me as rather odd.

'Have I ever been arrested for a crime involving moral turpitude?' I ask Henry.

'It sounds like a pudding,' he says helpfully.

Tonight I'm going to Ronnie Scott's and since there will be no trains running when the performance ends, I drive to London. On the way, I find myself in Balham, where we lived for a number of years. I make a detour so I can drive past our old house as there's something I want to see. It's the stained glass that we designed for the panels in the Victorian front door. I used to love the yellow and red light it cast along our hall on a sunny day. It also included a secret romantic gesture. Our initials were woven into the design. We liked the idea that in the future we could walk past and they would still be there.

I leave the car at Warwick Avenue underground station and meet up with Henry who has been having a day out. We've plenty of time until the performance starts so there's no rush, and a short walk away is a quirky cafe that straddles the Regent's Canal. I've been here with Emma and think Henry might enjoy it.

For the next hour or so, we sit here with an occasional barge gliding underneath us. The first one is full of jolly people all waving and raising their glasses in celebration. The next is much more sober with lots of men in smart jackets and open-necked shirts. They look like commuters on a compulsory night out. Big, gutsy garlic smells waft over us. A breeze blows on my face, and I enjoy the reflections of lights dancing around in the canal water. The pasta is hot and tangy with tomato, and the traffic roars relentlessly along Maida Vale. I try to take everything in. This week my counsellor talked about the benefits of using my senses more. I wasn't sure what she meant at first, but I'm beginning to get it. Spending time in my head, obsessing, is exhausting. A bit of time out, experiencing the smell of lavender, or the silkiness of body lotion on my skin, takes me away from the painful stuff.

While we eat, Henry and I chat about music. There was a time when it was very important to me but family life caused me to neglect my interest, and Shaun's tastes were very different from mine. He leaned towards sea shanties and Gregorian chant. Henry and I swap stories of favourite performers. I ponder for a while and then tell him who my top five would be: Dusty Springfield, Frank Sinatra, The Smiths, The Beatles and Amy Winehouse. Henry is more esoteric and chooses Tom Waits, Otis Redding, The Band, Jack White and, luckily enough given tonight's tribute gig, Ray Charles.

Henry says that he was born in the wrong era. The forties would have suited him, he thinks. I'd opt for the twenties with its cloche hats, drop waists and the abandonment of the Charleston. It's wonderful sitting here with my son. He's interesting and kind, and he isn't going to break my heart. I'll stick to this for the time being. I find it hard to ever imagine having a romantic relationship again.

We walk all the way to Ronnie Scott's. Edgware Road is lively and almost all the restaurants are Arabic in one form or another. It's a warm evening and the outdoor tables are filled with people toying with baskets of flatbread and puffing on hookahs. I drift along, taking in all the smells, sights and sounds. I'm wearing my favourite long blue and white dress. The design reminds me of a Chinese willow pattern plate. I'm also wearing strappy white sandals, the fronts encrusted with silver beads. I love them, despite the blisters they give me. Dashing around after children left little scope for playful footwear in the past but shoes are something I am learning to appreciate in my new life. Emma has an extensive, exotic collection; mostly very high and when she moved she left a few pairs in her wardrobe. I tried them on and although the dark blue suede ones with the little bow on the front *were* a size too big, I instantly fell in love with them. They made my legs look long and I realised that I'd just found another new pleasure to explore and enjoy.

We arrive at Ronnie Scott's half an hour early and are right at the front of the queue. I amuse myself by observing the 6 o'clock crowd coming out, and count how many are wearing suede shoes. I thought this was the sign of a true jazz aficionado but there are disappointingly few. The restaurant opposite is playing loud music. 'I'm a Believer' belts out and some women start dancing in the street. Then at 10.30 on the dot we're ushered inside the club. A pretty young woman ticks our names off on a list, welcomes us warmly, and shows us to our table. It's like going into a dim red cave and is even smaller and more intimate than I was expecting. The walls are covered with dozens of moody black and white photos of jazz artists; I only see one that's in colour. Henry tells me this is B.B. King and also gives me some background information about Ray Charles. He caused a scandal at the start of his career by fusing gospel music with the rhythm and blues that he heard in the street. Self-righteous critics denounced him for playing 'God's music in the devil's style.'

The band starts tuning up and then they play in the mellow light. There's a trumpeter, a pianist, a couple of saxophonists, a trombonist, a drummer, and a bass guitarist. Although I know very little about jazz I recognise immediately that this is the kind I like. Big and noisy. The musicians are really enjoying it. We're so close that we can even exchange smiles with them and I love watching how they interact. They tap their feet and the trumpeter moves his mouth constantly. When he's not actually playing, he pouts, licks his lips and puffs his cheeks out. Part-way through, the band is joined by a trio of female backing singers. They're attractive and charismatic and one has the biggest earrings I've ever seen: great round, golden discs. 'Hit the Road Jack', is particularly wonderful.

As I listen I wonder idly what a group of brass musicians is called. I like collective nouns and think back with affection to the 'twitter' of old ladies that we met in Edinburgh. Others I've enjoyed recently are a complex of psychoanalysts, a prickle of porcupines, and a flood of plumbers. I think the accepted one for brass instruments would be a 'flourish', and decide that in this case the musicians are an 'exuberance'.

The show comes to a big, joyful end and I feel completely satisfied. Henry has enjoyed it too. We have a drink and after a short break the late show starts. Unfortunately this is just the kind of jazz I don't like, and nor does Henry. There's a pianist, a double bassist and a drummer with brushes. It's all very twiddly with none of the drama that you get with brass. After giving it half an hour we decide that it's time to go home.

The loo is in the basement, at the bottom of a very steep set of stairs and as I go down, I meet the band members coming up, lugging their huge music cases. The trombonist is black with impressive dreadlocks.

As I pass him I say, 'It was great. Thank you.'

He looks at my feet and says in a deep, gravelly voice: *'Really nice shoes.'*

We pick up a night bus in Oxford Street. Annoyingly it breaks down twice on the way to Maida Vale but eventually we're in the car, and on our way home. Henry is fast asleep within minutes and a bit later I'm surprised to find myself in an unyielding traffic jam right next to Big Ben as it strikes 3am.

Many miles later I fall into bed with all kinds of jumbled thoughts. This was the twenty-fourth treat that I've engaged with: jazz and staying up late. These are things I would never have done with Shaun. I'm unfurling bits that have been packed away for years. Somewhere in there too, as I drop off, is a sleepy resolution to review my shoe collection.

PROCRASTINATION

Shaun has agreed, rather unwillingly, to instruct a local solicitor and is now pushing for our first meeting. The emails still come via his intermediary and I'm trying to get used to being addressed as if I'm the opposition in a legal case. I suppose that's what I've become, but I could do without his curt signing off: 'Please confirm you agree.'

I long to say, 'Lighten up a bit, Shaun,' but know this would annoy him, so don't.

Instead I do the only thing I feel able to do: I resist committing to a date. I'm managing to hold some things together adequately. I can work. I can get Molly to school on time and on some days I feel reasonably happy. But sleeping and eating are still a problem and the idea of having to face Shaun and talk dispassionately about the end of our marriage is overwhelming. I need time to develop a thicker skin: one that is not so fragile and easily knocked, exposing a raw, red, weeping weal underneath.

Then one Saturday evening, three and a half months after our separation, everything changes. An email comes direct, bypassing his intermediary. He tells me that we must get the divorce proceedings started this week. I am to issue them and to cite his adultery as the reason for the breakdown of our marriage. He will prepare all the papers and drop them off tomorrow afternoon. My part in all this is to sign in the places that he indicates and to take the papers to the local court. He will provide the court fee in cash.

That night I do not sleep at all. There have been many times in my life when it's been easy to exaggerate and to say that I've had a bad night and not slept. But this time I really mean it. I change position restlessly for hours. Shaun's wish to end our marriage is undeniable. I can't escape it any more. Images of him with another woman go round and round in my head.

The next morning Molly and I are up at six—we're doing a car boot sale. She has sorted out several boxes of books and other bits and pieces that she wants to sell. Any money we make will go towards our New York holiday fund. She's enthusiastic and I don't want to disappoint her. She also turns out to have a talent for haggling with customers. The grass is wet, our table collapses and we make £33. Molly is pleased. By midday when it's all over I'm more tired than I think I've ever been before. We go home and I get into bed, the curtains pulled to provide some cool, Sunday afternoon shade. But still I cannot shut the world out. Sleep is stubbornly elusive.

At about four there is the sound of papers being dropped through the letterbox.

On Monday morning I sign my name in the places where Shaun has put a post-it note. He has been very thorough.

On Tuesday I feel angry and unwilling to simply do what I'm told.

On Wednesday I get another email from Shaun. He reminds me that I 'must respect his timetable.' If I don't deliver the papers to the court by tomorrow afternoon he will issue proceedings against me. His implication is clear. He will cite my unreasonable behaviour: the knife.

On Thursday morning I ring my GP and book an appointment for a phone consultation.

On Thursday afternoon, at the last possible moment, I set off for the court with all the papers. Shaun has given clear instructions that once they are delivered I am to get a receipt. My solicitor must then fax this to him. When I get to the court there is a notice on the glass door telling me that during the summer months the reception desk will be closing early. I've missed the deadline for today. Despite my unwillingness to engage in the process, this is a genuine mistake. I ring my solicitor and explain. She says that she will contact Shaun. I know he won't believe me. As I walk home my GP rings. She says she will write up a prescription for anti-depressants and leave it at the surgery.

I sit on the edge of the pavement and cry as the cars go past throwing up dust. I don't care who sees me. I am worthless. I am sunk. I have no fight left in me.

On Friday morning I go to the court again. I hand over the papers and £340 in cash to the court clerk. As I put the wheels in motion for the official ending of our marriage, I can't help but think of the day it started: a sunny Bank Holiday Monday interspersed with the odd light shower. Two images spring to mind: a white tandem and a puddle in the aisle.

Shaun was an articled clerk at the time, and I was a student. We wanted to be independent and to pay for the wedding ourselves, but money was tight so we had to be creative. I did the catering for the eighty friends and family who helped us celebrate, and Shaun managed to borrow our wedding vehicle from one of his clients. But there was no Rolls Royce or horse and carriage for us. This was a white tandem belonging to a charity that took blind people out on bike rides.

I didn't have bridesmaids, but instead had my youngest nephews, aged five and ten, as pageboys. They wore dark green kilts and looked angelic. I walked down the aisle on my brother-in-law's arm to join Shaun, and the service began. The first five minutes went to plan—and then there was a big commotion behind us. I didn't dare to turn round as the vicar was earnest and solemn, but discovered later that a large puddle had appeared on the floor. My sister, Bonnie, had been so busy sobbing sentimentally on the way to the church that she'd forgotten to prepare the youngest pageboy and take him to the loo.

At the end of our wedding service we posed outside for photos until our faces ached from smiling. Then we hopped onto our tandem and prepared to set off to the reception at the rowing club where we'd met eighteen months earlier. I perched on the narrow seat and gathered my hooped petticoat around me. It wasn't an ideal cycling outfit but I'd planned to tie up my dress with an extravagant length of ribbon and hold it out of the way. I looked at my sister expectantly. She'd been entrusted with the task of bringing the ribbon to the church. But her tears had distracted her and she'd forgotten this, too. I gave up on all thoughts of elegance and did my best to keep the material away from the oily mechanism as we pedalled along and waved. That night I put my dress away inside a plastic cover. Despite the black marks it had gathered, it held such wonderful memories that I haven't taken it out of its bag since. I always thought that if I did I would break the spell.

Back in the court, the deed is now done and I have the receipt in my hand. As instructed by Shaun, I go to my solicitor's office. Melanie is out but has asked a colleague to talk to me when I arrive. I explain that the receipt has to be faxed to Shaun. She looks surprised. This in turn, surprises me.

'Is this unusual?' I ask.

'I've never come across it before,' she says. "You're the one starting proceedings against him. It's a bit strange that he wants a receipt.'

In my soggy state, I've not had the energy to question this. But now I remember how he has talked about his 'timetable'. Suddenly I realise there have been little clues in things he's said. The children and I are not the only ones going to America next week—he's going too. But he's not going to New York: he's going to see his girlfriend. And she clearly wants proof that he is done with me. Now I understand why my procrastination was inconvenient.

Later I file the receipt away in a shiny blue folder where it joins other painful paperwork. I am always careful to keep these divorce documents separate so they don't bleed over the rest of my life. Then I put the folder out of sight in the bottom drawer of my desk.

On the wall above my desk is my treats list, all white, black and pink. I'm inclined to ignore it. Like everything else, it is meaningless because I am worthless, sunk and without fight. But as I stand and stare in the midst of this wasteland, in spite of myself I feel something: not quite purpose, not quite promise— but some kind of commitment.

TWENTY-NINE

HAVING IT ALL

I've finally given into the lure of antidepressants so have another pill to add to my complex regime. Each afternoon at five o'clock I take a white tablet that looks like an innocent sweetener. It seems too tiny to make much difference but I'm told that I should begin to see an improvement in my mood within about three weeks. I desperately need to find some emotional equilibrium. The ups and downs are terrifying, and unfair on the children. They try their best to be kind and patient but they're suffering too. Not knowing how I'm going to be from one moment to the next only adds to their burden.

I'm pleased to say, though, that I've had more success at cheering people up. I nearly gave up after my recent attempt, but last week a friend asked me to have a chat with her sister. Her marriage is dying and we spent over an hour talking on the phone. I could relate to her distressing situation only too well and she said this was helpful. An unexpected bonus was that picking over our respective marital problems helped me to make progress, too. It reminded me that although it still feels awful, I'm a long way further down the road towards self-determination than a few months ago.

I've also added a new tactic to my arsenal. 180° thinking: turning difficult situations round and looking for the positive. I don't want to become a Pollyanna-like parody, but it *can* be very constructive. When I feel desolate it helps to remind myself that I can make a new start. I search for other pluses, too, and come up with several:

- I have a lot more wardrobe space

- It's now very unlikely that the children will be orphaned by both parents being in an accident together

- I can watch DVDs on my laptop in bed at 3am when I can't sleep

Treat #9 (Continued)

Although I still find it hard to concentrate during the day, I am extremely grateful for distraction in the tangled forest of the night. I've used many restless hours to finish my Mad Men treat. As the fifty-two episodes have unfolded, I've become more and more wrapped up in the characters and their various demons. Given my current situation, I'm particularly interested in the breakdown of the Drapers' marriage. Betty's lawyer tells her that if she wants a divorce in New York State she must prove Don's adultery. That's the only way of getting one. But if her husband wants to petition for divorce, he can just do it. He can take the children, too, if he wishes.

Fifty years on, I'm clearly in a much stronger position than Betty. In theory, Shaun and I have equal rights. But it's not straightforward. The reality is that we don't have equal financial status. I feel frustrated with myself for stumbling into a trap that I never knew was there. By having a traditional marriage in which Shaun was the major breadwinner, I've left myself at a disadvantage. Although his current work is well-paid, it's unstable and he could lose it at any time. A financial settlement can award me fair, or even generous terms, but it can't make him give me money that he's not earning. Financial insecurity would have been a continuing concern if we'd stayed together but its effects are magnified by having two households to run. Then there's the charity he is planning to set up with his girlfriend— and what will happen if he goes to live in America? If I'd spent the last thirty years building a professional career, I could be independent of him and not burdened with these worries.

I reflect on the reasons why Shaun kept his career going, and I didn't. The most compelling was his potential to earn a great deal more than I could. Everyone knows that London lawyers are generally well-paid, and sometimes extraordinarily well-paid. Shaun was ambitious and took pride in earning the money to provide a lovely family home. If I'd worked then a big chunk of what I earned would have been gobbled up in childcare costs. Then there were the complications brought about by our move to the countryside. It would have been a challenge to find a Mary Poppins who was both willing and able to cope with the complicated life we had created: a house several miles from the nearest shop; children at four different schools, and a menagerie of animals. These were the rational reasons. But the important one was simply emotional. I knew I didn't want to hand over the care of our children to someone else. I was grateful to feel that I had a choice and was therefore truly liberated.

My mother didn't have these options. With my father an unreliable, absent provider, she was constantly stressed about money and throughout my childhood she worked in a hotel bar. Until I was seven my sister was on hand to babysit, but when she left home to get married, the only way my mother could keep her job was by taking me to work with her. Every day after school I would have tea at home and then we'd set off for the hotel. My mother's financial vulnerability meant that she was pathetically grateful to her employers for this special 'favour'. My part in the arrangement was to be good. She made it very clear that if I was a nuisance, she would be sacked. I wasn't sure what this meant but although I hated this job of hers, I knew that the consequences of losing it would be worse.

This was an adult environment with a lot of heavy drinking and there was nothing much for me to do other than keeping out of the way. It was fortunate that I loved reading. We slept in various rooms, depending which were vacant, and all of them had bunk beds. I would sleep on the top one and when my mother finished serving in the bar, very late, she would slip into the bottom one and I'd see her when I woke up in the morning.

One night was different and very frightening. I got ready for bed as usual and when my mother came to say goodnight, she told me that she was going out after work with some friends but would be back by the morning. I read for a bit, then settled down in the top bunk and went to sleep. Several hours later, when it was dark, I was woken up by a fumbling noise at the door. It went on and on as if someone was trying to put a key in. But I knew the door wasn't locked—the rooms where I stayed never were. I sat up, thinking it was my mother coming in. Then suddenly the door flew open and a man staggered in. He was drunk. I knew this because I saw plenty of drunk customers in the bar downstairs. This one looked like all the others. His eyes rolled around slowly and his expression was preoccupied, like he could see things that I couldn't. He seemed to be in a different world. He looked at me and gave a lopsided, dribbly smile as if he was trying to be civil but couldn't see me clearly. He nodded, and I, brought up to be polite, nodded back at him like we were two adults passing one another in the park. Then he lurched over to the sink and started vomiting noisily. I was frozen. I lay very, very still. I tried not to exist. After lots of groans and erratic splashing sounds he rolled backwards and fell into the bottom bunk. I stayed motionless and quiet. It seemed like hours passed as he snored. The sound was ugly, but helpful as it told me he was unconscious. And if he was unconscious then he couldn't hurt me.

Eventually, I forced myself to sit up by making tiny movements. Nothing that might wake the sleeping giant. Step by step I went backwards down the ladder to the ground. I could hardly breathe and I wanted to cry but didn't dare. Then more slow steps to the door. When I touched the door handle it felt solid and reassuring. I was scared that it would squeak when I pushed down but it didn't betray me. I closed the door silently as I made my escape.

I was relieved to be out. But now what? I decided to keep

walking. I wanted to look normal at all costs. If I sat down it would be obvious something was wrong but if I kept on the move, looking purposeful, then everything would seem fine. Just an eight-year old girl in her nightie wandering around a hotel corridor, alone at 3am. Up and down, up and down—still wanting to cry but knowing I couldn't or I'd draw attention to myself.

Then after a long while Margy appeared. She was a young barmaid who worked with my mother and lived in the hotel. She wore pale pink lipstick and had long dark hair. It rested on her shoulders and flicked up at the ends. I thought she was beautiful. She was kind, too, and one of the only adults who took any notice of me when I hung around downstairs. I was glad it was her who found me. Margy took me to her room and said that my mother would be back later. She was there by the morning but even though I tried to tell her what had happened I know that she never understood.

There was another time, too, when I was alone in my room and something happened. This time it was a much older man. He came in through the open casement window. I have a memory of him in brown trousers and a candy-striped shirt, squatting on the surface next to the sink. He looked like a frog—a drunken frog. This seemed very strange. I can't remember what happened next: I've blotted it out. But I know that he didn't take any notice of me. He didn't harm me, at least not physically. He was well known at the hotel. His name was Mr Rainbow and I remember thinking it was odd that his shirt matched his name so well.

These experiences unconsciously but inevitably shaped my motivations in raising our children. I wanted them to feel safe, and to always know there were adults who had time for them and valued them. Shaun shared my sentiments. He'd had a tricky childhood too. His mother suffered from schizophrenia and he felt that from an early age he'd been emotionally abandoned. We both wanted to create a different kind of family from the ones we'd grown up in.

Although I was always the main carer for the children, I still did bits and pieces of work throughout their childhood. I'd started my PhD before Will was born and continued to work at it on and off for a number of years. By the time I finished it, I had three children and much of it was written at the kitchen table in the evenings after I'd put them to bed. Eventually it all came together and I had the requisite four bound copies made. Three copies had to be delivered to the University of London so they could be passed to my examiners and the library; the other copy was for me. So one afternoon I got Henry up from his nap, put him in the car and we drove to Russell Square. Then Henry sat in his buggy whilst I pushed it with one hand and struggled to contain the three very thick tomes under the other arm. It didn't take long to realise that their combined weight was considerably more than my two-year old son, so I got him out of his seat and stuck him under my arm. Progress from then on was considerably less awkward. I wheeled my finished PhD work into the grand university building in a child's buggy, with a wriggling toddler under my arm. It was only some time later that I realised how well this summed up all the hurdles I'd encountered in completing it.

However, it had not only been the arrival of the children that delayed this work, but also the fact that Shaun started a business. It was another of his grand, lateral-thinking ideas and for several years I ran it, never quite sure what I was doing, but wanting to support him nonetheless—to help him to be successful in his dreams. Eventually we sold it, for a pound, complete with its debt.

After being awarded my PhD, I got a two-year fixed-term contract to do some part-time research work. It was at the end of the first year that we made our move to the country and for that second year I drove up to London a couple of days a week. There was a nursery right next to the village primary school so Henry went there and the older two joined him at the end of the school day. This was stressful when I got stuck in traffic, but it worked pretty well most of the time. By the time the contract came to an end, though, and I'd written up the results, I was pregnant with Molly. The idea of further commuting and juggling was just too much to contemplate, and it was then that Shaun and I agreed it was best for me to stay at home. What was mine was his and vice versa. For the next four years I spent a great deal of time driving children around, rounding up recalcitrant goats, painting walls, furnishing our newly extended house, and trying to create a garden. But once Molly went to school, I felt I should start to contribute again. And it wasn't just about the money. There were times when Shaun was really unhappy at work. He had a number of ups and downs and I felt guilty about being at home.

The logistics of returning to my former employment seemed insurmountable so I took what work I could find. I did a number of different jobs. One involved visiting dozens of opticians in the South East as a mystery shopper. I carried an innocent-looking handbag but inside was a secret camera which I used to film conversations with the staff in the shops. Each visit involved having an eye test too. It's just possible that I hold the world record for the number of times I've had my eyes tested. And then there was the job that required me to sit at my computer and produce rapid answers to questions that people texted in. My image of having interesting topics to research was soon dashed. I realised quickly from the lewd nature of the questions that most of the punters were probably on a night out, and drunk. Another job involved visiting local council planning departments and carrying out personal searches. Doing this within school hours led to some complicated time management as I covered nine different councils, and even more when colleagues were on holiday. And more recently I was intimately involved with the business that Shaun set up after he was made redundant. I helped with the marketing and did all the bookkeeping. I also wrote a training course and ran it with a couple of banks and law firms.

Latterly when Shaun became ill, I trained as a careers adviser and have juggled several jobs since then in order to get maximum flexibility.

Because Shaun was the main earner and made the significant financial decisions, I lost a lot of confidence and felt that I didn't contribute as much as he did. But I'm beginning to see this differently. And I'm beginning to realise that I made fundamental errors. I didn't set up my own pension or make other astute moves that would have given me financial independence. At the time, I never thought I would be swept aside. This was naive as I don't anticipate our forthcoming negotiations to be either straightforward or amicable.

The days of 'what's mine is yours' are gone.

THIRTY

DISPLACEMENT

It's 29th August and I wake up full of confused emotions.

Twenty-nine years ago, today, my wedding ring was placed on my finger and even though it's three and a half months since I took it off, there are still tell-tale lines where it sat for all those years.

Today is also the day that Molly, Henry and I are off on our New York trip. For me, this treat is primarily about avoidance of a significant date. But it's important to the children, too. The last few months have been demanding, and they deserve some fun—so I'm not taking any chances with our travel arrangements and we arrive at the airport with a ridiculous amount of time to spare.

TREAT #25

Twelve hours, several films and over three thousand miles later, we're emerging from the subway directly opposite the New York Times building. In perfect synchrony we all look up, and up, and up, mouths like goldfish. Then, trundling our awkward luggage, we negotiate our way into the fast-moving stream of pedestrians. It's like trying to filter onto a busy motorway.

Thankfully, the hotel's not far and it's a relief to dump our bags in our twelfth-floor room. We don't stay here long, though, as we're keen to get started on some sightseeing and are in agreement that we'll start with the Brooklyn Bridge. Several friends have told us that it's the best way to get a view of Manhattan for the first time. We go south on the subway and since Henry and Molly are in charge of map reading on this holiday, we find it easily. Hundreds of tourists amble slowly along the pedestrian walkway whilst grit-faced homeward bound commuters cycle aggressively in the opposite direction. Molly holds a guide book and tries to identify the imposing buildings we can see in the distance.

'Is that the New York Telephone Company building? Perhaps it's the Woolworth Building—or is it the Manhattan Municipal Building?'

Henry interrupts. 'I know what *that* is,' he says wryly, pointing to the left. There, undeniably, at the mouth of the Hudson River is the Statue of Liberty.

The bridge is nearly two kilometres long. It was daylight when we set out, but it's dusk when we reach the other side. It's been a long day and we're starting to feel disoriented. We're hungry, too, and Little Italy sounds romantic so we head off there to get some pasta.

It's familiar from countless films. The streets are lined with tenement blocks, each with a metal fire escape zigzagging down the outside. The sound of an accordion comes from inside a small restaurant which has red and white checked cloths on the tables. It's just like the scene where Lady and the Tramp share a bowl of spaghetti. As we sit at an outdoor table and wait for our food we're entertained by two yellow cab drivers having an altercation. One gets out of his vehicle and yells through the other's window, '*Say* you're sorry'. I can't hear what the reply is, but it's clearly not the right one.

Next morning we prepare for the day and set off, passing through Times Square on our way. It's only nine in the morning, but it's already ridiculously busy. This is the most-visited place on earth with over 360,000 pedestrians passing through each day. Somewhat dazzled by the flashing lights and whizzing images, we turn down a side street towards Fifth Avenue, and then, just a few yards from the fluorescent clamour, we come to one of the most peaceful places I've been in ages. St Mary the Virgin, Times Square, entices me in. I got through yesterday's anniversary but this morning I feel raw again—and very aware that somewhere on this continent my husband is with another woman. The children wait patiently whilst I sit for a few minutes in a side chapel and pray for strength. This time, unlike in Heptonstall, I feel that someone is listening and a thought slips into my head: 'I must let go of the hurt. Until I do that I cannot heal.' I'm not at all sure what this means or how to do it, but it gives me something to hold onto.

We eventually reach Fifth Avenue and its stunning architecture. Wildly different styles stand side-by-side and then as we wander along we come to the New York Public Library. It's a beautiful neoclassical building with marble columns and white stone lions guarding the entrance. Signs outside advertise a free exhibition called Lunch Hour NYC, and I think this sounds promising. Henry and Molly look doubtful but as it's early in the holiday they're in an amenable mood.

It tells the story of how New Yorkers over the ages have enjoyed that most important of meals: lunch. We learn how immigrants brought street food to the city. Pretzels were introduced by the Germans and were considered disreputable because of their association with beer drinking. Hot dogs had a poor reputation, too, in their early days. They were the kind of food that mothers would warn their children not to eat. 'Dog' was a term of contempt for the poor quality meat that thrifty butchers used to put in them.

One of my favourite exhibits is a reconstruction of an automat from the 1950s. These had rows of compartments with glass doors and inside each was a portion of food on a plate: honey pie; Manhattan cheesecake; baked macaroni, and even fancy dishes like lobster Newburg. Diners would drop a nickel in the slot, open the door and pull their plate out. This gave the impression that the food was untouched by human hands. It also kept the customers from interacting with staff and made it easier for restaurants to hire 'women, people of colour, immigrants, and anyone else that diners might find objectionable'.

As we wander around, I realise that there's something about

American food that seems both familiar, and at the same time pleasingly exotic. Some of the old hotel menus list odd-sounding dishes such as canvasback duck and fiddler crab lump. And I love the description of the sharp literary meetings that took place over lunch at the Algonquin Hotel, and which led in 1925 to the birth of The New Yorker magazine. There's a picture of Dorothy Parker in the exhibition. I expect her to look old, grumpy and frumpy, but instead she looks gamine and surprisingly modern. Her acerbic book reviews in the New Yorker were said to delight everyone except the unfortunate authors. I enjoy her cynical take on romance:

> *Oh life is a glorious cycle of song*
> *A medley of extemporanea*
> *And love is a thing that can never go wrong*
> *And I am Marie of Romania*

Our next stop is Central Park. The weather is warm but just the right side of sweaty, and as we stroll along I hear puzzling bursts of humming. At first, I think it must be an insect or bird, but the park is such a strange mix of urban and bucolic that I don't want to ask what the noise is, in case I sound idiotic. I imagine a park attendant telling me dismissively that my 'pastoral symphony' is in fact, just a car alarm.

We sit at outdoor tables and relax over bratwurst and root beer. Later, there's plenty of music to entertain us as we explore. The buskers are all out today. There's an Irish fiddler, a lone saxophonist, a cellist, and a small jazz ensemble complete with a tuba. My favourite, though, is a Korean guitarist, who drones so dreadfully that it's fascinating. He's playing Simon and Garfunkel's 'America' very slowly and miserably. It takes me quite a while to recognise what it is.

On Literary Walk we come across four statues of writers: William Shakespeare; Robert Burns; Sir Walter Scott, and Fitz-Greene Halleck. 'Fitz-Greene Who?' we all think. Then we read that despite being almost completely unknown today, he was once known as the 'American Byron'. The unveiling of his statue in 1877 attracted ten thousand spectators.

The following day we set ourselves up for a busy schedule by having breakfast in a diner. The waitress is grumpy as she takes our order. I try some English charm but it doesn't penetrate. She remains deadpan and brusque. Afterwards, we pass St Mary the Virgin, Times Square again, and I go in for another shot of spiritual comfort.

Our main trip today is a visit to the Statue of Liberty, and after filing through airport-style scanning we get on a boat. The wind blows in our hair as we take in Manhattan from the water and when we arrive at the island an excellent audio-guide provides us with all the background information we could ever wish to know. Close up, the statue is magnificent. 'Liberty Enlightening the World' was donated by the French in recognition of the friendship that was established between the two countries during the American Revolution. Gustave Eiffel advised on the design some time before working on his eponymous tower. Liberty posed similar problems to the bridges that he was known for, as she has to withstand winds of up to 60mph and can only do this by having parts that allow some movement. Without these she would break. She has an iron frame with 310 pieces of shaped copper bolted onto it. The seven spikes of her helmet represent the seven seas and seven continents.

The dedication ceremony took place in 1886, but despite the overt femininity of this symbol of liberty, women were banned from attending. Outraged suffragettes hired boats and bellowed through megaphones that even if Liberty were able to get off her pedestal, she would not be allowed to vote in either France or America.

Next morning we spend a puzzling five minutes looking for the hotel reception desk. There's major building work going on and it keeps being moved. Eventually we locate it and ask for directions to Grand Central Station. It's about a twenty minute walk, and on the way we take in the Mad Men's Madison Avenue.

At the station, light streams in through the high windows. It's wonderfully uncluttered, with the food stalls all out of sight in the basement. There are no throbbing trains, either, as they, too, are well away from the main concourse. It's surprisingly calm and serene. I like ranking things, and decide that this is now number one in my list of favourite buildings.

Henry and Molly want to spend the rest of their morning exploring vintage shops in SoHo. I'm keen, on the other hand, to visit Greenwich Village, so we part at the subway and make plans to meet later. I stride off confidently in the wrong direction and forty minutes later arrive back where I started, hot, sticky and very cross. I can't quite get to grips with Greenwich Village when I do eventually find it. I had visions of sitting in a charming café munching on a delicious pastry and watching wealthy Bohemians living out their fascinating lives. It may well be delightful, but I lack the insider knowledge to make the most of it, and don't find what I'm looking for. It simply feels like a residential area with a lot of rather expensive shops.

In the evening we go to a jazz club. It's Charlie Parker's birthday and the band are playing his music, in tribute. It's vibrant and noisy with lots of brass, and there's an abrasive barman who reminds me of Humphrey Bogart.

The following day, after MOMA and Ground Zero, our stay in New York comes to an end. The displacement is over, the avoidance complete, and it's safe to go home again. It's been up and down. More up than down, though, and like so many of these recent treats, it was there just when I needed it.

TREATS COMPLETED THIS SUMMER

Eye make-up

The Races

Roses

National Media Museum

Jazz club

Mad Men

New York

TREATS IN PROGRESS

Compost

Life on Earth

North Downs Way

Jane Austen

AUTUMN 2012

THIRTY-ONE

SIGHS

September is my favourite month. I love that sense of changing seasons and fresh beginnings. In the past it's been the time when I've started courses and taken up new hobbies: Indian cookery; photography; goat keeping; church history; patisserie; counselling; vegetarian cookery, and the ill-fated picture framing with the drunken tutor. September has also paced out the children's progress, year by year, from their first day at nursery school through to university.

But this year I'm not sure if I like September. In fact I'm not sure if I like anything very much.

Reflecting on our trip to New York, it was exciting and enjoyable, but also sprinkled with horrid pangs. I was so used to travelling with Shaun that despite recent events, his influence clung to me like a shadow. I realised to my surprise that I was conditioned to do even the most mundane things in a particular way. Thoughts snuck into my head all the time. This is how we'd stow our luggage in the overhead lockers—this is what Shaun would say to reassure me when the flight got bumpy—this is how we'd wait in our seats before joining the scuffle. At the hotel it started all over again. This is how we unpacked—this is what we ordered at breakfast—this is how we decided what to do each day. These routines seed freely during a long partnership and like weeds they are hard to eradicate.

Something else that has bothered me recently is the paired-up nature of the world. On the flight to New York, a couple sat in front of us. They were about my age. I can't remember what they looked like, but I can still picture very clearly the way he placed his hand gently on her shoulder as they stood up to get off. It was such a simple gesture. And it said so much. Then there was the woman ahead of me when I got off the train the other day. She was about my age too. When we got outside the station she walked straight to a red car and got in, leaning towards the man in the driver's seat. He kissed the top of her head. I was envious of these women. I'm grieving the loss of what they seemed to take for granted: the ordinary day-to-day confidence that they are at the centre of someone's world, and that the 'someone' is at the centre of theirs.

I read an article about divorce the other day that did little to lighten my mood. It warned that it takes a year of healing for every four years of marriage. A quick calculation told me that I should therefore expect the next seven years to be challenging. This dreadful thought left me teetering on the edge of a new emotional plummet, but fortunately I had the presence of mind to text Rita and tell her about my unwelcome prognosis.

'No,' she said firmly and reassuringly, 'they've put the decimal point in the wrong place. You'll be fine by your birthday.'

There are undoubtedly a few hurdles to negotiate before that, though. Shaun and I are due to meet together with our solicitors at the end of the month and I'm dreading it like nothing else ever before.

By the time we meet, we won't have seen one another for three months. Not since the knife incident. Although this lack of direct contact has been at his instigation, I've not been sorry about it. His reactions are unpredictable and hurtful and I feel like I no longer know him. My friend, Bernadette, observed that he's probably done me a favour, since if he'd been kind and caring it would have been even harder for me to let go.

I had a phone call with my solicitor the other day and by the time we'd finished I was really upset about Shaun's latest tactic. I sat on the stairs and a comforting thought flashed through my mind: 'I'll tell Shaun about it when he comes in'. This peculiar state only lasted a moment.

Other peculiar states are proving to be more persistent though, and I'm keen to find some activities this autumn that will provide distraction from the intrusive, obsessive thoughts.

After much deliberation I come up with a self-help package for the next few months. I've got my six-week divorce recovery course starting soon and I'm continuing to see my counsellor every couple of weeks. There's also a new interest to explore thanks to my swearing, doggy friend Dot who has suggested I join her choir. This also seems an excellent time to start a treat—riding lessons.

I've never been very sporty and actively loathed PE at school. Our games mistress was nicknamed Hitler and she was dedicated to her calling. Her preferred method of humiliation was to stand eyeball to eyeball with us, whilst grinding her hockey boots into our feet, and spitting venom. I hated her. At the start of the fourth form I was thrilled to see that her name had disappeared from the timetable. My joy did not last long, though, as I soon discovered that she'd married during the summer holidays and was back with a new name, and as much spite as ever.

Gym lessons in our voluminous, navy blue knickers were particularly detestable. Mainly because we girls had to file past the boys who loitered around waiting to stare at us. They didn't have to suffer the traumas that we did. Their games master was good-natured and so obsessed with basketball that it made him absent-minded about everything else. Those of an idle disposition could get away with doing very little.

Other sporting activities didn't hold any more appeal for me than gym did. I could run quite fast, though, and always played right or left wing in hockey. This seemed to involve endlessly rushing up and down, whilst trying to look enthusiastic about capturing the ball but not really caring—I've got no competitive spirit. The memories I do recall with fondness were the sensuous ones: the crisp noise of hockey sticks cracking against the ball on a frosty morning; the sulphurous coal fumes that belched from the steam engines as they chuffed past on the preserved branch line, and the delicious, green smell of the grass.

These days I detest getting hot and sweaty, so swimming is

my preferred exercise. I enjoy it once I get into the pool, but I still find it hard to overcome my inherent resistance to exercise for its own sake. Some weeks I decide that I will swim three times. Anyone sensible would make the days go along the lines of 'swim, no swim, no swim, swim, no swim, swim, no swim'. In my case what always seems to happen is 'no swim, no swim, no swim, no swim' and then 'swim, swim, swim' all packed into the end of the week.

Whilst 'PE with Hitler' did nothing to make me love organised sport, I do nonetheless enjoy being active. And I'm hoping that riding will put me far enough outside my comfort zone to be a bit exciting, but without being the kind of hearty challenge that I would hate. As a teenager I rode a few times and a couple of years ago I got the chance to try it again. Shaun, Molly and I were on holiday on the Scilly Isles, and rode along the cliffs and beach on St Mary's. My horse trotted along obediently, following the one in front. He was clearly so used to this routine that he needed no input from me. We ambled along shady lanes with scratchy stone walls, and clumps of purple agapanthus. Then we made a steep descent alongside dramatic views of sea, sand and coves: sapphire, white and boulder-strewn. I was disconcerted, though, when I realised that I didn't know how to stop, start or even steer my horse. This is how some equestrian driving lessons made their way onto my list.

I'm not sure where to go, and dither about for a while. Then a friend recommends her daughter's riding instructor, Debbie. I get in touch and explain that I'd like to have six riding lessons but that 'I don't know if I like riding and I don't even know if I like horses.' She doesn't seem offended by this and we book a date for my first lesson.

Highs

Despite the inevitable bumps, some things have got easier. Last week, Shaun texted Molly to say that since she and the other children have not visited him as much as he expected, he is moving from his local flat to Notting Hill. I'm taken aback by his hasty decision. He's only been there a few months, and everyone needs time to settle down and find new routines; time to let bruises heal. I'm interested too in his choice of area. We have no links there and it's extremely expensive. He says it's so that he can be near to clients, and to the hospital in case he gets ill again. It crosses my mind that the film Notting Hill was very popular in America. It portrayed the area as just the kind of place where a perfect English gentleman would choose to live.

Whilst this makes life more difficult for Molly as she has to travel to see him, it has definite benefits for me. I can now visit the supermarket without worrying that we'll lock horns over the freezer cabinet, or that I'll pass him in the car. It might also prolong my life. I was waiting at a junction recently when he turned in past me. I pulled out into the main road in panic and was nearly ploughed down by a car coming from the right.

Emma is also living in London and sharing a flat near London Bridge with a school friend. And they seem to have struck lucky with their landlady. She's moving to Bolivia for a year, but instead of focusing on the tedious details of inventories and rent deposit schemes, she's anxious to pass on the news that she's registered them for free tickets with the local theatre.

Treat #26

It's a sunny Thursday morning in the second week in September and I'm heading towards my first riding lesson, along a mile or so of uneven track with sheep chewing in the fields on either side. As promised in Debbie's instructions, I eventually come to an isolated farm where a picture-book farmyard goose glares at me suspiciously whilst balancing on one leg. Tiny, fluffy, brown chicks scurry along, desperate to keep up with their mother, and cockerels crow in the distance. Everything looks clean and orderly and there are horses all around, standing still and quiet, watching patiently from inside their wooden stalls.

Debbie comes out into the yard to greet me, smiling warmly, and as far removed from 'Hitler' as it's possible to be. My anxieties disappear and I know immediately that I can trust her. She explains that I'll be having all my lessons on Twilight, an elderly chestnut mare who is steady and experienced. She introduces us to one another, and then they both wait patiently while I go to the equipment room to look for a hat. Shaun has a huge head—no doubt full of brains—but mine seems to be worryingly undersized. I keep trying smaller and smaller hats and eventually end up with a child's one.

The next forty minutes in the sand school pass quickly and by the end I've mastered the basic controls; the equine equivalents of ignition, brakes and steering wheel. I've even tentatively used the accelerator. We've done some satisfying manoeuvres round a group of buckets and I've been introduced to the rising trot. Debbie assures me that moving up and down in the saddle is more comfortable than just sitting, but I'm not yet convinced. Riding is turning out to be surprisingly rhythmic and I can't quite get the 'up-down' sequence. My recent enthusiasm for jazz has left me with a passion for the off-beat, so at the moment I'm riding with a syncopated 'down-up' which is not quite right. Despite this hiccup I'm surprised how much I've enjoyed my first lesson.

This is turning out to be a busy day as I have work afterwards, and then my first session at Rock Choir in the evening. Dot offers to pick me up so that we can go together. We met about seven years ago on a course. When we moved to a flat and had to rehome our animals, she offered to take our elderly labrador, Harvey. This was a perfect solution as he had the company of her three dogs, and a large sunny garden in which to spend his final year. It also meant that we could carry on seeing him. This is why I think of Dot as my 'doggy friend', but more recently in my time of need she has become a swearing ally too. We exchange regular texts and follow the general principle that there's no point in saying, 'Having an awful day' or 'Had a great time,' when a couple of profanities would make it so much more expressive.

When she arrives to take me to choir I get into the back of the car as she's also giving a lift to an elderly lady called Sarah. We chat politely at first, and then Dot asks how my week has been. The urge to include a few strong words is irresistible and so we explain to Sarah that we are 'swearing partners'. She's very interested and asks us lots of questions.

The singing is fun. We start with the Bee Gees classic, 'How Deep is Your Love' and I sit with Dot's alto group. Apart from singing lullabies to the children I haven't sung for many years, so make this choice because my fellow altos are friendly and welcoming, rather than because I know this is where my vocal range lies. The different parts are confusing but everyone keeps telling me that with practice it all comes right in the end.

We also sing Adele's 'Rolling in the Deep', but my favourite bit of the evening comes when Dot drops me outside my house. Sarah jumps out of the car, flings her arms round my neck and says warmly, 'Sodding bugger off.'

A few days later I set off for the first divorce recovery course meeting. I'm early and sit in the car outside the church hall where it's being held. I scrutinise the people going in to see what my fellow walking wounded are like. They all seem to be in their twenties and are dressed in Lycra. I'm a bit daunted by this but eventually pluck up courage and go in. One of the organisers greets me warmly and immediately makes me feel at ease. Fortunately, he is not dressed in Lycra. It's a relief when he leads me past the pulsating hall where an aerobics class is in full swing, and into a quiet side room full of people who are mostly my sort of age. We introduce ourselves, watch a short film about the stages of loss, and then break into small groups to talk about it. The facilitators have all been through major relationship breakdowns and have plenty of empathy. I'm tearful but glad to have come.

Unfortunately, though, however much I enjoy these distractions, I can't ignore the fact that my meeting with Shaun is looming and I've been putting off filling in my financial statement. This will be used to agree how much maintenance he will pay for me and Molly in the interim period until the settlement is finalised. Eventually on Saturday morning I can procrastinate no longer. I make a large pot of coffee and shut myself away to get the beastly job done. In the event it's not that awful, and facing up to the issue of money makes me feel less panicky about it. After several hours, all the boxes in the 28-page document are completed and I reward myself with a juicy nectarine which I eat whilst sitting in the garden and inhaling the scent of the roses.

It's a beautiful afternoon. Suddenly things seem less bleak and as I step inside the house I say out loud, 'All's right with the world.'

'Where on earth did that come from?' I think and immediately a text arrives.

It's from Rita. She says, 'Out for the day in London—just lit a candle for you in St Botolph's—prayed for the pain to go and strength to come.'

THIRTY-TWO

FIRMER THIGHS

The meeting with Shaun and his solicitor turns out to be much easier than I was expecting. It's wonderful to have my solicitor dealing with the issues on my behalf. No longer do I have to try in vain to get my point across. I look dispassionately at Shaun across the table and ask myself, 'Was I really married to this man?' He seems like a total stranger.

My friend Sheila told me that she sat on a train recently and realised that her ex-husband was sitting a few rows away. He didn't see her but she looked at him and felt how odd it was that she had slept next to him for forty years and had three babies with him. She wanted to nudge the passenger sitting next to her and say, 'Would you believe I was once married to that man over there?'

We make some progress towards an interim settlement, although now that Shaun is living in such a smart part of London, his outgoings are astonishingly high. The other gulp comes when he announces that I can no longer be the sole beneficiary of his life insurance policy because he now has 'other responsibilities.' He's not prepared to elaborate. We fix a date for another meeting in a month's time.

I keep remembering the thought that I had in the New York church: 'Let go of the hurt. Until I do that I cannot heal.' I have moments of serenity when I am able to let it all wash over me. Rationally, I can see that we had a satisfying marriage for many years and most importantly we gave our four children a good start in life. He can't be blamed for falling out of love with me. But there are many moments when the pain of rejection overpowers my attempts at detachment. Gradually, though, I *am* beginning to believe that the balance will shift towards acceptance. Keeping busy and having new experiences helps.

And the anti-depressants have started working too. I don't feel numb but I do feel a lot less prone to being tossed around on stormy emotional seas.

Choir continues to be entertaining but puzzling. This week we're not only singing mysterious harmonies but are also putting moves to the music. I can sing—I can move—I can't do both together. But it's fun and the best bit is that concentrating takes my mind off things.

Treat #26 (Continued)

It's week four at the stables and I'm surprised to find myself standing, feet out of the stirrups, with no reins, whilst Twilight trots along steadily. I didn't expect to ever feel like a circus performer, but I'm loving it. I've also got the hang of the rising trot, although I can only do it by thinking about something else. Then it seems to happen naturally. Twilight snorts and sneezes a lot, nodding her head vigorously so that I have to loosen the reins in order to stay steady. But she's wonderfully responsive. As soon as I tweak her accelerator by pressing down in the saddle and squeezing with my legs, she does a little bounce and steps up a gear.

I'm out in the autumn sunshine and using my body to communicate with her. I feel her warmth and power. She smells of hay. I lean forward and sink into the saddle so I can move with her rhythm. For now, there is nothing else.

Later in the day, I remember how it felt. I've been frozen for weeks but this was a brief, warm reconnection with life. It crept up on me when I wasn't expecting it. And this treat also has another benefit as I discover when I go shopping with Molly. She tells me off several times for walking too fast, but I don't seem able to slow down. All this riding is giving me powerful thighs.

Another positive aspect to life at the moment is my divorce course. This is going well now that we're getting to know one another, but when I mention it to friends they all have the same reaction. They put on sad, serious and sympathetic faces. Then I have to tell them that it's not like that at all. We talk about difficult things, but we're not completely miserable. There's lots of support and laughter. I sit next to Rachel. We discover so much in common that we wonder if we've been married to the same man for all these years. She's dealing with her pain by baking, and brings her produce for us all to share. People come up with various distractions that help them cope. For one it was yoga, for another it was cycling, and I realise that for me at the moment, riding and singing are making a significant difference.

I'm enjoying the good moments. It's reminiscent of emerging from a very severe illness and edging back to normality. In the first week of the divorce course, one of the facilitators said, 'Divorce is not the worst thing that can happen.' I agree.

CONFUSION

Since sharing a room with Maud in the Pennines I've been curious about her friend, Isla. It seems that we have a lot in common. I send her an email and introduce myself. Maud has mentioned me, so she's not surprised and her reply is warm and friendly.

We arrange to have a chat and later as I sit on the stairs in my preferred phone position I hear her story. She and her husband were happy for a very long time—people would comment on how devoted they were and how well matched. I remember that, too, about my marriage. Then her husband got ill and changed, like mine did. The details are so similar: leukaemia, a bone marrow transplant, complications, suffering, and then a complete rejection of what he seemed to love and value for so many years. And now like me she is bemused. She's a successful, intelligent, independent woman but these events have knocked the bottom out of her world.

This is the first time that I've talked to someone who really understands what it's like when your partner changes. It starts with the feeling that you must be imagining it. Their reactions, once broadly predictable because you knew one another so well, are now sometimes surprisingly angry or antagonistic but you tell yourself that this is just temporary. Then you realise that while you've been trying to just get on and cope with day-to-day life, the 'sometimes' has wrapped its roots around your marriage and is strangling it. There's a gradual cold dawning that they no longer want what you want.

Towards the end Shaun used to talk about our 'misunderstandings'. I thought we communicated well. If I didn't understand what he said then I was confident we could talk about it and thrash it out until we did. I just simply didn't see that there was a problem. But now I'm beginning to realise that I was communicating with the old Shaun. There were things that the new Shaun couldn't talk about because they were too shocking; like that he no longer loved me. Or perhaps he was just too confused to know what he thought.

I wonder constantly whether I failed him in some way. I witnessed the pain and fear that he went through. I saw him being diminished and vulnerable. But even though I was there with him throughout it all, I cannot ever understand what it felt like for him.

It's easy to see why people reassess their lives after surviving cancer; why they feel that life is too short not to be happy and pursue their dreams. The trouble is that we've ended up with different dreams. He wants to be charitable and give thanks to God—to cycle through mountains and test himself physically. I just wanted to get back to a normal family life and to help our children through their challenges as we watch their lives develop. To have long, noisy lunches enjoying their silly humour. To spend time with friends and have weekends away with my husband. To support him in taking up new interests and to have him do the same for me. I believed we would get on with life afterwards and appreciate what we had, more than ever.

So much has happened to Shaun that it's difficult to disentangle influences and to understand the processes that brought us to where we are today. The drugs may have played a part. He used to complain that they affected his memory and ability to think. Then there was the radiotherapy. And the constant fear that the cancer would return—as it did. There were insecurities, too that he carried from childhood and his mother's mental illness, and recently there was the financial turmoil that caused so much worry and threatened his self-esteem. And there was the fact that for years he was the focus of concern for our family and friends. When he got better and life started to get back to normal he seemed to find the loss of this attention difficult to accept.

Any, or all, of these factors may have been culpable. No doubt there were others too. But in the end all that matters is that he was unhappy. He became increasingly distant from me and the children, and lost his sense of humour. He may even have had something akin to post traumatic stress. That can make you turn against the person you are closest to; to mistrust them and to become detached and numb. Maybe that was what enabled him to hurt me so much, and not to care.

I'm grateful to have had the chance to talk to Isla about the confusion that whips and twists inside me, and to have heard about hers. She's insightful and generous. We agree to stay in touch.

Ten Pounds Buys Me

I'm having some problems with my self-image. I suppose this isn't surprising as I'm still struggling to come to terms with the oddness of waking up one morning a wife, and by the end of the day being unexpectedly single.

Several other things have happened recently to make me wonder who I am now. I assumed that if I took Shaun off my car insurance then my premium would go down. After all, it's one less person to insure. It hasn't done, though. It's gone up. Apparently by not being in an orderly married state, I'm more of a risk.

The next reminder of my changed status comes when I'm invited to a get-together and am cautioned in advance by the hostess that there *'will* be husbands there.' I know she is trying to be sensitive, but I never thought I'd be the kind of woman who can only face other people's husbands with prior warning.

The final blow to my self-image comes when I'm shopping at Sainsbury's with Emma. I'm perusing the dozens of varieties of porridge on offer but can't see properly as there's a trolley in the way; a small girl is sitting in the child seat without any sign of a parent. They've presumably gone to hunt down something that is not porridge-related. I gently move the trolley a few inches to the side so that I can get by. The child looks at me in terror and whispers huskily, 'Please don't steal me.' Not only am I now an insurance risk and in purdah, but I'm also a potential child abductor.

The finality of our split and the chasm between us has made me think about another aspect of my identity, too. I've begun to toy with the idea of changing my name. I no longer want to be linked to Shaun in this fundamental way. Once the divorce is complete I will quickly become the discarded Mrs M, replaced by a new model. However, this is a delicate issue as we share four children who have his name. There's also the question of what to choose. I don't want to go back to my maiden name as that feels like a step back into an unhappy phase of my life. I suppose I could make up a name. But what?

One evening I have a few friends over and we noisily exchange suggestions for my new identity. It all seems terribly funny, but when they've gone and I go to see Molly in bed, she has overheard and is cross and unhappy.

'You can't change your name.' she says. 'That's rejecting all of us, and you're just going to have some stupid made-up name.'

I feel so sorry for having upset her, and ashamed for being insensitive. 'It's fine,' I say, 'I won't change it.'

I don't want to do anything to hurt her so I shelve the plan indefinitely. The need to have my own identity is visceral, though, and I can't help fantasising about new names, and trying them out in private. Nothing seems right. They're all too dull, or have the wrong rhythm—or bad associations. Then one day, I'm on a long drive when a name takes up residence in my head and won't leave me alone.

At first I wonder where it's come from, but when I say it out loud it fits like a favourite dress: 'Farley-Rose.' This is a union between my favourite flower and the middle name of my enigmatic grandmother, Esmeralda. The two surnames I've had in life, so far, have been rather plain, so a bit of fanciful floweriness is welcome. So what, if it's a 'stupid made-up name'. I love it.

I decide that I'll use it for any creative work I do, but will keep my married name for everything else. I talk it through with Molly and she is content with this arrangement. Then a few weeks later, we're in the car, and out of the blue she says, 'I like Farley-Rose. It suits you. I think you should change your name properly.' I ask Will, Emma and Henry how they feel about it. They all understand and so with their blessing, I go ahead and start the process.

An internet search on 'changing your name' comes up with a number of companies who provide a deed poll service. One offers the opportunity to ask questions of an adviser, using instant messaging. I'm very sceptical, but type in my question just to see what happens.

'I'm in the middle of going through my divorce. Does it matter if I change my name before it's concluded?'

Within ten seconds I have an answer: 'No, you can go ahead.'

This is impressive so I try another question, and another. Each time I get a prompt and helpful response. I end the conversation by saying that I want a fresh start and hope that a different name will help.

Back comes the response, 'I understand. Good luck.'

It costs just ten pounds to order the deed poll form. I provide details of my old name, my new name, and my address, and everything arrives within a few days. I double-check with all the children, then I ask Nicky if she would be the witness to my momentous change. She has been unwavering in her friendship despite becoming increasingly troubled by numbness and frightening bouts of dizziness. These have worsened in the few months since she helped me transform my garden and I want to mark the contribution she has made. She gives her trademark conspiratorial chuckle and says that she would be delighted.

I'm in excellent company as many famous people have chosen to change their name: Fred Astaire was originally Frederick Austerlitz; Jennifer Aniston started out as the lyrical, but difficult to spell, Anastassakis, and David Bowie was born with the unspaceman-like surname of Jones. Others change both, which is understandable in the case of John Wayne: 'Marion Morrison' simply doesn't conjure up virility. 'Stefani Germanotta' isn't as instantly memorable as 'Lady Gaga', and 'Mark Feld' lacks the glamour of 'Marc Bolan'. Would Michael Caine have been as successful if he'd stuck to his birth name of Maurice Micklewhite? Elton John was originally Reg Dwight, and Elvis Costello was Declan MacManus. But my favourite is Doris von Kappelhoff. This doesn't immediately make me think of 'the girl next door'. Changing to Doris Day was a wise move.

I go over to Nicky's house on Sunday morning and we sit at her kitchen table. It's surprisingly easy and feels absolutely right. I sign the form, rejecting my old name and embracing the new one. Then she countersigns it. David takes a photo of us; we beam and look like we've just got married and signed the register.

How strange it is to wake up in the morning with one name, and go to sleep with a different one. I even managed to do this without promising to love, honour and obey.

THIRTY-THREE

A Mystery Holiday

Although it's not on my list, I've always wanted to go on a
mystery holiday. Molly thinks it would be fun too, so we plan
one for half-term. Actually, I suppose it's more accurate to
say that 'We don't plan one', as planning it rather defeats the
object. Instead we decide which days we'll be away, settle on a
budget, and come up with a starting point: Monday morning at
Victoria Coach Station. Unlike London rail terminals, it offers
up transport that could potentially whisk us away to any part of
the UK.

Going away with no idea of where we're going or what we'll
do is a useful metaphor for my life at the moment.

It's hard to pack when you don't know where you're going, so
we prepare for all eventualities by each including a dress and a
raincoat. Our final act of preparation, the evening before, is to
paint our nails purple.

A Steamy Interlude

The first thing we do in London is to buy a guide to the UK.
We're careful in our choice, though. We don't want a 'family'
one that has just commercial attractions; we want real cities,
history, and a bit of grit.

It's the Monday of half-term and Victoria Coach Station is
exceptionally busy. Big boards display the destinations of all
buses due to leave in the next couple of hours. It's exhilarating
to feel so free. We could go to Penzance, Aberdeen, or anywhere
in between. The whole country is a potential playground.

We spend a few minutes thinking; each choosing three places
that we'd be happy to visit. Our combined list is Manchester,
Glasgow, Sheffield, Manchester, Newcastle and Scarborough.

Molly wrinkles her nose and says that she doesn't like the sound of Scarborough, although the truth is that she knows absolutely nothing about it. Despite it getting two votes on our list, we reject Manchester and settle instead on Sheffield. This is mainly because our cousin Catherine went to university there and speaks highly of it.

I leave Molly with our suitcases and brave the automatic ticket machine. This involves pressing umpteen options and getting all the way through the selection process only to be told at the final stage that the next bus is full. I go through the rigmarole all over again and discover that the one after that is also fully booked. I'm beginning to think that Sheffield is not such a good idea, so call to Molly across the heads of the dozens of people who are standing between us. We shout back and forth for a while and eventually settle on Leeds. A couple of years ago Will was studying for a master's degree there and we visited him. We didn't get to see much of the city, though, as Shaun was in pain with his hip.

There's a bus leaving soon, and I finally feel we're on our way when the driver makes the first of many announcements in a broad Yorkshire accent. We must not smoke. We must not drink alcohol. There are many other things that he forbids us from doing but fortunately, he does not mention eating and drinking, as we have our lunch with us. Inevitably we start by spilling the coffee, but eventually we get settled and eat our sandwiches. Travelling by coach turns out to be very relaxing, and as we are higher up than we would be in a car, we can peer into the cabs of the lorries that we pass.

Before long, we get a text from Emma, who is eager to follow our progress. I decide not to make it too easy for her, so come up with a riddle: 'Take a representative of the Templar. Make him cross the river, then send him up-country.' I painstakingly enter this convoluted message on my phone, and send it, smugly confident that it will keep her perplexed for ages.

After five minutes a text arrives: 'Leeds. Knightsbridge of the

North. Emma xx.'

I'd copied Henry in on my text too, and after an hour he sends a message. 'What? My head hurts.'

The driver hasn't said anything since his initial onslaught of health and safety announcements. As we approach Leeds, however, he winds up again. He starts with, 'Do not stand up as we will be pulling off the motorway soon.' Then as we get near the bus station he adds, 'Do not try to get your own luggage out as this is due to health and safety matters.' He comes into his own as the bus stops and he tells us that it's now safe to stand up. 'Mek sure you 'aven't left your false teeth,' he adds as a final flourish.

We spotted a budget hotel as we pulled into the bus station and so decide to try our luck there. It's certainly basic, but it's clean and convenient and leaves us plenty of money with which to have some fun. We book for three nights.

I'm very much looking forward to a cup of tea. But when we reach our room, we're dismayed to discover that there's no kettle. That's a double blow as we've also come prepared with hot water bottles. Later, as we walk through the city centre on our way to see Skyfall, the new James Bond film, we spot an electric kettle in a shop window. It's only nine pounds so I nip in and buy it.

The film is thoroughly enjoyable and makes me realise how much I adore Judi Dench. There's something elusive about her, like a deer that's easily startled. It's been a good evening but by the time we come out of the cinema it's gone eleven, and I'm frustrated to find that the nearby supermarket has closed. I'd been planning to buy some teabags there. Since I can't bear the idea of not having my early morning cup of tea, there's no alternative but to resort to some crime.

When we get back to the hotel, there's a solitary security guard on duty in reception. I distract him by chatting about the weather whilst Molly nips round the corner to the breakfast area and steals one teabag. I justify this by telling her that we're just borrowing it and will replace it when we buy our own supply tomorrow. She looks quite pleased with herself as we go up to our room, and I feel guilty for leading her astray.

The next morning I wake up, looking forward to my cup of tea. I remember cheerfully that we have a kettle and a teabag—then I realise that we have no cups.

After croissants and coffee in an attractive Victorian shopping arcade we take a bus to nearby Bradford and then another to Saltaire. This is an industrial model village that was built next to a textile mill, along similar principles to Port Sunlight. In the 1850s when it was started, Bradford was overcrowded and had the reputation of being the most polluted city in England. The housing is built next to the River Aire. It's made of honey-coloured stone and is very pleasing. We stroll around the streets which are each named either in honour of Queen Victoria's family or the children of Sir Titus Salt, the founder. Ada, Albert, Victoria, Whitlam, Edward, Harold, Fanny, and Jane are all there. But I'm a bit disappointed that there's so little information about the history of the area that could bring it to life.

Later we explore Bradford's curry district. Our guidebook recommends the Kashmir, which is the oldest Indian restaurant in the city. It started in 1958 to cater for the Asian textile workers who moved to the area. The lights are very bright, the tables are basic, the chairs don't match, and the china is a hotchpotch, but none of this matters. The food is spicy and fragrant. We particularly enjoy the crispy mushroom bhajias, sheekh kebabs and chapatis. There's more than we can eat and the bill is only £17.

The next day we decide to have a day trip to Harrogate as it's only forty minutes away. We get on the train and start settling down for the journey but as I try to take my coat off, the zip sticks and I have to turn to Molly for help. After a bit of tugging she releases me, and when I say tenderly, 'What would I do without you?' she replies, 'You'd be stuck in your coat.'

In Harrogate we head straight for the Royal Pump Room Museum. We learn that there are dozens of springs and wells in the area which originate from an ancient sea far below the earth's surface. They rise up through faults in the rock and for several hundred years from the seventeenth century onwards, they were believed to have health-giving properties.

In the early eighteenth century, the area was visited by Celia Fiennes, an enthusiastic traveller who explored England, keeping a diary as she went. Her entry for Harrogate recorded that the water had such an offensive odour that her horse wouldn't go near the well. Molly and I noticed a revolting smell when we arrived, but we assumed it was the drains.

The Harrogate season lasted from May to September. Visitors stayed in the town to focus on their health: they would drink an early morning glass of spa water at the Pump Room and the rest of the day would be taken up with cards, gentle exercise, afternoon tea, theatre visits, balls, and more of the foul-tasting water. I ask the museum assistant whether the water has genuine restorative properties. She says that any health benefits for the spa visitors probably came from the purgative effect of the water and the fact that they were taking more exercise than normal.

By the end of the nineteenth century, Harrogate was facing competition from spas in mainland Europe, so in 1897 the Royal Baths opened. There were Turkish baths for visitors to enjoy and they could also choose to have their limbs immersed in molten paraffin wax, their muscles stimulated with electricity or their spines massaged with needle-like jets of water. In 1910, an exciting innovation was introduced: peat baths. These were heated to about 100°F and clients could select from a menu of optional extras such as salt water or electric current.

By 1912 the Royal Pump Room had about 2000 visitors a day. You could pay to drink inside, or there was a free tap outside for the poor. Its popularity continued right up until the Second World War, but then the spa trade declined and Harrogate re-invented itself as a conference town. Today, only the Turkish baths remain and we decide to spend the afternoon there.

Everything is very grand. We get changed into our swimming costumes in cubicles with solid mahogany panelling and thick, red velvet curtains. The floors are decorated with Roman-style mosaics and the walls have huge Victorian stencilled designs.

We shower as instructed and then spend ten minutes in the steam room. It makes the inside of my nose very hot. Then we shower again and get into the cold plunge pool—at least *Molly* does. She immerses herself in the chilly water, whilst breathing in and out very fast, and squealing. I immerse the lower part of my right leg, and my left toes. That's enough for me. I feel like a failure as we move to the first of the warm rooms, called a tepidarium. We move through progressively hotter areas: the calidarium, and the laconium where the floor is decidedly hot. Then we shower and go for a lie-down in the long, thin relaxation room, languorously reading magazines and imagining that we're Victorians. Then we start all over again. This time I force myself to get into the plunge pool. Once I'm in, it's surprisingly enjoyable; very cleansing and invigorating. It's funny how the bit I was dreading turns out to be the most rewarding. We go through the complete cycle three times and agree that it's been a perfect way to spend a rainy Yorkshire afternoon.

We like the next bit too: tea at Betty's with waitresses in black dresses and long white aprons; chocolate cake, and a pot of tea that seems to last forever. There's the polite chink of teaspoons on bone china teacups, and the rattle of the cake trolley as it's wheeled around seductively. Waitresses can be heard saying, 'Of course,' every now and again through the babble of contented chat. We sit engrossed in writing postcards and consulting our guidebook.

Suddenly, there's a loud noise outside. We look up and realise that it's grown dark whilst we've been in here. The rain is hammering against the window and the big trees outside are covered with red, white and green fairy lights.

A House That's Totally Stuffed

We've spent three nights in Leeds and need to decide where to go next. I suggest to Molly that we might visit Chatsworth as taking her there is on my list. I visited with Shaun five years ago and thought then how much she would enjoy it. At that stage he was responding well to the gene therapy drugs, and going away for a few days together was like surfacing for air after holding our breath underwater. We did some walking in the surrounding area and I was amazed that I'd managed to get to my late forties without discovering the beauty of the Peak District. I thought we were happy in each other's company, but now I look back and wonder.

Molly and I check out of our hotel, but not before replacing the stolen teabag. My conscience immediately feels lighter. Then we head for Chesterfield by coach and take a local bus to Bakewell, where we plan to stay overnight. I've phoned ahead and have made a booking at a B&B in the village. When we arrive, our hosts take us to a charming room which, happily, comes with a kettle, teabags and cups.

The next morning we browse in the vintage shops and I do a bit of day-dreaming about how to make my small entrance hall more feminine. Nothing too obviously pink, but I'd like old-fashioned overblown roses to figure somewhere in the scheme.

Treat #27

By mid-morning it's time to get on the bus to Chatsworth, along with various holdalls containing bits and pieces that we've accumulated. These include the electric kettle, which is an awkward shape so gets trailed along noisily in its own bag. The driver tells us when we reach Baslow and gives us directions, so we clatter off the bus and begin to make our way along a boggy footpath. We keep getting waylaid by puddles, but eventually, we emerge on the long main drive that leads to Chatsworth House.

Nearly everyone that we've come across on our holiday has gone out of their way to be helpful and the security staff at the house are no exception. They store our bags and tell us, much to our relief, that we can get a bus back to Baslow for our return journey.

After a lunch of local sausages and red cabbage, we join a guided tour of the house. There's been a family home on this site for over five hundred years, and sixteen generations. During that time the occupants have built up a huge collection of treasures, and as the Dowager Duchess, the former Deborah Mitford, says, 'This house is totally stuffed.'

It was originally home to Bess of Hardwick and when she died it passed to her son, William Cavendish. He wanted to buy a title and the only one available at the College of Heralds was the Earldom of Devonshire. It cost £10,000, the equivalent of four million pounds today.

The original house stayed put until the fourth Earl came on the scene. He pulled it down and replaced it with the one we see today. Everyone knows that Mr Darcy was on £10,000 a year. Well, the Earl of Devonshire was on £120,000, quite a few years earlier. He had no hesitation in installing marble floors and the best of everything, throughout his house. In 1694 he received an aristocratic upgrade when he was rewarded for his loyalty to William of Orange during the Glorious Revolution. He became the first Duke of Devonshire. We see the huge, intricate, silver chandelier that would travel everywhere with him. It would be set up over his desk, wherever he was, to set the standard and remind everyone that he was a very important person.

There's something going on as we get to the top of the main staircase. The current Duke is showing Chatsworth's priceless Chinese porcelain collection to the Chinese Cultural Ambassador and his retinue. We stare as politely as we can and recall how the last time I was here, Shaun and I saw the

Dowager Duchess. A new exhibition about the life of her late husband, the 11th Duke, had just opened in the house, and she was strolling around, pointing out items of interest whilst being interviewed by a radio reporter. Later that day we saw the current Duchess darting through the house with her dogs. It's like trainspotting; I can now tick off three members of the family.

We could stay for days and not see everything, but by mid-afternoon we have to leave. It's been a fascinating visit, and we're both glad to have come. We're very glad, too, of the bus that takes us, our luggage, and the electric kettle, back to Baslow. From there, we take another one to Chesterfield, and then after quite a bit of hanging around, we join the coach for Victoria. It's very late when we get home, and I'm relieved to fall into my own comfortable bed.

Next morning I wake up and remember that it's six months to the day since my marriage ended. I feel different. Something has shifted. New York with the children was stimulating and I'm glad I did it. But throughout those four days, excitement and tears jostled with one another for prime position. On this latest trip I was able to enjoy the entire experience. Sharing Chatsworth with Molly was happy and gave me confidence. I know that I can choose to let things unfold and wait to see what happens. There's lots in my life that feels uncertain at the moment but, as with our holiday, I hope that one day I'll be able to say, 'It worked out alright in the end.' There's a chance it might even be fun.

THIRTY-FOUR

Grappling with Fish

The success of our mystery holiday has filled me with optimism and I convince myself that the bad bits are over. I appreciate these moments of believing that it's all going to be easy from now on. But not far below this rosy surface I know only too well that ups are followed by downs.

Moves like changing my name and taking up new hobbies have been helpful, but nothing changes the basic facts that:

- I didn't want my husband to change

- I'm sad about the impact on the children and their experience of family life

- I feel a failure

- Being discarded is horrible

- Much of the time I don't feel steady enough to face the divorce proceedings, whilst also working full-time

The anti-depressants help to even out my emotions, but they don't mitigate the sharp stabs in the accusatory correspondence which comes via Melanie now that the legal process is underway.

There are potentially three routes that we could choose to go down in order to agree our divorce. The first is to go to court and have a judge rule on what should happen. We're both keen to avoid wasting our limited resources on this because of the high costs involved. The second is to negotiate via our solicitors. I'm not keen on this as Shaun's affairs are so convoluted. He has overseas investments and shares in lots of small companies. I think there's great scope for misunderstanding if we try to sort these issues out by letter. It will be slow and laborious and I might never get to the bottom of what he has.

Guided by Melanie's pragmatism, it seems to me that the best option is the third one: collaborative divorce. This requires us to sit round a table with our solicitors and to talk. That way we each have the chance to state our wishes and to negotiate fairly. The solicitors aim to smooth issues where possible, and to look for solutions rather than fuelling antagonism. I don't relish the prospect of spending time with Shaun, but Melanie says that collaboration often helps people to resolve differences, and to feel better about the divorce. She adds that provided I can face the meetings—and not everyone can—it's much less daunting than the cold formality of solicitors' letters or the officialdom of a court.

Our meeting last month was based on this approach, and I thought it went well. But now we've hit a barrier. The next step is for us both to sign an agreement saying that we'll engage with the collaborative process and commit to make it work. The overall aim is to make it less likely that the negotiations will break down and end up in court. If this does happen then both parties have to start again and instruct a new solicitor. This is a sticking point for me.

Shaun has been single-minded about the divorce right from the start, but it has gone much faster than I would choose. If it was my decision alone, then I would have waited a good few months longer, like most people in my divorce group. The main thing that's helping me to engage with it at all, is that I trust Melanie. This makes me nervous of signing the collaboration agreement as that would risk having to use a different solicitor at a later stage. I discuss my concerns with her and she says that we can continue to have round table meetings but without the agreement being signed. I'm happy with this arrangement.

Shaun, however, is not. He is furious and once again accuses me of being manipulative. I wish he could understand that I can't help finding the annihilation of our marriage difficult.

He sacks his solicitor and informs us that he will act for

himself in future. The next thing that will happen is that he will put forward a financial proposal. In the meantime there are still many things to address. I pass many profoundly depressing lunch hours listening to holding music whilst waiting to talk to 'advisers' about disentangling our joint bank account, our life insurances, our mortgage, and a multitude of household bills. As we spent so many years deftly weaving our lives together, I suppose it's inevitable that picking them apart will take time. There are still a lot of knots to untangle.

I'm back in a state of confusion and wondering what the next twist will be. The clarity I thought we'd got in our first meeting has now evaporated. Dealing with this divorce feels like trying to hold onto a slippery fish. Just when I think I've got hold of it, the darn thing does a flip and is off again, flashing and glinting like quicksilver.

YAWNING

I'm yawning a great deal at the moment. Not polite little yawns that can be hidden behind a fluttering hand, but huge ones so big that I think I will fall over or dislocate my jaw. I worry that I'll end up alone because all my friends will have given up on me, offended by this relentless and antisocial habit.

THIRTY-FIVE

EVERYTHING TASTES LIKE CARDBOARD

The changes that have taken place may have been difficult for me and the children, but they've definitely benefited the cat. There's now a vast expanse of empty bed to claim. Although I could stretch out if I wanted, I always stay glued to my old, familiar, 'married' side. It's where I've always slept, and I'm not yet ready to embrace the wilderness. What might one day feel like a gain is still too suffused with loss to be enjoyable. The other night I woke up and felt lonely. I put my hand out in the dark and found a warm bundle of fur. She chirruped contentedly as I stroked her.

As well as being allowed to sleep on my bed she's enjoying extra rations. I've struggled to cope with everyday tasks, and weighing her food out, as recommended, is one that's been neglected. Now the fierce vet has referred her to the weight control nurse and she's on a strict diet of biscuits that make her feel 'fuller for longer'.

Normally, I have an enthusiastic attitude to food, just like my cat. When eating one meal I'm already planning the next. But the last six months have been different. I've felt nauseous and acidic. Everything has tasted uniformly dull. Each morning I've sat at the table, picking at my porridge with a teaspoon, and when I've managed to get half of it down, I've pushed the bowl away with relief. Eating out has been no better. I've left plates of toyed-with food all over the country, causing distress to waiting staff who look unhappy and ask, 'Is there something wrong with it?'

When the children are at home, though, it's not fair to drag them into my dietary depression. So I've been grateful for the convenience of pasta, despite it tasting like soggy cardboard whatever treatment I give it.

During all the years of raising a family, churning out meals day after day has often got tedious. I get stuck in a rut and can't think what to do. But cooking for special meals with friends and family has always been a pleasure. Sadly, since the separation my hospitality spark has dimmed. I've managed to have a few friends over, but the cooking has been a joyless chore and I've felt unhappy about entertaining on my own. This is an emotional reaction, rather than a rational one, as when I think back over the past I realise that I always did the cooking and shopping and was usually the one who organised it in the first place. Shaun would pour the drinks and make the coffee.

This seems a good time to bring in my Italian cookery treat. I can cook lasagne, risotto and spaghetti carbonara fairly competently, and when I made my list I was enthusiastic about cooking and keen to discover a few clever 'restaurantv' tricks. I knew that Ruth Rogers' and Rose Gray's River Café has had praises heaped upon it because of its authentic Italian fare so I decided that I would include 'Make ten recipes from the River Cafe Cookbook'.

I can't carry on getting sustenance from half-eaten bowls of porridge, the odd banana, and forkfuls of cardboard pasta. I also want to give back some of the hospitality that friends have shown to me. And there's another motive, too—I want to discover if I can cope with making the coffee myself.

ZEN AND THE ART OF GRATING PASTRY

My second-hand copy of The River Café Cookbook has already provided me with several evenings of bedtime reading when Cousins Maggie and Philip email to say that they'd like to pop in on Friday evening. They suggest taking Molly and me out to a pub but I tell them that we'd be delighted to feed them here.

I flick backwards and forwards through the book and manage to summon some enthusiasm. For our starter I'm going to do char-grilled peppers with anchovy and capers. I already have ordinary tinned anchovies, and capers in vinegar, in my store cupboard. However, the book tells me very firmly that these will not do—I must use salted anchovies and salted capers. I put these on my shopping list but have no idea whether I'll find them. The main course is to be risotto with mushrooms. I've already made some chicken stock as prescribed and add 'a lot of' dried porcini and flat field mushrooms to my list. Then there are the seven lemons, six whole eggs and nine egg yolks that are required for the lemon tart. Fortunately Waitrose comes up trumps with all the ingredients, although I'm a bit surprised at my exorbitant porcini bill.

On Friday afternoon I finish work early and get down to some cooking with the radio as company. The pastry for the tart turns out to be interesting. The ingredients are similar to those I usually use, but there's a clever twist: it has to be chilled and then grated into the tart tin. When pressed gently into place and baked, the pastry is crisp and biscuity which is a great improvement on my usual dense results. I get impatient with the length of time it takes to char-grill the peppers, though, and give up too early. They're a bit firmer than they should be, but still taste good, and the risotto is intensely mushroomy.

We have a very happy evening and I manage to make the coffee quite competently. There's lots of food left and I pack some up for Maggie and Philip to take home. Despite this, there's still enough mushroom risotto to provide me with lunch for three days in succession. This is a benefit that comes from our separation. Shaun frequently worked from home so I used to cook lunch for us both. He'd moan if I made the same meal too often but now I can eat the same thing day after day if I choose.

It's not long before I'm ready for my next River Café experiment. Two friends come for dinner and I make penne with a slow-cooked sausage sauce. This involves taking the meat from Italian-style pork sausages and cooking it with red onions, garlic, chillies, red wine, tomatoes and nutmeg. Towards the end of the slow process, cream and Parmesan are added. I have to substitute goat's cream and Pecorino instead, but the results are delicious. For the first time in ages, pasta tastes interesting. I use the grated pastry trick again and this time make a pear and almond tart.

As I sprinkle basil on the pasta, I breathe in the fragrance and remember how this helped me out of a tricky situation some years ago. I had an academic paper to write, but the deadline was getting close and I hadn't even started. For two and a half days I sat despondently and, like the schoolboy Churchill, had little more to show for my efforts than a blot and a few smudges. On the third day I went to the local deli to buy a sandwich and noticed some lovely basil plants so I bought one of those too. All the way home I kept absent-mindedly picking the leaves off, squeezing them, and breathing in the aroma. Then I ate my lunch, settled back at the computer, and wrote the entire paper in one continuous flow, stopping only now and then to sniff another basil leaf. A few months later an aromatherapist told me that basil helps you concentrate.

The next week I ask Nicky and another friend, Anne, over and plan to make chocolate nemesis. The book promises that this is 'the best chocolate cake ever'. I check I have all the ingredients and then notice that the recipe calls for a 30cm cake tin. No problem, I think and get out my tape measure to check the diameter of my favourite round one. I'm very poor at judging dimensions so am disappointed to find that it's only 23cm. I need to go into town for various bits and pieces and add a new cake tin to my shopping list.

The local department store has nothing larger than 25cm but fortunately Lakeland has just what I need. I pay for the tin and lug it home. It's only when I get back to the house that I realise just how enormous it is. It's the size you would normally use for the bottom tier of a wedding cake. Still, I want to do things properly so I get on with melting a pound and a half of dark chocolate and a pound of butter. Then I whisk ten eggs with almost a pound and a half of sugar. It has to quadruple in volume. Eventually, it's thick and luscious so I pour it into the tin and level the top. The problem comes when I read the next instruction which is to place the tin in a bain-marie. It is apparently essential that the water should come right up to the rim of the tin, or it won't cook evenly. Who on earth has a bain-marie that's big enough to take this titanic cake tin? Emma, Molly and I all scratch our heads as we try to puzzle out a solution. Then the girls simultaneously have a partial brainwave. We could use the grill tray. It's not very deep so the water won't come up to the rim, but never mind, we'll just have to put up with unevenly cooked cake. By the time the tin is sitting in the grill pan it's so heavy that it takes all three of us to lift it into the oven.

This makes me smile and remember the Christmas when we accidentally acquired a giant turkey. We had two geese at the time, named Edwina and Tarquin, who hissed like snakes and patrolled the front garden with all the dedication of presidential security staff. We'd been raising them with Christmas dinner in mind, but as the festive season loomed large it became clear that neither Shaun nor I was prepared to do the dreadful deed. A week before Christmas I asked the village butcher if he would help us out. He agreed, but then became increasingly inventive with his excuses—his assistant had gone to Australia—his mother-in-law had suffered a stroke—he'd sprained his wrist plucking turkeys—Eventually, two days before Christmas, with no lunch solution in sight, and the butcher and I no longer able to make eye-contact, I bumped into a local turkey farmer at a drinks party. I told him about our dilemma and not surprisingly he recommended that we abandon our plans for goose, and enjoy the pleasures of turkey instead. He was keen to tell me that he had just one bird left, and that I was welcome to have it for a bargain price. I agreed to go and collect it the next day. However, he'd failed to mention that it was a 40lb superturkey. Shaun and I had to get up in the middle of the night to put it in the oven and it took both of us to lift it in. I still wonder whether it was a misplaced ostrich.

To precede the chocolate nemesis, I decide to do pork cooked in milk. It sounds intriguing. The addition of lemon rind is supposed to make the milk curdle so that it forms a rich sauce, but unfortunately this dish is not a success. I'm a bit slapdash in peeling the lemon and include some pith which makes it taste very bitter. Also, the sauce fails to materialise as promised. Maybe it's because I've used lactose-free milk. I can't serve this; but fortunately I have some beef stew left from earlier in the week so I eke that out. The smashed celeriac cooked in chicken stock is good, though I lack aplomb and spoil the general effect by explaining that 'It's meant to have lumps in it.'

We have small pieces of the chocolate cake with some fresh raspberries. It's very good indeed, but also very rich. Given its size, I estimate that there are about 25 servings there.

There's still plenty of cake when Rachel from my divorce group pops in for lunch the next day. She makes me laugh by telling me about her husband who is a 'narsecissist'. I make penne with tomato and balsamic vinegar. It's a pleasant dish— but not a great one. This is possibly because I've disobeyed the book's strict instructions to use a ten-year old vinegar and have instead tossed the pasta in the ordinary balsamic stuff that I had in my cupboard. I give Rachel some cake to take home. And she's not the only one. Everyone who comes to the house this week gets a parting gift of chocolate nemesis.

As the final part of this treat I make some espresso ice-cream. I have Henry in mind for this, as it's one of his favourite flavours. The ingredients include a whole jar of coffee and fifteen egg yolks. The next evening I have a very small bowl.

It's deliciously bitter, but turns out to be lethal. I'm still awake at 3.30am. It probably contained the equivalent of about eight cups of coffee.

In the classic 'Zen and the Art of Motorcycle Maintenance', Robert Pirsig says that routine tasks may be either dull and tedious drudgery, or enjoyable and pleasurable pastimes. It all depends on attitude. I'm indebted to this treat for reawakening my appetite and taste buds. I've discovered once again that cooking can be an enjoyable and pleasurable pastime.

MANSFIELD PARK 2

TREAT #10 (CONTINUED)

I've had another go at reading Manfield Park but had to start at the beginning again because I'd forgotten who all the characters were. This time I got through the first fifty-three pages.

My concentration for reading is poor but many other things are tricky too. Simple tasks like unpacking the shopping are peculiarly overwhelming. I can't sustain my attention long enough to complete them. Then I hit upon the 'rule of three'. Instead of the impossibility of focusing on the overall job, I can manage if I break it down into stages. Randomly picking out three items from the bags and putting those away is achievable. Then I do another three, and so on. It's a kind of game, though I have to admit it's not a very exciting one. This helps in other situations, too. I can cope with a list of three small actions, like getting dressed, putting the washing on, and feeding the cat. Then another three, and so it goes on until I either forget where I've put my list or the phone rings and distracts me. I spend a lot of time talking on the phone these days.

There's still no further progress with my North Downs Way walk. But I do manage to keep feeding the compost bin.

BEAVERS

My sleeping pattern is erratic and since finishing Mad Men I've needed something new to distract me in the long, slow hours of the night. Life of Mammals, the next series in my Life on Earth treat has fitted the bill well and I've enjoyed it, in a dozy kind of way. David Attenborough is easy to watch and listen to. Sadly, with my poor concentration there are few bits from the ten episodes that lodge in my memory, but the handful that do are very pleasing.

TREAT#7 (CONTINUED)

One highlight was watching the sloths with their Beatle haircuts. They live high in the trees, hardly moving apart from once a week when they make their way down to the ground for a loo break. No-one knows why they do this as it's a great deal of effort and also puts them at risk from predators. A stoat killing a rabbit that's ten times its size was remarkable. And it's been satisfying to discover that sealions differ from seals by having external ears. Then there was the moment when a crocodile jumped out at a herd of wildebeest. It was like a horror movie.

My favourite mammals, though, are beavers. They're so focused. Everyone knows that they build dams, but I'd never wondered why; now I know. The programme shows a huge and precisely engineered dam that extends across a stream, creating a pool that extends for a mile or so. The beavers eat twigs and tree bark and in order to have an ongoing supply when the pool is iced over in winter, they collect large branches in the autumn and stick them in the mud. The pool keeps the food fresh. It's the beavers' fridge.

After one of the divorce group meetings I was telling Rachel about this and also what the beavers do when there's a leak in the dam. Several of them swim out to it, and plug it up with mud and twigs. They're remarkably good at teamwork. We stood outside my car in the dark and chatted about beavers for more than twenty minutes. By the time we'd finished swapping stories and enthusing, it was raining and we were both completely soaked. I looked at Rachel and said, 'That's the first time we've talked about something that's not related to divorce.'

Treats completed this autumn	Treats in progress
Riding lessons	Compost
Chatsworth	Life on Earth
River Café recipes	North Downs Way
	Jane Austen

WINTER 2012

THIRTY-SIX

MAGIC

It's good to stay busy so I'm keeping up my riding and singing, and I select something new from my list. This time it's a 'Meet the Magic Circle' event in London. I heard about these a few years ago and have wanted to go ever since. I book tickets to go with Molly and Emma.

Magic has always fascinated me. When I was a child there was a big oak wardrobe in my bedroom. It had belonged to my maternal grandfather and was a rather imposing piece of furniture. There was a full-length cupboard on the left hand side and on the right there were drawers with double doors above. These were divided into square wooden panels and I used to spend hours tapping carefully at the edges. I longed to find just the right point to press. I imagined one of the panels springing open and admitting me to a network of secret passages and a Narnia-like world sprinkled with snow.

LITTLE BLACK DRESSES

I'm at work when I get an unexpected phone call from school. Molly has had an accident. She was whirling round, holding hands with friends, when she decided for some inexplicable reason to let go. She went flying across the room and banged her head on the floor. The school receptionist says there's nothing to worry about but as she passed out briefly I should take her home and keep an eye on her. When I arrive to collect her, she's sitting in a wheelchair, quite chatty but looking a bit dazed.

At first it's not clear whether she'll be fit enough to go to the Magic Circle tonight but after several hours of regular observations, I'm confident that she's fine. Her only regret is that she wasn't able to see what happened.

'Amy says I flew,' she reports proudly.

As usual, planning what to wear is a big part of any outing for Molly. 'We could wear our black dresses,' she suggests. I've had my one and only little black dress for about twelve years and am very fond of it. I used to think that I always had fun when I wore it, but in recent years, I'm not sure I can say that. It's time to inject a bit of happiness back into this favourite dress. Molly got her first LBD this autumn and wore it for her murder mystery birthday party. It's waif-like and simple, and she looks lovely in it. My initial reaction is to say that we'll be overdressed for this evening's event, but then I think better of it. In my single state, I'm unlikely to go to many smart occasions this year. Tonight, we'll dress up—never mind if everyone else is in jeans.

In the car on the way to the station, Molly reflects, 'I'm sure the world would be a happier place if people wore their little black dresses more often.' I have to agree with her, although I do remember Will asking curiously about the mysteries of female clothing. 'Why doesn't anyone talk about little green dresses or little yellow dresses? And there's no male equivalent. No-one talks about little black trousers.'

TREAT #29

The Magic Circle's home is in a cobbled street just behind Euston station, and we're delighted to be welcomed at the door by several gentlemen in evening dress. It seems safe to assume that they're magicians. Emma has come straight from work and we meet her there. She recently ordered a carpet for her flat and had it sent to her office. It arrived today and so she has brought it with her. She hands it in for safekeeping at the cloakroom.

The attendant looks at the large plastic-wrapped cylinder and asks, 'What is it?'

'It's a carpet,' says Emma, nonchalantly.

We're directed upstairs and handed a drink. Then we sit in small groups whilst magicians circulate amongst us, doing short performances. I'm in the second row and there's a very tall woman blocking my view. I feel irrationally furious with her. Fortunately, the first magician calls her out to help him. But as soon as I can see her face, which is sweet and friendly, I feel horrid for having directed so much venom towards the back of her head.

She's a passive assistant in a number of card tricks; spades, hearts, clubs and diamonds appear and disappear all over the place. Then the magician places a pack of cards between his assistant's hands and asks if she would be surprised to find a block of glass there instead. She separates her hands and that's exactly what has happened.

The next part of the evening takes place in an intimate little theatre. A senior member of The Magic Circle tells us about the history of magic, going right back to Ancient Egypt where there were accounts of magicians severing the heads of geese and ducks. After they had waddled around for a while their heads were put back on.

We learn, too, that The Magic Circle started in 1905 after a small group of magicians met in a restaurant. They were keen to start a club where they could share their ideas and one of the founders was a young man named Martin Chapender. When he died suddenly from meningitis at the age of 25, his peers suggested that the new magic society should be named after him. The objectives of The Martin Chapender Society may have been a bit opaque, however, so someone came up with the idea of calling it The Magic Circle which honoured him by having the same initials.

After this entertaining session there's a break for refreshments. Emma tells me that I'm a bit garlicky so when I go to the bar and ask for a coke, I keep my mouth closed. The assistant has to ask me to repeat my order. She probably thinks that I've come to the wrong group tonight. I should be at the

Ventriloquists' Society gathering.

During the break we all sit around large tables and help ourselves to tea, coffee and sandwiches. Magicians mingle amongst us doing close-up magic; it's charmingly old-fashioned. Then for the final stage of the evening we troop back into the theatre for a live magic show. The compère appears every now and again doing tricks with lengths of rope as he introduces the magicians. They all have distinctive styles and are excellent. The tall, smiling lady gets called out again for some audience participation, as does a giggly, elderly lady. We don't get chosen but one man is so popular that when the third magician points to him and asks what his name is, I'm tempted to shout out, 'Dave!'

As we make our way out of the building there's an opportunity to have a brief look at the museum. We chat to the curator and ask him to tell us about his favourite object. He shows us a nineteenth-century clock which keeps perfect time but appears to have no moving parts.

'How does it work?' asks Emma.

'Very well,' says the curator, inscrutably.

The motto of The Magic Circle is 'Indocilis Privata Loqui', which means 'Not apt to disclose secrets'. Any member of The Magic Circle who does this is expelled.

I don't want to return to the real world, but at last we have to leave and Emma goes to collect her carpet. As we walk round the corner onto the main road we see a parked coach with lots of elderly people in it. It's a reasonable assumption that they've been to the same place as us since there's a man standing at the front, doing unusual things with lengths of rope. We stand and stare rather rudely. Then we realise that the people on the coach are staring back at us; so we all wave at one another. The magician looks peeved that his audience seem to find us more interesting than his tricks.

Emma travels back on the Tube with us to London Bridge. There, Molly and I say goodbye to her and she sets off happily with her magic carpet under her arm.

I'm annoyed with myself. I applied for a promotion that's well within my capability; then I messed up the interview and an external candidate got the job. I'm probably not as ready for this big step as I thought I was but it would have helped me to be more financially independent.

It's a great strength, however, to have positive people around, and those who are going through their own trials have particularly insightful advice. Rachel and I swap texts regularly. Hers are supportive and wise. One I find particularly useful is 'Fear is that the worst thing will happen, faith is that the best thing will'. I can relate to that. Fear days are dark and terrible. I imagine that I will lose the house in the divorce and end up living rough, with no friends. My children will have disowned me because I smell of meths. On faith days I begin to believe that I can do anything.

Despite her usual clarity of expression, Rachel's texts are occasionally perplexing. I'm aware that the twelfth of December 2012 is a special date. It's been in the news recently as it's the last repetitive date in this century. This is seen as lucky by many, and a pondering good day on which to marry. Others are gloomy, and because it's the final date in the Mayan calendar they expect it to herald the end of the world. On the morning of the much anticipated 12/12/12, Rachel texts, reminding me to wear my 'suspicious underwear'. I think hard:

'Is she suggesting that I try to attract a new man today?'

'Am I ready for this?'

'Do I have any suspicious underwear?'

'Even if I come across any likely males, how will I alert them to my suspicious knickers?'

After careful consideration I conclude that her spell checker is having a joke on this auspicious day.

Shaun is still trying to 'move on' as fast as he possibly can, and puts in a proposal for the divorce settlement. He would like me to look at this before Christmas when he'll be off to America to see his girlfriend. But I need to be in a good frame of mind for the holidays, as the children have been through a lot. A passably calm mother and a welcoming home is the least I can offer them. I tell Melanie that I'll look at the proposal in the New Year.

THIRTY-SEVEN

KITTENS

The holidays are fast approaching and the children are due home. We're all a bit apprehensive about this first Christmas without Shaun. We decide it would be good to keep to our traditional ways of doing things, but to add a few fresh ideas too, to mark the start of a new future.

I'm not at all organised this year, but somehow things get done in time and we even manage to host a Christmas Eve lunch party for my sister and other close relations. With them, we are twelve. In the evening, the five of us go into town for a drink at a seventeenth-century coaching inn. The walk there and back is atmospheric and the roads are quiet; there's that sense of the world slowing down and holding its breath, that you only get late on Christmas Eve, or when it snows.

Apart from being together, one of the best things about this Christmas is that we've recently got kittens; two beautiful Bengals called Emily and Lola. They adore one another, and everyone else too. Our older cat, Mimi, is not impressed, however, and swears at them. We have to give her space and plenty of time to get used to them. She retains her place on my bed and they sleep snuggled up together in another room, twitching as they dream. They take regular naps, but when they're awake they rush around bursting with curiosity and are so affectionate that it's impossible to feel miserable. I spend a lot of time at my computer, lost in thought, and keep discovering that whilst I've been distracted, two warm little bundles have curled up on my lap and are fast asleep with their paws tucked neatly underneath them. Getting them has been miraculously therapeutic. The first morning after they arrived, I woke up and instead of immediately thinking of 'the issue', my heart leapt and I thought of kittens instead.

RESOLUTIONS

It feels good to leave 2012 behind and to enter 2013 with hope. I'm not sure quite what it is I'm hoping *for*, but I think stillness, strength and fun are all somewhere in the mix. On New Year's Eve I reflect back over the past twelve months: 'What an awful year.' Then I wonder whether I'm thinking this because it's what I *expect* to feel. A year in which my marriage ended was never going to be a great one. With the help of some 180° thinking, though, I remember how much kindness I've been shown and how I've begun to explore what an independent life might have to offer. It's not what I would have chosen but it *has* been a remarkable year.

Feeling out of control has been my biggest problem recently and I need to start reining my life in a bit. It's been difficult to get organised, partly because everything has been different from when I was with Shaun, and partly because I've felt so emotionally exhausted.

The first resolution I come up with is for Molly and me to do a bit of fun shopping together, once a month. A new pair of earrings, some knickers, and a magazine we haven't tried before, won't break the bank, but will cheer us up. I balance this frivolous resolution with a purely functional one. Having my groceries delivered will save me several hours each week. At least it *will* so long as I bear in mind that it's all too easy to make mistakes when ordering. I once nearly placed an order for 234 bags of salad, and recently a friend was astonished to unpack her Christmas Eve delivery and find one Brussels sprout placed carefully in a plastic bag.

A third resolution is about relationships. Internet dating sounds terrifying and I rarely meet men who aren't married to one of my friends. Relationships make me wary and suspicious and I resolve not to get into one unless it makes me really happy.

While I'm at it with resolutions I decide that this is a good opportunity to get to grips with technology. I used to look to

Shaun for help with this, but now I need to know how to deal with things myself. I want to be independent, and confident that I can cope.

There's a link here with one of my treats: I want to '*Learn what to do with digital photographs*'. Although I did a photography course twelve years ago, I spent all my time messing around with chemicals in a dark room, and I've not yet managed to make the leap to digital photography. On the rare occasions that I've taken photos using Shaun's camera, I've had no idea what to do next. He would always deal with the cables and connectors and print off the photographs. At the time I put this treat on my list it was just from a general wish not to be clueless, but now there's a more compelling need: I want to have photos of my family around the house.

This is also a good opportunity to explore a few other technological mysteries. I come up with a list of equipment which confounds me and resolve to study the relevant manuals. There's the oven, the kitchen radio, my iPod, and most baffling of all, the dishwasher. Why does it display a different number of minutes every time I switch it on?

SOLVING MYSTERIES

I want to be like my friend Tilly. 'I'm so glad I can take a dishwasher apart,' she said the other Sunday over a delicious lunch at her house, 'and the tumble-drier—I did have seven screws left over, though—but it seems to work OK.' I happened to know, too, that just before I arrived she'd been grouting the shower.

I decide to start with the oven. It has lots of mystifying symbols and buttons that I've never got round to understanding. Half an hour of reading the manual and pushing various dials and knobs, though, and I'm a whole lot wiser. I now know that pressing that funny little button with 'i' on it, reveals what temperature the oven has reached in its heating-up process. It's not life-changing, but it *is* satisfying. Molly likes baking and so it's also pleasing to find that the oven has a special setting for dough-proving. The manual is easy to understand, but at times it does state the obvious. In the FAQ section I read, 'What should I do if the meat starts to burn during cooking?' The answer is wise: 'Reduce the temperature.'

I'm annoyingly smug that the 'Oven Project' went well, so move straight on to my 'Kitchen Radio and CD project'. As with the oven, I know how to switch it on and off, but have a hunch there's a lot more I could be getting from it. One of the problems is that the controls are so small that I can't see them. I grab my glasses and settle down to concentrate. The manual is clear for the most part and before long I'm dabbling with pre-set radio stations and discovering how many there are to choose from. I'm a bit fed-up with waking to the miseries of the world in the Today programme; it would make a wonderful change to start the day with some jazz. I decide to move the radio to my bedside table and to throw out the current clock radio which is not only chipped and tatty, but is also a reminder of my old life. 'Oh joy, tonight I can listen to whatever I want in bed. I can have it as loud or as quiet as I please, without having to worry about what someone else wants.' I hit a problem, though, when I try to set the alarm. But there's no need to struggle on my own as the manual has a technical helpline number at the bottom of each page. I ring and it's answered immediately by a calm woman who knows exactly what to do. Stoically, she takes me through the process of pressing a particular combination of buttons for just the right length of time and then letting go. She also tactfully introduces me to the concept of (learning point here), being patient and not just pressing random buttons.

Next on the list is my sat nav. I've had it for several years and know that I'm supposed to connect it to the computer every now and again so it can update itself with new roads and speed cameras. This proves to be very straightforward. More smugness.

As I spend a lot of time driving I'd love to know how to use my iPod in the car, and how to download podcasts from Radio 4. I rarely get the chance to listen to The Archers on a Sunday now, and am also keen to explore the huge Desert Island Discs archive. I discover that Henry has left a cassette contraption in the car that will let me connect my iPod and play it through the tape player. That bit's easy. The podcast downloading is surprisingly easy too. Things are going well.

I update my iPod music collection and download 'Ain't No Mountain High Enough'. It gets completely stuck in my head and I sing it down the phone to Henry who winces, audibly. He says he wishes there was a mountain high enough where he couldn't hear my singing.

As I'm on a technological roll, I decide to take up a special offer from Virgin which will give me a new phone to replace my seven-year old model. However, when it arrives it takes me two weeks to pluck up courage to open the box. In the past, Shaun would have set it up for me. There's no excuse now, though, and I'll have to do it myself; another manual to grapple with.

I manage to get the new phone sorted out adequately, and then Emma helps me with the fine tuning. The speaking text feature is particularly exciting as it means I don't need to fumble with the keys and rely on having my glasses with me. I experiment by sending late night texts to all the children. They are much more accurate than my predictive text. However, the phone clearly disapproves of swearing as when I try to text a friend whose husband ignored her on her birthday, it sends the polite, but incomprehensible message, 'Bar starred.'

TREAT #30

The digital camera was Shaun's, so I no longer have one; but fortunately my shiny new phone provides me with the solution to my photographic dilemma. I discover how easy it is to take photos with it and to send them to my computer. Rather than attempting to print them myself, though, I decide it's much easier to put them on a memory stick and get this done professionally. Recently, I gave myself a budget of ten pounds and bought a number of photo frames in local charity shops. I'm looking forward to filling them with photos I've taken and had printed.

I don't know about all this technology, but my brain certainly seems to be wired badly at present: it's got a bug. Repetitive thoughts go round and round my head in a loop. The first thing I think of in the morning is the breakdown of my marriage, and it's the last thing I think of at night. It's there in the background when I'm driving and in just about everything I do. I really want to conquer these thoughts so I come up with a new technique for getting rid of them. I tell myself again and again that it's a tedious subject and whenever thoughts about Shaun waft across my mind, I make myself yawn. It takes quite a lot of vigilance to stop the thoughts creeping in, and I have to warn friends that I might suddenly say, 'Boring boring boring,' quite violently in the middle of a conversation.

I'm not sure how effective this will be in the long run, but one thing which has really helped my sanity is to limit contact from my solicitor. In recent months I've begun to dread getting home from work in case there's an email from her with some new Shaun-related bombshell. I ask Melanie if she would be willing to only make contact with me on Tuesdays, then at least I can feel safe on every other day of the week. She agrees to do this unless there's something that needs a pressing answer, when she will text in advance to warn me. This makes a huge difference to my anxiety level.

THIRTY-EIGHT

The Mysterious Affair of the Dishwasher

The dishwasher is next. And after spending just a few minutes with the manual I solve the mystery of why the display always shows a different number of minutes: there are umpteen programmes available, each with several options. To my delight I discover that it offers a short economy programme that at half an hour is considerably quicker than the one I've so often ended up with over the past two years; that cycle lasts 143 minutes. I use the economy programme and after only thirty minutes the dishes are all spotlessly clean.

It's time to progress to the trickiest task on my list: the TV. Several months before Shaun left, he bought me a very sophisticated model. I know that it can do Skype and connect to the internet, but have never worked out how to do it. I set aside a whole Monday evening to sit down with the manual and start out full of enthusiasm; but after going through all sorts of strange instructions and prohibitions to do with 'illegal actions', 'widgets' and 'HDMI CEC', I feel exhausted and remember that it's a TV. Why would I want it to do Skype or connect to the internet? I'm sure it's very big and very bright but I've got a PC that will do the job adequately. What I want the TV to do, is to *be a TV*, just like when I was young. I put the manual away with relief and get on with the rest of my life.

I feel a lot more in control now that I've mastered some of the features of my equipment. But it's not long before there's a new independence challenge. We have a heavy fall of snow and after a quiet weekend at home I need to get to work. The wheels of the car go round and round on our hill and I make no progress whatsoever; there's no option but to start digging myself out. I put on my wellies and grab a shovel. After about fifteen minutes a man comes past on the way to school with his young son. He says that if I'm still here when he returns in twenty minutes that he'll help me. I thank him and ask whether my car is front-wheel drive or rear-wheel. He tells me that it's front-wheel drive. This helps as I now know to concentrate my efforts on clearing the snow and ice under the front wheels. I make very slow progress, but after a while I really get into it, and thoroughly enjoy getting rid of some divorce venom by flinging snow onto the pavement. By the time the helpful man comes back, I'm so proud of my progress that I refuse his offer of assistance. After about an hour of digging I'm on my way; late for work, but pleased to have limped over another hurdle.

I've learned quite a lot about technology in the last few weeks. I now know what the 'i' button does, I can wake up to jazz in the morning, I've solved the dishwasher mystery, and I'm well on the way to having a new collection of photographs. I also have a contentedly undemanding relationship with my television.

In the death throes of our marriage, Shaun said bitterly to a friend that, 'Lynn wants the old Shaun back and the old Shaun's not coming back.' At the time I was bruised and confused, but now I think it's just as well. If the old Shaun were to come back he might not recognise me.

MANSFIELD PARK 3

With my new technological confidence I decide to try Mansfield Park again, but this time by downloading an unabridged audio version onto my iPod.

TREAT #10 (CONTINUED)

I start out enthusiastically, sure that this new medium will help me make progress. I play it in the car whilst thinking about other things. I settle down at the kitchen table to listen whilst doing some knitting and thinking about other things. And I sit in bed to listen and almost immediately fall asleep.

I've no quibbles with the production. Juliet Stevenson reads it beautifully but I simply can't concentrate and keep forgetting who all the characters are, who they're in love with, and who the focus of their passion is in love with (they rarely coincide). I get as far as the point at which the young people are due to stage a play and then I can't sustain my interest any longer.

Not being able to get any pleasure from literature is a real loss. It's been indispensable to me since I was first able to read, 'Look, John, look. Run, Janet, run', aged five. Before the separation I'd never go anywhere without having a book in my handbag just in case I had a few spare minutes. And I was obsessed with reading book reviews and hanging around bookshops. Now there's an empty void where there used to be excitement.

I worry that maybe I can't appreciate literature because I've stopped caring about other people and have become completely self-absorbed. A bit of this was inevitable at first, but I don't want to find I've turned into the kind of person who only thinks about their own needs and only stays with people so long as they are useful to them.

On that subject, I had a dramatic realisation, the other day. I suddenly replayed the moment at which my marriage ended and remembered how I'd said, 'I don't make you happy, do I?' It hadn't occurred to me before, to wonder where *my* wishes were in all of this. Maybe he didn't make me happy, either, towards the end, but somehow this seemed irrelevant. Our family dynamics were focused entirely on Shaun's health and happiness.

HECTOR HUGH MUNRO

I'm still rattled about my inability to finish Mansfield Park, or any other fiction, and rack my brains to think of something that might win me over. This complete loss of enjoyment in reading is comparable to my loss of interest in cooking—it's like a vital part of me has fallen into a deep sleep and I can't wake it up.

Recently I dipped in and out of a social history of the post-war period and that was fine because I could skip chapters and it didn't really matter that I didn't finish it. But there seems no point in starting a novel because I know I'll lose the essential thread that ties it all together. Maybe I could ease myself back into reading by tackling some short stories, and as it happens there's something on my list that might fit the bill.

For a long time I've been curious about the Edwardian short story writer, Hector Hugh Munro, whose pseudonym conjures up such an air of mystery. He's the kind of writer that people in the know, nod and smile about. When I wrote my list I wanted to find out why, so I included 'Read some of Saki's stories'.

TREAT #31

I order 'The Collected Short Stories of Saki' and start to read the first few at bedtime. Most are only two or three pages in length, and there are dozens of them. They're acerbic little portraits of Edwardian society, more often than not with a malicious twist at the end. I try my best to enjoy them, but am disappointed to find that yet again I'm struggling. I can't say I actively dislike these stories; I just don't care about them.

Night after night, I pick up the book without enthusiasm, feeling that I have to get through it. Then I remember that one of my fundamental rules is that treats are different from goals: they're there to be enjoyed. I've done what I set out to do, which was to read some of Saki's stories and I've gained a general idea of what his writing is like. I put the book to one side with relief.

A couple of weeks pass, but I still have a niggling curiosity about Hector Hugh Munro and one afternoon find myself browsing the internet to read about his life. I discover that he was born in 1870 in Burma, where his father was in the military police. He was very young when he came to England, but when he was two his mother was chased by a cow. This resulted in a miscarriage, and shortly afterwards she died. For the rest of his childhood he was raised in North Devon by his two maternal aunts and grandmother. By all accounts it was a strict household without much fun. Suddenly this begins to make sense and I understand why aunts crop up so often in his stories and why they are usually such unsympathetic characters.

I also do some reading about his literary influences, and those whom he in turn influenced. There are similarities with Oscar Wilde and PG Wodehouse; perhaps he is an acquired taste. I decide to give him another chance and one wintry Saturday afternoon, I dip into a couple of the stories that are recommended in online reviews. This helps as there are a great many to choose from; previously I just started at the beginning and read them in order. The first one I try is 'The Open Window'. This is a study in how to get rid of unwelcome visitors and I'm surprised to find myself really enjoying it. It reminds me of Richmal Crompton's 'Just William' stories.

I read a few more, picking out those that have been suggested as the best. My favourite is 'The Phantom Luncheon' which recounts how Lady Drakmanton deals with the free-loading Misses Smithley-Dubb. 'The Philanthropist and the Happy Cat' is satisfying in its depiction of middle-class self-satisfaction, and there's real food for thought in 'The Reticence of Lady Anne'. An elderly husband potters about and gets increasingly annoyed because his wife of many years is not responding. He fails to notice that the reason she's not answering is that she is dead.

Many of the stories are about dark goings-on in the English countryside and there is nothing cosy or safe about them. Ordinary creatures like cats, otters and polecats become sinister under the influence of his pen. This all becomes rather fascinating now I know that his mother's death was caused by a cow.

The final thing is to find out why he chose the pen-name, Saki. I'm surprised to discover that no-one knows for certain, but the most likely explanation is that it comes from the 'Rubáiyát of Omar Khayyam'. This eleventh-century Persian poetry caused a stir in the nineteenth century when Edward Fitzgerald translated it into English. One of the characters is a cupbearer called Saki. Cupbearers were people of high rank whose job was to pour the king's wine and taste it to make sure it wasn't poisoned.

Unfortunately, I don't think that reading these stories has cured my disengagement from literature but I'm still glad to have had this treat. I had to work a bit at enjoying it, but knowing something about the writer's life nudged me into finding his work more rewarding. Also, I can see that there's a time and a place for everything. These stories are not bedtime reading. They're the kind to keep out on a table and to dip into occasionally when I'm in the mood for a brief blast of caustic wit.

I've made some progress in understanding an Edwardian writer who died many years ago in the First World War, but I'm struggling to fathom out the man who is still, at least for the time being, my husband. Perhaps there are things that I just can't admit to myself. It helps to talk to Isla and we have regular chats on the phone, as we pick over the debris of recent years. She is wonderfully insightful and generous-spirited and I hate to hear how much she has been hurt.

One evening I'm sitting on the stairs with the phone to my ear, when she asks if I'd be interested in meeting a friend of hers. He's called Mike and she thinks we might get on. I'm a bit surprised as it's the first time in over thirty years that I've come anywhere near having a date with a man who's not my husband. My initial reaction is cautious interest. I trust her judgement and it could be fun.

'OK,' I say, and agree to send a photo.

Then a few days later I get cold feet and tell her I'm not ready to meet anyone.

THIRTY-NINE

MORE GRAPPLING WITH FISH

Over the past few months the shock has worn off and I've begun to get a clearer perspective on my marital breakdown. Up to now, I've not said anything to Shaun in response to what has happened but I'm starting to feel that it's time to speak. I find the idea of this difficult—like he has a right to say things, but I don't.

I'm shocked that I've let myself drift into such an unhealthy pattern. I think that it first took root several years ago, when Shaun's illness made it difficult to be emotionally robust with him. Then it became ever more difficult in the months after our split: I was weakened by a gaping wound which hurt with every move. I couldn't challenge him or criticise because I was afraid of the pain he could inflict. Now the wound has formed a fragile scab and although it sometimes itches and I pick at it until it bleeds, I'm feeling stronger overall.

I write a carefully worded email and ask Melanie to send it to Shaun. I also ask her to read it through first and to let me know if there's anything controversial or foolhardy in it. Her opinion is that it's heartfelt but entirely calm and reasonable.

Very soon after sending it, I get a reply. Shaun says to Melanie that he read the first line and could see that it was a 'rant' so he didn't read the rest. Intriguingly, he then goes on to say that he 'refutes everything I say.' This response helps to confirm what has been clear to me for a while: he's not interested in hearing me.

Shockingly, given our initial intentions, it has also become increasingly clear that we're not going to make any headway in negotiating our divorce through solicitors' letters. We're going to have to go to court and let a judge decide our financial arrangements. My sister generously lent me the money to pay my solicitor's fees, and now offers to add to this so that I can fight my corner in court. We agree that I will pay her back if, and when, I sell the house and downsize.

I know that I am very lucky.

LIME MARMALADE

I had a thought the other day that was enormously helpful. It was a 'lime marmalade moment'.

This thought took me right back to when I was about eight and had some toast and lime marmalade. It was the one and only time in my entire life that I have ever eaten lime marmalade and later that night I was violently ill. I don't think the marmalade was to blame for this but ever since then even the sight of the vile, pale-green, translucent stuff has induced a stomach-sinking nausea.

For the past eight months I've struggled to understand why Shaun wanted to end our marriage and the good things that we'd built together. I've come up with all kinds of theories to try and explain something that I don't think even he understands. One strong contender is that he developed an aversion to me. I think that I am somehow linked in his brain to all the bad things that happened; a bit like me and the marmalade.

It reassures me to think that the lime marmalade just happened to be there. It didn't really do anything terrible, so maybe I didn't either.

BIRTHDAY

While Christmas and New Year still feel very recent, we're into February and there's another hurdle to cross in this first year of uncharted loneness: my birthday.

I try hard to remember how we marked it last year but my memory is curiously empty. Elusive images of Shaun fade in and out like shadows. I can't remember what we did or where we went, although I do know that he gave me the impossibly complicated television. He'd undoubtedly given up on our marriage by then and was trying to find a way out. This has become clear with hindsight, but was impossible to face at the time.

I want to mark the passing of another year by celebrating. Also, as the boys are both away and Emma will be in San Francisco on a work trip, Molly is the only one of the children who'll be here for the actual day. I don't want her to feel responsible for making me happy, so as my birthday falls on a Sunday I decide to have a lunch party. I invite cousins Rita, Eric, Maggie and Philip, as well as my nephew Dan, his wife Wendy, and their children. They have all in their own ways been significant in helping me stumble my way through the past nine months. The adults have offered kindness, wisdom and patience; the children have helped by just being themselves.

The day begins with breakfast in bed provided by Molly, whilst we chat to Henry via Skype. He sits on the end of the bed enclosed within a little screen, and makes encouraging comments while I open my presents and eat my porridge. Later, I spend an enjoyable morning listening to The Archers, cooking roast chicken, and making the table look festive.

Lunch is lively with the focus of chat on the present and the future rather than the past, and Rita produces one of her expertly decorated cakes for pudding. I manage to blow out all the candles in one puff. I hope that's a good omen for the coming year.

It's very special to have a family gathering like this. After growing up in such isolation, I appreciate my family and extended family beyond measure. My sister would have enjoyed being here too, but she's away.

Afterwards, when we're having coffee, Wendy hands me an envelope. Inside are two tickets for next Sunday's matinee performance of Cirque du Soleil. I think that Emma did some spying on behalf of her cousin, as she asked to look at my treats list a few weeks ago. As with Derren Brown, I'm not at all sure whether I'll like this kind of extravagant production, but for years I've seen adverts for the shows and put it on my list so I can find out what the fuss is all about. Like many of my treats this is about coming out of the fog and feeling connected with life.

My birthday passes cheerfully. It's sobering but comforting to realise that it's been a definite improvement on last year. I end it by sitting at my computer and replying to an email that arrived this morning. I respond to questions about what kind of books I enjoy, what music I listen to, and what I like doing in my spare time. I'm careful to keep off the subject of treats in case I seem insufferably self-indulgent but I do enthuse about noisy jazz. I also avoid the subject of my distressing relationship with Mansfield Park, but instead mention books I've loved in the past: The Great Gatsby; Remains of the Day; Far from the Madding Crowd, and 101 Dalmatians.

My correspondent seems interesting and I'm learning a bit about him. What I already know is that:

- He's an academic

- He grew up in South Africa

- He's four years older than me

- He enjoys sailing, swimming, reading, travel, and a wide range of music, particularly jazz

- He has more patience with reflective, twiddly jazz than I do

This interchange is all thanks to Isla, who completely ignored me when I got cold feet and said I wasn't ready to think about dating. She went ahead and gave my email details to her friend Mike, and vice versa. We got off to a cautious start but over the past ten days or so, we've had a couple of friendly exchanges.

Negotiation

There's a new problem to solve, though I have to admit it's a lot less challenging than some I've had to deal with recently. Emma gets back from her trip this week and as I only have two tickets, I have to decide which of my girls to take to Cirque du Soleil. I don't want either of them to feel left out and am not sure how I'm going to choose.

I can truthfully say that I love my children all the same, which seems a miracle as they're such different characters. I heard the other day that 'very few parents love one child more than the other, but at different times in raising children, favouritism is unavoidable'. Mine have all tried my patience at times, and have each had the honour of being the most and least favoured child an equal number of times. Or so it seems to me. I hope they remember it the same way.

I decide to use the strategy I resorted to so much when they were all young and squabbled endlessly: 'Sort it out yourselves.' Realising I could say this and walk away was a great discovery. And when there was no parental audience to annoy, they always *did* sort it out.

This time is no exception. I overhear them trying to work it out.

'You go with Mum,' says one.

'No, you go,' says the other.

For a moment I think that neither of them wants to come with me, but then realise that the miracle of maturation has worked its transformational magic. Instead of childish bickering, they're being thoughtful towards one another. After some discussion, the girls decide that Molly will come with me, but that we'll all have lunch together beforehand at one of our favourite places: the gloriously ornate café at the V&A Museum.

FORTY

UNBENDING

Today is Sunday and we're going to the circus. I wake up to feel my hair being pulled and my right ear nibbled. It takes a while to come round and realise what's happening. Sadly, there is no passionate lover next to me—it's the kittens, Lola and Emily treating my head like a playground.

I've done some preparation for today's performance and have found out that Cirque du Soleil is based in Quebec and was founded in 1984. Its defining characteristics are 'dance, daring, dexterity, grace, imaginary worlds, acrobatic performance, acting, and art forms from around the world'. The company has a social conscience and works with troubled young people in many countries. And another thing that I spot on the website is the recent launch of a 'career transition programme' for employees who have reached the end of their performing life.

'What does a retired clown or trapeze artist go on to do?' I wonder.

One option that was open to previous generations was to set up home in Gibsonton, Florida which for many years was a favourite out-of-season resting place for American circus and fairground workers. It started in the 1930s when Al Tomaini and his wife went to visit and fell in love with the area because of its excellent fishing. They made an unusual pair as he was 8ft 4in, and she was only 2ft 6in but they started a trend in the town and gradually it adapted to a wave of new residents. Nowadays, the post office has a special counter for little people, and the byelaws allow residents to keep Ferris wheels on their front lawns and elephants in their back yards. Some of the characters who have lived in Gibsonton include the Anatomical Wonder, Siamese twin sisters who ran a fruit stall, Lobster Boy, and Percilla the Monkey Girl.

Molly and I meet Emma for lunch at the V&A. She tells us that her chest is hurting and then owns up that this is probably because she's joined an aerial pilates class. This involves doing pilates whilst climbing up silk ropes.

TREAT #32

A bit later Molly and I settle in our seats at the Albert Hall and the show begins, with lights, dancers, dazzling costumes and loud music. There's a great deal of what I can only call 'Pzazz'. This particular production is called Kooza and supposedly there's a story that ties all the different acts together. However, very soon I've completely lost the plot. It doesn't matter, though, as there are plenty of astonishing things to watch.

A dancer stands on a large ball. Then he places another one on his head and a second dancer wiggles about on top. It looks deceptively simple. Next, a performer rides a unicycle whilst a girl stands on his head. Then he stretches out his hand and she lies spreadeagled across it. He carries on riding. Then four men appear and launch into a sword fight on a tightrope. When that's done, one of them walks along with another on his shoulders, and stands nonchalantly on one leg half-way across. After that they trundle a couple of bicycles across the wire.

I particularly enjoy the group of three dancers whose costumes are so tight that they look like they're painted onto their skin. They move gracefully like cats and bend themselves into amazing shapes. I'm fascinated at the contortions that the human body can put itself through. It's not just the body, though: I remember how Shaun used to talk about life 'bending him out of shape.' He meant that he was forced to do things he didn't want to do in order to keep food on the table and the people in his life happy. I often wonder whether he's content now that he no longer has to do this.

I'm also learning how to unbend as I, too, did a lot of

contorting over the years. This period since our separation has been about discovering what makes me happy, and no longer having to do so many of the things I dislike. For one, I hate skiing: it's cold, wet and terrifying—you have to wear Michelin Man clothes—spend hours queuing—and you're surrounded by hearty people who are enjoying it much more than you are, which enrages me. Now I never again have to feel guilty that I don't like it, when Shaun does. Unbending helps in discovering who I am.

The show comes to an end and I clap enthusiastically. Molly tells me off. She says I'm on the off-beat and out of sync with everyone else. I've enjoyed the performance very much, but I still don't have a clue what the story was about. Later, I look to the website for some guidance. It tells me that 'Between strength and fragility, laughter and smiles, turmoil and harmony, Kooza explores themes of fear, identity, recognition and power.' Perhaps it was about marriage.

The Clock at Waterloo

Today I'm going up to London to meet Mike for the first time. During our email exchanges over the past couple of weeks, I've got to know a bit about him. But I'm cautious and wary of getting involved with someone who is going to add to my problems. I'm beginning to manage quite well on my own and don't need an emotional numbskull, an arrogant control freak or a sloppy kisser. I quiz Isla. I tell her that the key values for me are a sense of humour, generosity of spirit, curiosity about life, and an open mind.

'He has all of those in spades,' she says, 'and lovely eyes too.'

I'm reassured and so when he suggests we meet for lunch and go to an exhibition, I agree. London's the obvious place for this; he'll come up from Southampton and I'll travel in from Kent. We arrange to meet under the clock at Waterloo at 12.30.

On the train I suddenly remember that this is a popular rendezvous point and panic that there'll be hundreds of people all meeting there under the iconic four-faced clock: crowds of long-lost relatives; walking groups; international business travellers; illicit lovers; spies; friends having a day in London, drug dealers— He's given me his mobile number in case of problems, so I text him.

'How will I know you?' I say. 'I'll be wearing pink shoes.'

'Well I won't,' he replies. 'I'm tall and dressed in black.'

By the time the train arrives I'm very twitchy. It shouldn't really be such a big deal, but I'm just not used to this. I'm scared that I won't like him—scared that I will—scared that he won't like me—scared that he will. I get rid of some nervous energy by striding vigorously up the stairs and along the corridors that lead from Waterloo East. Then I go down the escalator onto the main platform at Waterloo, take a deep breath and make for the clock. I look for the crowds of people, but there underneath is just one man. He's tall and slim in black jeans with a black corduroy jacket. He's looking at the ground and paying careful attention to the feet of any woman who comes near.

Suddenly he spots my shoes and looks up. His expression is tentative. He's clearly wondering whether I'm the right 'pink shoes woman'. I smile briefly to acknowledge him and then feel awkward and very shy.

'This is my first date in over thirty years,' I say, and immediately realise this is not a cool way to start. I'd wanted to give the impression of being a woman of the world, confident and unfazed. I've blown it. He nods and smiles cautiously.

We've got a booking for lunch in an Italian restaurant in the Strand so as we've already established that I'm the one who knows London best, I start to lead us towards Waterloo Bridge. Then after several minutes of intense talking and walking I realise that we're lost. Somehow we've ended up in a back street on the Southbank amongst some dustbins. I explain that I have a very poor sense of direction and in just a few moments he has us back on track.

When we get to the restaurant I delve around in my bag and

pull out a book: 'Mrs Palfrey at the Claremont' by Elizabeth Taylor. It's one of my all-time favourites.

'I brought this for you,' I say.

He rummages around in his backpack and pulls out Kazuo Isiguro's 'Never Let Me Go'.

'And I thought you might like this,' he says.

After lunch we go to a Man Ray exhibition at the National Portrait Gallery. We wander round separately but every now and again he puts his hand gently on my shoulder and points out something that interests him. I like that he's not arrogant and pretending he knows more than he does. We each have a rather disjointed knowledge of the era and share our varied impressions and scraps of anecdotes. Towards the end he says, 'I realise that you probably need to get back home, but do you have time for a cup of tea first?' We chat nonstop until the café closes and throws us out. He tells me about his struggle to rebuild his life after being widowed three years ago. I tell him about my separation. Our experiences are very different, both of lost love but through different channels. He also tells me about his upbringing in apartheid South Africa and his hatred of racism. As we go out onto the pavement and I envisage setting off to Waterloo he says, 'I realise that you probably need to get back home, but do you have time to join me for dinner?'

Later, we walk across Waterloo Bridge to get our respective trains. The lights of the city cut their way through the dark, and dance in the black of the water underneath us. We both enthuse about London, and as I listen to his gentle South African inflections, I wonder what it would be like to kiss him.

TREATS COMPLETED THIS WINTER	TREATS IN PROGRESS
Magic Circle	Life on Earth
Digital photographs	North Downs Way
Saki	Jane Austen
Cirque du Soleil	

SPRING 2013

FORTY-ONE

COURT

Shaun and I took a step nearer to divorce this week when we had our first meeting in court. It was brief and its purpose was simply to agree which financial questions we are allowed to ask one another. This was the first time we had breathed the same air for over five months, but despite being in a small room with our solicitors and a judge, we didn't speak or even make eye contact. I'm not proud of behaving childishly but we see things so differently that there's nothing constructive left to say. Melanie assured me that she's seen this many times before.

A measure of the gulf that divides us is the fact that Shaun thought it necessary to bring up the knife incident in the papers that he submitted to the court. He said it was an 'attempt to emotionally blackmail' him into staying with me. The judge read this and then looked at us sternly over the top of her glasses. She told us to go home and try to negotiate our divorce, causing as little damage to our children as possible.

Overall, this court appearance was much less disturbing than I thought it might be. But there are still plenty of things that floor me. Anniversaries, for example, continue to be a problem. I've expected this, so have planned ahead where possible. For our wedding anniversary, Molly's birthday, Christmas, New Year, and my birthday, I made sure that the children and I had plenty of distractions lined up. I was surprised, though, when Henry's twentieth birthday took a swipe at me. I phoned him in the morning and then felt irrationally miserable all day. At first I couldn't work out what was wrong, and then I realised it was the contrast with twenty years ago that was so poignant.

Compost

Compost making was one of the first treats that I made a start on, but it's taken a long time to complete. I was married when I started and am nearly divorced before I have anything to show for it.

Treat #4 (Continued)

After the 'rodent setback' last year, the first bin filled up quickly and I was pleased when a friend offered me another identical bin that they had no use for. Now, I'm half-way through filling this second bin when I check progress with the first one. There are a few twigs and other bits and pieces that are indigestible to the worms, but other than this they've done a fantastic job. At last I have a large quantity of wonderful rich compost to spread over the garden.

When I started on my second bout of compost-making I had no idea that my marriage was about to end. In the time since we separated, natural processes have transformed the vegetation into something completely different. A miraculous process of nature has worked its magic on me, too. I try to find an analogy between the two processes but realise quickly that this is both trite and simplistic. Vegetable peelings transform into compost. It's as simple as that. People, on the other hand, keep transforming throughout their lives. Within the course of the last ten months I've gone through many stages. I've been unhappy, confused and married. And I've been shocked, sad, desperate, pessimistic, optimistic and separated. Now I'm nearly divorced.

One thing I do know, though, is that I can cope. I'm a lot less scared than I was.

DATES

I've now had several dates with Mike and am getting to like him very much. The second date was a couple of weeks after our meeting in London. We met in Guildford and walked five miles along the river to a romantic pub where we had lunch. Ten days later we were due to meet for a drink and dinner at a pub half-way between us, when it started to snow. I texted in the afternoon to say I may not be able to get there and he replied, 'This is very bad news.' Later the storm cleared and we managed to meet up. The next day my boss asked, 'What was the pub like?' I tried to give a sensible answer and then realised that I hadn't noticed.

DECLUTTERING

I've recently had a cathartic sort-out for the second time since we separated. The first was last June, when I felt compelled to sweep through the house after Shaun moved out; I delved deep into cupboards, leafed through dozens of files, and braved the most remote corners of the garage. With single-minded fervour I filled up a succession of carrier bags and passed them to him, via the children. They contained a miscellaneous collection of rowing cups discovered at the back of the larder, books I knew he especially liked, tedious but essential bits of official paperwork, and a shirt that had lain for days in the ironing basket; *that* went back unironed. I did a comprehensive job and eventually the flood of plastic bags ceased. There was nothing more to pass on; all tangible traces of him were gone and everything in the house belonged either to me or the children.

Then a few weeks ago I had a new urge to sort through all my worldly goods. This time it was about getting rid of things that represented my old life. There were earrings Shaun had given me, a suede jacket, and an evening dress; all perfectly nice but I'd feel uncomfortable wearing them now. The charity shop did well from my unsentimental decluttering.

There is one item, though, that has created a dilemma: I can't decide what to do with my wedding dress. For years it has stayed encased in its plastic cover. Although I haven't taken it out since our wedding night, I'd imagined it lying with happy memories entwined in its fibres. Now it's no longer a symbol of the promises we made to one another, but it's too important, to simply throw out. I work through the various options:

- I could keep it just as I have for the past twenty-nine years. But that doesn't feel right—in my new life I don't want to be weighed down by tainted love.

- Would a charity shop want it? I don't think so. When we rode our tandem between the church and the reception it got smeared with bicycle oil.

- A friend suggests I use it to clean the car. That's a tempting idea, but on balance, I decide I'd prefer a more positive solution. Destroying or discarding it would feel like I'm denying the importance of my marriage.

Memories have preoccupied me for some time now and I find them confusing and complicated. Recent difficult events should not invalidate what came before, but whilst I'm trying not to rewrite the past, I'm finding it hard. So many of the happy memories I thought I'd hold forever, have evaporated. Others remain but have now lost their meaning or gone sour. I thought I knew Shaun, but now I can't help questioning what he was really thinking and feeling. So, in one hand I have the memories that were happy at the time and are now tarnished. In the other are those that were difficult in reality but gain a sheen with hindsight. I think of my trip to New York with Henry and Molly last summer with great fondness despite knowing that I was still struggling with profound grief and spent some of the time crying and desperately searching for spiritual relief in a church near Times Square.

Another contradictory situation at the moment concerns the number twenty-nine. I've had an excellent relationship with it for much of my adult life. I got married on 29th August and became a mother when I was twenty-nine. Recently, though, its glint has been dulled by my marriage failing in its twenty-ninth year. Pinning such significant life events to a mere number may be unusual, but it helps me to work through the conundrum of how to deal with memories. Do I go through the rest of my life feeling negative about what was good, because some of it ultimately went bad? The truth is that my marriage was good, but it changed and our family has taken on a different form from the one I expected. The eventual failure of our marriage can be seen as a new opportunity. Each of these 'twenty-nine' milestones are life events that signify transformation from one state to another.

Somehow I'd like to find a way to keep the good associations my wedding dress has and not throw them out with the bad ones. Then one day I'm in the car in that strange semi-automatic state that accompanies long drives, when the solution hits me: patchwork.

What appeals to me about this craft is that no two creations are ever the same. Scraps of treasured baby clothes, flowery skirts, and little girls' party dresses can all be reassembled into something completely unique. One of my favourite places is the American Museum in Bath, where there's a room full of patchwork quilts that were made by early settlers. Life was very hard for them and they had to make good use of their limited resources. When their bedcovers became worn they were patched with scraps of old clothing. By the eighteenth and nineteenth centuries, however, patchwork was becoming an art form in its own right. Women would hold quilting bees where they gossiped and sewed. Nothing was wasted; the backing papers that kept the fabric pieces in shape were often made from old letters.

Visiting the American Museum got me interested in doing some patchwork myself. I don't have any sewing talent so when I made my list I knew that a quilt would be too ambitious, but that a cushion cover was probably achievable. I imagined myself at my own private sewing bee, stitching serenely whilst listening to Radio 4.

Unfortunately, I've downsized so many times in recent years that I don't have any surplus baby clothes, flowery skirts or party dresses. However, I do have a wedding dress that's going spare. When I initially thought about my cushion cover, tired white cotton adorned with bicycle grease was not my fabric of choice. However, I could transform it by cutting it up and dying it bright colours. I think I'm onto something promising but the idea needs time to mature.

A Stitch in Time Saves Twenty-Nine

It's Saturday, several weeks later and I've set aside the afternoon to get started on my patchwork. I spend the morning doing household chores and then just before lunch, the post arrives. My heart always sinks when I see my solicitor's address on the envelope. This time it's a letter from the legal assistant who has been helping Melanie. She starts by saying, 'I am pleased to tell you that your decree nisi has been granted.' This doesn't seem quite the right way to put it and I cry. It's a curious situation for which there's no obvious social convention; 'I regret to tell you' or 'I am sorry to tell you' wouldn't be right either. Sometimes the simplest words are the best ones: 'I am writing to tell you—'. Just tell it like it is.

We have to wait at least six weeks but can then apply for the decree absolute which is the final stage of the divorce. We won't do that, though, until the financial issues are resolved in court.

In the spirit of being positive I get on with the business of transforming my wedding dress. I get it out of the garage, take a deep breath, and unzip its plastic cover for the first time since my wedding night.

It has moved house many times, in a box along with other sentimental bits and pieces: there's the white lacy shawl I wrapped our babies in; the multicoloured playmat they all lay on; the blue spotty dress I wore when I first met Shaun, and the pale yellow quilt cover with clowns on, that I made for Will's cot.

I breathe in deeply and hold the moment. It smells of something I recognise from long ago. It's elusive but not unpleasant: previous houses, maybe.

There's a deep, gathered flounce along the bottom. This is ideal for patchwork as it's straight, so will make measuring and cutting much easier. As I snip and tug gently at the fine stitching that holds it together, it feels like a supreme act of destruction. This is the moment when I finally realise there's no going back. My marriage is well and truly over. At times over the past months it has felt like a dream and I've half expected Shaun to pop out from behind a door and tell me it was all a joke.

It takes several hours to complete this phase but when it's freed I have nine metres of heavily textured cotton fabric. I stick it in the washing machine, then while it dries in the garden, I set off to the craft shop to get some dye. I spend ages lining up packets and finally settle on yellow, red, orange, green, and violet.

The next day is Sunday and equipped with a large amount of salt, rubber gloves and a bucket, I get to work. I cut the fabric into six strips and one by one the dye transforms them. They hang on the washing line looking like miniature Indian saris. Later I cut them into squares and machine them together whilst listening to old editions of Woman's Hour. It's all going quite well and I even feel I've achieved my desired state of serenity. Then Molly appears. She purses her lips.

'It's very nice—but I'm not sure if the colours go together.' She picks it up and examines it closely. 'Perhaps you could give it to someone you don't like very much,' she suggests kindly.

I carry on regardless, but am not sure how to finish it off. Molly's right about the colours being a bit 'hot' together so I use some plain cream fabric for the backing. This calms everything down slightly. I sew steadily and listen to The Archers, determined to get it done. Then much to my surprise, after several hours, there in front of me is a brightly coloured cushion cover. No-one would ever guess it started life as a wedding dress. It's very flawed, though. Some of the seams are wobbly, the dying is streaky and the edge is a bit puckered. Transformation is a tricky process and it's not always possible to get things right the first time. This has not been my favourite treat, but I *have* got something to show for it. Perhaps one day I'll sign up for a patchwork workshop that will give me tips for a more professional finish. For now, though, this will do and I put it on the chair in my study. Molly comments that it looks better than she thought it would and I am pleased that I've resisted the urge to throw the wedding dress out with the car wash water.

FORTY-TWO

The Meaning of Treats

It's nearly two years since I wrote my list and I've now completed half of the treats. They started out as a simple way to reconnect with the world and to fill in some gaps. But they have become so much more. In the dazed early days after the separation they were something firm to hold onto whilst the rising waters eddied around me. I was traumatised, the children were in shock, and friends and family were all impacted by the events. The treats, though, stayed steady.

I mentioned early on that I wanted them to sit in the wings of my list like characters in a play. Then when the time was right, they would make their entrance. And that is just what happened. I got to know them and like the best of friends, they revealed hidden depths. The New York treat was a sassy friend who took me out on a painful anniversary and provided stimulating distraction. My eye make-up treat was an older female friend who gave me some confidence when I'd lost it all. Italian cookery cajoled me to eat, the photographs encouraged me to explore coping alone, and the patchwork was a step towards resolving difficult memories. Then there was the moment when the sheer physicality of being on a horse counterbalanced the unhappiness and I tipped into joy.

Through the treats I've also stumbled upon all kinds of pleasing treasures. I now know about jumpology, how silk is extracted from spiders, why Oliver Cromwell welcomed Jews to England, why beavers build dams, how to gamble, and how to identify the song of the chaffinch. I've also discovered the wit of Dorothy Parker, loud brassy jazz, River Café chocolate cake, and Sebastian Flyte. Rather unexpectedly, at the same time, I've learned how to get divorced.

303

At the beginning, the dips and dives were terrifying, but with time, they've become less frequent and I've got over them quicker. Counselling has helped me to reflect on what happened, and joining a divorce recovery group has made a huge difference. Rachel said that she didn't want to sit next to me at the first session as I looked like I was going to cry. She thought that would set her off. I did cry of course. Now we laugh a lot. The other day I asked what her ideal party outfit would be. Quick as a flash she replied, 'Biker jacket; tutu; very, very pointy shoes; suspicious underwear, and a carpet bag.' Every girl needs a friend like that.

New friends have opened up the doors to alternative lives I'd not considered before, whilst old friends have listened and offered constancy. And anti-depressants were invaluable during the worst bits. They helped to level out the emotional rollercoaster which was so exhausting and terrifying. I've just come off them, but am doing it very slowly under the guidance of my GP. So far, I've had no problems.

One of the best steps was getting our kittens. It's hard to be relentlessly miserable with a trusting, purring bundle on your lap. The only drawback is that they love pretty, sparkly things, and steal my earrings.

Forgiveness has been a testing but important conundrum. One of the divorce recovery sessions dealt with this topic, and for a long time I didn't get it at all. Why should I forgive someone who hurt me so much? Then quite a few months afterwards I began to understand. The act of forgiving is not so much for the other person's sake, but for yourself. It allows you to move on and leave the poison behind. It's not about saying you were to blame for everything if you don't think you were. Nor is it about wanting to rekindle some kind of relationship. Instead it allows you to say that you played a part in things going bad and to stop putting energy into being defensive. Hardly anyone could say that they never did anything wrong in a relationship. I eventually decided to send Shaun a message. I said I was sorry that I couldn't give him the things he wanted, and that I knew he'd been through very difficult life-changing events towards the end of our marriage. There was a long silence. Then after three weeks I got a furious reply. Rather than feeling upset as I once would have done, my main feeling was relief that I no longer have to try and understand his emotions.

Over the past year the repetitive thoughts have been exhausting. Now at last I spend less time trying to understand what happened. Much of the experience remains mystifying and I'm beginning to accept that this may always be the case. Not only were we not on the same page towards the end—we weren't even in the same library.

Throughout all of this, I've been aware that it's very easy to become wrapped up in my own misery and I've needed to be jerked out of this at times. My dear, loyal friend Nicky has recently been diagnosed with motor neurone disease. This explains her fall when we were working on my garden, and the peculiar dizzy feelings that she's been having for some time. Like her family and the many other friends who love and value her so much, I find it hard to take in. Then, too, there was a report I heard on the radio news early one morning, about ten little Afghan girls who were blown up on their way to collect water for their families. These awful things have helped to bring my troubles into perspective and to make me wonder what right I have to expect things to be fair. I may have been struggling, but at least I have the luxury of hoping for a better future.

Although I'm grateful to be happier, I'm frustrated to be feeling physically drained at the moment, and to have all kinds of annoying minor ailments. At first the emotional issues scream for attention, but eventually the body gets a look in too, and requires care. I fantasise about staying in an old-fashioned convalescent home in Worthing. My comfortable, rather faded room looks over the sea and kind staff bring me tempting little meals on a tray. I just sleep, read, stare at boats bobbing on the sea, and watch old episodes of undemanding television like Bewitched, Fawlty Towers, All Creatures Great and Small, and the Adventures of Twizzle.

In Thackeray's story, The Rose and the Ring, there's a character called Fairy Blackstick. With a wave of her ebony wand she grants gifts to her godchildren. One is given a ring and the other a rose. Both of these objects make their wearers look beautiful. But they don't make them happy. The fairy is saddened to see that they are grumpy, vain and lazy. The next time she has to bestow a gift, she is more circumspect. She decides instead to grant something that will give her godchild the strength to get through life, and to be happy: 'The best thing I can give you,' she says, 'is a little misfortune.'

Rita texted me some other words of wisdom a while ago: 'When pain stops, whether physical or mental, you are in a state of true pleasure, more so than the pleasure that comes with indulgence.' Over the past months there have been stunning moments when I've begun to unfurl my wings. Contrasted with the raw grief, they have made me feel fully alive. This has been more exciting than anything I've done for years. Maybe a little misfortune does turn out to be a gift in the end.

There are certainly reasons to be happy right now. An important one is that I'm enjoying getting to know Mike. He's proved to be none of the things I was worried about. He's not an emotional numbskull or an arrogant control freak. Nor is he a sloppy kisser. And then there are my remaining thirty treats; somehow I have to find a way to get to Japan and to cross America by train. Closer to home, I want to finish the North Downs Way and to visit the Norfolk Broads. There are plenty of wildlife delights to discover in the remaining David Attenborough programmes, and I'm looking forward to some Hitchcock. I've now made three attempts to read Mansfield Park but am not giving up on it yet, and Glastonbury beckons too, if I can only manage to get hold of some tickets. I can't yet know how these and other experiences will unfold but I'm all prepared with my walking boots, reading glasses, paintbrush, dictionary, passport and fish filleting knife.

TREATS COMPLETED THIS SPRING	TREATS IN PROGRESS
Compost	Life on Earth
Patchwork cushion	North Downs Way
	Jane Austen

EPILOGUE

Old Smells and New Beginnings

Shaun and I finally agree our financial settlement on a hot day in July. I have the help of a clever, charming young barrister who was born the year we married, and together with Melanie's assistant, she and I sit for most of the day in a small bare room at the local County Court. 'The other side', as I learn to call Shaun and his solicitor, are in another room further down the corridor. There's a lot of toing and froing as my barrister and his solicitor thrash out various issues: maintenance—Shaun's pension—his life insurance— the house and its contents—

It's no surprise when Shaun brings up the knife incident again, but something that does come out of the blue is the news that he no longer plans to go and live in America. His relationship with the cancer nurse is over.

As my barrister and I wait for 'the other side' to reply to our responses, we pass the time by chatting. We compare notes on shoes and she tells me about the recent Stones gig that she went to in Hyde Park. My day in court is turning out to be companionable and far from the stressful experience I'd been dreading.

Eventually, all the issues are negotiated and our legal representatives are ready to draw up an agreement. Shaun has won on some points and I've won on others. After more than a year of uncertainty, I'm so relieved to have everything resolved that I startle myself with an unexpected burst of bonhomie. At the final exchange I ask my barrister to tell 'the other side' that I wish him well in his new life. He responds through his solicitor with a similar sentiment.

Later, Shaun and I sit near one another while the judge reads through our agreement and rubber-stamps the end of our long and mostly devoted marriage. Then we nod at one another in a reserved manner, and it's all over. I walk home to see Mike. He's come to stay for a few days. We sit in the garden chatting and watching the kittens chase one another round the tree.

Two days later it's Saturday and I get the train to London to have a day on my own and to mark the start of my new life. As so often, the idea has grown out of a treat and blossomed into something bigger. Someone in a perfume shop once told me that the key to smelling gorgeous is to layer different products on top of one another. I've never been quite sure what this means but am fascinated by scent so put *'Understand how to layer perfume'* on my treats list. Like with all the others I had no idea when or how this treat would come to life, but then I came across the website of a rather fabulous young woman who calls herself Odette Toilette. She organises talks about the social history of perfume, and I signed up for an afternoon of exploring 1930s scent in the basement of a smart shop in Marylebone.

When I realised that this was going to be two days after going to court I thought I may as well celebrate my new beginning by stimulating not just my sense of smell, but all the others too: I planned a five senses day. In other circumstances it would have been fun to do this with someone else, but on this occasion I know I have to do it alone. It's about independence, indulgence and feeling fully alive.

I start by visiting the BP Portrait Award exhibition at the National Portrait Gallery. There's such a range of styles and subject matter and so much to see. I love it. And something I read makes me think about portraits in a different way. When the subject looks directly at you, it's like they invite you into their world. But when you cannot meet their eyes, you can only be an onlooker.

Then it's a short walk to Wardour Street and Paul A. Young's chocolate shop. In there, behind the purple paint and the blinds drawn to shut out the meltingly hot sunshine, I discover a new world. There are truffles flavoured with goat's cheese, rosemary and lemon; ginger pig black pudding, sourdough and rye whiskey; sea salted caramel cooked with cigar leaves, and the signature Marmite dark chocolate truffle dusted with gold. The assistant offers me a sea salted truffle to try. It is quite simply the best truffle I've ever tasted. I stand in the middle of the shop and groan with such abandoned ecstasy that she looks embarrassed and backs away. When I recover my composure I choose nine chocolates to take home and share with Henry and Molly. The assistant packs them into a smart box and then puts this inside a classy bag.

TREAT #34

After a quick lunch of spicy Malaysian noodles I walk to the perfume shop in Marylebone and make my way to the basement. There I'm greeted with a glass of prosecco and together with lots of other women and one man I spend a fascinating couple of hours hearing about the aspirational perfumes of the 1930s. These accompanied the new age of cars and planes and were an antidote to the mass poverty of the 1920s. We have a chance to smell many of them too, as Odette buys up old bottles of perfume from house sales and auctions. Provided they've been kept in a cool, dark place they can survive well. At the end I ask her advice about layering perfume. She says that she doesn't do this as the effect can be overpowering. Instead she uses unscented body lotion which helps the scent to sink in.

After this thirty-first treat I swim at Marshall Street Baths. The pool has recently been restored to its former Art Deco glory; I swim up and down, looking at the barrel vaulted ceiling and the green marble walls. While I do this I try to concentrate on the feel of the cool water as it rushes past my skin.

I end my sensory day with a Vivaldi concert at St Martin-in-the-Fields. A long-haired violinist bows The Four Seasons wildly as the windows reflect the candlelight.

The next day I wake up feeling cheerful and full of

impressions of a stimulating day. But by lunchtime I'm sobbing inexplicably and feeling desolate as I stand at the supermarket checkout. I'm going to have to accept that it will be like this for at least a while longer.

There are things to look forward to, though. Mike and I have booked to go to Berlin for a few days later in the month. This is on my treats list and was on his wish list too. It's surprising how much our lists overlap. It will be our first holiday together, and we're taking Henry and Molly with us. And then the other day he asked if I would consider going to South Africa with him for his brother's wedding in December. It's not on my list—but somehow I'll cope.

The Complete List

	Completed	In Progress	Yet to Start
South West Coastal Footpath			*
Jewel in the Crown			*
Family tree			*
Brideshead Revisited	Autumn 2011		
New England in the Fall			*
America by train			*
Dublin			*
River cruise			*
New York	Summer 2012		
Old-fashioned roses	Summer 2012		
Clock with a nice tick			*
Japan			*
Poundbury			*
Dennis Severs' House			*
Tate Liverpool	Autumn 2011		
Jewish Quarter	Winter 2011		
Saki	Winter 2012		
Stratford	Spring 2012		
Norfolk Broads			*
London walk	Spring 2012		
The Carmargue			*
Burgh Island Hotel			*
The Races	Summer 2012		
Jazz club	Summer 2012		
Berlin			*
Knit a jacket			*
Patchwork cushion	Spring 2013		
Greenwich market	Winter 2011		
Ten fish			*
Truffles	Winter 2011		

	COMPLETED	IN PROGRESS	YET TO START
Birdsong	Spring 2012		
Compost	Spring 2013		
National Media Museum	Summer 2012		
North Downs Way		*	
Elizabeth David recipes			*
Perfume	Summer 2013		
Eye make-up	Summer 2012		
St Petersburg			*
Magic Circle	Winter 2012		
Cirque du Soleil	Winter 2012		
Derren Brown	Spring 2012		
Glastonbury Festival			*
Jane Austen		*	
Middlemarch			*
Hitchcock			*
River Café recipes	Autumn 2012		
Edinburgh	Autumn 2011		
Chatsworth	Autumn 2012		
Wrap treatment	Winter 2011		
Digital photographs	Winter 2012		
Mad Men	Summer 2012		
Zara	Winter 2011		
Tallinn	Spring 2012		
Riding lessons	Autumn 2012		
Cryptic crosswords			*
Life on Earth		*	
Holland alone			*
Produce a piece of art			*
Port Sunlight	Spring 2012		
Billy Wilder			*

Acknowledgements

My heartfelt thanks are due to the many people who have helped me through a difficult time, and during this project. In no particular order, they include Sue Crocker, Tilly and Denis Christie, Melanie den Brinker, Frances Plummer, Dan and Wendy Tall, Nick and Sarah Tall, Rita and Eric, Maggie and Philip, Iram, Steve and Liz, Rachel Gay, Helen Nash, Helen Davison, Frances Morrish, Cookie Dakin, Ursula Ellwood, Stella Carswell, Anne Tuite Dalton, Mandy Shanahan, Anne Catliff, Caroline and Peter Norman, Chris and Angela, Debbie Strang, Dot Lawson, Marion France, Sue Goode, Margot Pagniez, Anne Stanton, Kate Brignall, Bernadette Donoghue, Corinne Gaskell, Jason Sadler, Claire Elizabeth Jackson, David Briffa, Esther Kieboom, Shirley Martin, Bill and Audrey Rodi, Colin Marriott, Paula Tadmore, Lynne Spencer, Sam Selby and Fiona Ingham. My sister Bonnie has always been there and I value her support more than I can say. She and her husband Jeff, are very dear to me. Will, Emma, Henry and Molly provide sunshine, and Mike is a matchless treasure. Special thanks to Jo Dalton for the illustrations and cover design, to Kate White for publicity, to Bidisha for her encouragement at an early stage when I most needed it, and to my brilliant editor, Robert Peett whose wisdom and support has been inspirational and transformational. And lastly, in spite of everything, I want to thank Shaun for the good times. When they were good they were very good indeed. Without them this would not be a story worth telling.

About The Author

Lynn spent her childhood in Devon and then went to university in London. She spent some years working as a research psychologist before a move to Sussex resulted in a complete change of lifestyle. At one point she was responsible for the welfare of thirty-two animals and eight species including her four children. She now lives in Hampshire. This is her first book and she is working on her second, which is about English cities and independent women. She writes a regular blog: treatsandmore.com.

Lightning Source UK Ltd.
Milton Keynes UK
UKOW01f0046120516

274023UK00005B/94/P